Welfare States
Under Pressure

Welfare States Under Pressure

Edited by
Peter Taylor-Gooby

Sage Publications
London • Thousand Oaks • New Delhi

SAGE Publications Ltd
6 Bonhill Street
London EC2A 4PU

SAGE Publications Inc
2455 Teller Road
Thousand Oaks, California 91320

SAGE Publications India Pvt Ltd
32, M-Block Market
Greater Kailash - I
New Delhi 110 048

British Library Cataloguing in Publication data

A catalogue record for this book
is available from the British Library

ISBN 0-7619-7198-X
ISBN 0-7619-7199-8 (pbk)

Library of Congress Control Number available

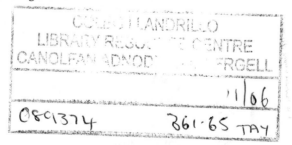

Typeset by SIVA Math Setters, Chennai, India
Printed in Great Britain by Athenaeum Press, Gateshead

Contents

List of Figures and Tables

Figures

Tables

Notes on the Contributors

Dr Frank Bönker is Assistant Professor at the Department of Economics, European University Viadrina, Frankfurt (Oder) and Research Fellow at the Frankfurt Institute for Transformation Studies. Recent publications include *Privatization, Corporate Governance and the Emergence of Markets*, (Macmillan, 2000), *The Political Economy of Fiscal Reform in Central-Eastern Europe: A Comparative Analysis of Hungary, Poland and the Czech Republic* (forthcoming) and various articles with Hellmut Wollmann on social services and social policy in Germany.

Dr Giuliano Bonoli is a Lecturer at the Department of Social Work and Social Policy, University of Fribourg. Publications include: 'Switzerland: adjustment politics within institutional constraints', (with André Mach) in F. Scharpf and V. Schmidt (eds), *From Vulnerability to Competitiveness: Welfare and Work in the Global Economy*, (Oxford University Press, 2000); *European Welfare Futures: Towards a Theory of Retrenchment*, (with Vic George and Peter Taylor-Gooby); (Polity Press, 2000) and *The Politics of Pension Reform: Institutions and Policy Change in Western Europe*, (Cambridge University Press, 2000).

Professor Luis Moreno is Senior Research Fellow at the Spanish National Research Council, CSIC, in Madrid. Social policy publications include: *Precarious Citizens: The 'Safety Net' of Social Protection* (forthcoming); *The Federalisation of Spain*, (Frank Cass, 2000); 'The Spanish development of Southern European welfare', in S. Kuhnle (ed.), *The Survival of the European Welfare State*, (Routledge, 1999); *Unión Europea y Estado del Bienestar* (ed.), (CSIC, 1997) and *Social Exchange and Welfare Development* (ed.), (CSIC, 1993).

Dr Bruno Palier is a member of CEVIPOF in Sciences Po Paris. He organized the comparative programme on social welfare systems in Europe for MIRE in the French Ministry of Social Affairs (1994–1999) and is now a member of COST Programme A15 on 'Reforming Social Protection Systems'. His publications include: 'Defrosting the French welfare state', *West European Politics*, (2000); 'Phénomènes de path dependence et transformation des systèmes de protection sociale' (with G. Bonoli), Revue Française *de Science Politique*, (1999); and 'Changing the politics of social programmes: innovative change in British and French welfare reforms', (with G. Bonoli), *Journal of European Social Policy*, (1998).

Peter Taylor-Gooby is Professor of Social Policy at the University of Kent. Recent publications include: *European Welfare Futures*, (with Vic George and Giuliano Bonoli), (Polity, 2000); *European Welfare Policy*, (with Vic George), (Macmillan, 1996); *The End of the Welfare State?* (with Stephan Svallfors), (Routledge, 1999), *Risk, Trust and Welfare*, (Macmillan, 2000) and *Choice and Public Policy*, (Macmillan, 1998).

Virpi Timonen has worked as researcher at the University of Turku, for the Council of Europe and for Lawson Lucas Mendelsohn in London. She is currently completing her PhD at Magdalen College, Oxford. Recent publications include: 'A threat to social security? The impact of EU membership on the Finnish welfare state', *European Journal of Social Policy*, (1999), and 'What explains public service restructuring? Evaluating contending explanations' *Journal of European Public Policy*, (2000).

Hellmut Wollmann is Professor of Public Administration at Humboldt-Universität, Berlin, Germany. His recent publications include: 'Germany´s trajectory of public sector modernisation – continuities and discontinuities', *Politics and Policy* (forthcoming), 'local government modernisation in Germany: between incrementalism and reform waves' (with Frank Bönker), *Public Administration* (forthcoming), 'The rise and fall of a social service regime: marketisation of German social services in historical perspective' and 'The development and present state of local government in England and Germany' (with Frank Bönker) in H.E. Wollmann and Schröter (eds), *Comparing Public Sector Reform in Britain and Germany*, (Ashgate, 2000) and 'Incrementalism and reform waves: the case of social services reform in the FRG', *Journal of European Public Policy*, (1996).

Preface

The welfare state in Europe is like guaranteed annual pay rises, nine to five working and family meal-times – traditional, much-loved, but not quite the modern style. Welfare states developed during the period of secure growth, male bread-winner family systems and stable labour-markets. Globalization, technological unemployment, fewer children and more older people, new patterns of migration, shifts in political ideology – all these developments call the traditional settlement into question. Recent studies of the response to these challenges have reported that – surprisingly – the European welfare state is in much better health than might have been expected. Welfare spending continues to increase, privatization is relatively unimportant in most countries and most people express enthusiasm for the maintenance of existing standards of provision. Reforms are best summed up as an adjustment or 're-calibration' of the welfare settlement, not a fundamental restructuring.

This book examines welfare policy-making in detail in seven key European countries, chosen to represent the main welfare regimes, political configurations and policy-making frameworks – Finland, France, Germany, Spain, Sweden, Switzerland and the UK. Each country chapter is written by a leading national expert to an overall conceptual structure developed through a lengthy collaboration, helpfully financed by the UK's Economic and Social Research Council under grant number R000222914. Special attention was paid to ensuring that the book is accessible to an undergraduate audience. The distinctive features of the work are two. First, it focuses on the welfare politics and on the policy-making framework in each country (the particular configuration of constitutional factors and institutions through which the relevant social actors interact), as well as welfare regime-type, in its account of the national trajectory of policy. Thus, it includes Switzerland, a country that is often not considered as a major welfare state, but of considerable interest in policy-making debates because it represents the polar case of consensual democracy in Europe. Second, it builds on the evidence of both the recent development of policy and the changes in the roles and opportunities open to the various political actors to construct an account of the factors likely to influence policy in the future. Much research in this field pays considerable attention to regime type and policy development but gives less weight to political and institutional factors which, we believe, are changing rapidly in a number of countries.

This approach produces a rather different picture of the sustainability of the European welfare settlement from that derived from accounts which assume continuity between the future and the pattern of recent years. The welfare state has so far been relatively undamaged by the challenges it has faced. However, current reforms and continuing pressures are likely to shift the balance of forces among policy actors, so that adjustment will develop into much more substantial reforms. The detail of these shifts will vary according to national context, but there are changes that are likely to challenge current welfare development in all the countries reviewed, from the most consensual to the most majoritarian, from federal to centralized, from social-democratic to liberal. All European welfare states are subject to the 'competitiveness imperative' which drives a determination to activate policies to sustain higher levels of productive employment and lower state spending on dependent groups, so that benefits are targeted and the private sector expands. The obstacles to movement in these directions in the policy-making frameworks of most European countries have now been eroded. Opportunities for radical change in welfare systems that were not available in the past are now opening up through institutional changes in France and the 'neo-liberal turn' of the SPD in Germany, and the liberal consensus in the UK reinforces a similar policy direction. The past and the present are unlikely to be a good guide to the future of the European welfare state.

Peter Taylor-Gooby
University of Kent
June 2001

Acknowledgement

This research was financed by the UK's Economic and Social Research Council under grant number R000222914 (1999–2000).

1 The Politics of Welfare in Europe

Peter Taylor-Gooby

Welfare under altered circumstances

The future direction of the European welfare state is hotly debated. This book reviews recent developments in welfare and in the institutional, constitutional and cultural frameworks within which policy is made in seven major European countries. It concludes that, while welfare policy has so far resisted pressures for retrenchment and radical reform with considerable success, shifts in policy-making, made possible by changes in institutional structure, the organization of welfare and the modernization of social democratic parties, imply that the European welfare state is set on a new trajectory. Current (and recent) experience is not a good guide to the future.

The European welfare state developed as a distinctive solution to the problem of securing social integration within competitive capitalism (or 'civilizing the economy' as Streeck puts it – 1996: 300) in the three decades of secure growth following the Second World War. Pressures emerged towards the end of the 20th century. The labour market and family structures which the welfare state was designed to support are undergoing rapid change: increasing numbers of older people confidently expect high quality pensions, health and social care, globalization is undermining the authority of the nation state and the expansion of the EU is creating an increasingly unified and competitive market in Western Europe with further prospects of expansion to the East and around the Mediterranean basin. The welfare state faces a more severe challenge than at any time in its 50-year history. This book examines its response.

Current problems attract much attention. Analysis of recent developments supports five points. First, despite the concerns of the 1980s and early 1990s, the European welfare state is not contracting, nor is it obsolete. Indeed, 'the clear and sober message' is that 'survival is possible and likely – and desirable', as Kuhnle concluded his study of the 1990s in Europe (2000b: 237). Similarly, Beck and colleagues stress the essential value and viability of the European solution to the problem of achieving a measure of social justice within a capitalist market system (Beck et al., 1998). Ferrera and Rhodes conclude from their study of developments across Europe that the welfare state is a largely successful solution to the 'problem of reconciling growth with social cohesion' (Ferrera and Rhodes, 2000a: 279).

Second, reform and restructuring have had limited impact on convergence. Indeed, as Scharpf points out, because welfare states differ in vulnerability to international pressures, structures of provision and specific immediate problems, 'there is no one best way by which advanced welfare states could maintain their economic viability without abandoning their employment, social security and egalitarian aspirations' (1999: 39). Studies of specific areas such as social dumping (Alber and Standing, 2000), social security policy change (Daly, 1997), or the impact of EU policies (Geyer, 2000) reach similar conclusions.

Third, while welfare states do not march in step down the same highway, it is possible to identify a number of common trends. The EC's official biennial report sums these up under two general headings – cost containment and 'activating policy to reduce the number of people dependent on social transfers' (CEC, 1998: 19, 2000b: 19). Ferrera and Rhodes decompose these: cost control involves adjustments in response to socio-demographic developments, mainly in pensions and health care, and also a trend to more accurate targeting of resources on those in need. Activation policies include the general shift from a passive to an active approach in the management of unemployment and the modification of financial arrangements to promote competitiveness by containing labour costs (CEC, 2000b: 4–7). Kuhnle (2000b: 234–5) and others identify similar developments.

Fourth, pressures from the same sources generate different problems and opportunities in different welfare states. Writing in the mid-1990s, Esping-Andersen argued that the Nordic universalist welfare systems enjoyed a high degree of citizen support, but faced real difficulties in balancing the costs of generous provision against the 'growing tax burden that a huge public sector entails', unless high productivity could be secured (1996: 13). Conversely, neo-liberal, market-driven systems (the US and to some extent the UK) are good at creating jobs, but face increasing social polarization. The corporatist social insurance systems that characterize much of continental Europe provide good protection for labour-market insiders, but not for those without access to secure employment, and also risk inertia since current arrangements generate a strong political constituency opposed to change.

The view that differences in the nature of welfare provision lead to differing agendas for policy change is endorsed in more recent work. For example, Scharpf concludes his analysis of the impact of globalization on welfare systems that while

> there is no reason to think that economic viability should be incompatible
> with [welfare] aspirations … welfare states differ greatly in their vulnerability
> to international economic pressures … in the specific problems … they need
> to address … and in the policy options that they could reach under the
> constraints of existing policy legacies and … veto positions. (1999: 38–9)

These points add up to the suggestion that welfare systems are successful in adjusting to a changed environment in ways that reflect differences in their current structure and organization and the political and cultural characteristics of the national context in which they developed. Welfare is being 'recalibrated', 'recast', is 'in transition', 'adapting', 'restructuring', 'evolving' or being 'modified', as the titles of recent work suggest. The fifth point focuses on the processes that underlie change. Most commentators agree that the political processes that drive current reforms differ from those that provided the basis for the earlier expansion of state welfare.

Pierson (1994) argues that a 'new' politics of welfare is developing, characterized by 'blame avoidance' and the attempt to achieve changes in welfare by stealth. The new politics is distinct both from the traditional politics of growth, in which all interests can be satisfied as the welfare state expands, and the neo-liberal politics of cuts and marketization, which confronts welfare spending directly and offers voters lower taxes (see Ross, 2000: 15–18). The key point is that the 'welfare state now represents the status quo' (Pierson, 1994: 181). Any attempt to dismantle it affects entrenched interests and will therefore provoke unpopularity, so governments who wish to contain spending must act indirectly. This approach has generated considerable interest and been reinforced by a number of empirical studies (for example, Clasen, 2000; Hinrichs, 2000; Palier, 2000).

Analysis of the processes influencing current changes raises questions about the limits to the successful adjustment identified at the beginning of the chapter. One influential approach, closely linked with Pierson's and Esping-Andersen's arguments about the entrenched nature of current provision, argues that welfare regimes, once established, tend to advantage particular groups and thus generate policy feedback – an in-built pressure for their maintenance. This leads to an emphasis on 'path-dependency' (Hall and Taylor, 1996, Immergut, 1998, Pierson, 2000) in analysis: all things being equal, current welfare systems by the very fact of their existence inhibit change. Provision runs the risk of becoming increasingly inappropriate to new needs as they develop. For example, Esping-Andersen concludes that current arrangements lead to 'median voter support for anachronistic modes of welfare production' (1999: 184). This raises the question of whether European welfare states, which are adapting to meet the pressures they face, will continue to do so in the longer term.

Our contribution is to argue that, alongside the external and internal pressures, and the different opportunities and obstacles provided by the various welfare state regimes, the institutional and constitutional apparatus within which policy-making takes place varies between countries and these differences must also be taken into account. Welfare state policy changes are, in the first instance, the direct result of decisions made by political actors. Political decisions can only be understood as the result of political processes. Those political processes are currently becoming more complex and less transparent, as governments and political parties face the task of restructuring welfare provision to meet altered circumstances, and as they seek to escape blame for retrenchment. We will argue that, while the review of current policies supports the impression of resilience, analysis of changes in the political basis of policy-making implies that the way is now open for radical changes in welfare, which would not have been politically feasible in many countries in the recent past.

Welfare policy-making takes place primarily within national contexts which are characterized by individual circumstances. Theory-building can proceed from analysis of general categories, abstracted from the particularities of given examples, or from observation of the detailed interaction of the factors influencing reform in specific contexts. This book provides accounts of policy-making in seven countries (Finland, France, Germany, Spain, Sweden, Switzerland and the UK), and focuses on three key areas of welfare policy (pensions, employment and unemployment, and the finance of welfare). The different countries are used as 'markers' to represent different policy-making contexts. They enable us to contrast the various policy-making frameworks, welfare traditions and labour-market structures found in the EU.

The list includes four of the five largest EU countries, with double representation on the Commission. The countries account for about 70 per cent of the EU population and almost exactly the same proportion of EU domestic product (OECD, 2000a, Tables 1 and 4). The group also includes Switzerland and the UK, the polar cases in Lijphart's influential analysis of patterns of democracy (Lijphart, 1999), and major representatives of the dominant models in academic categorization of European welfare states (corporatist France and Germany; social democratic Sweden and Finland; Mediterranean Spain and liberal UK – see Esping-Andersen, 1999; Ferrera, 1996). The chosen policy areas enable us to discuss the chief differences between the different welfare systems in the design of services and patterns of entitlement, and also include financial arrangements, much debated since they are often seen as directly related to economic competitiveness. Thus, the book will review the processes generating the political choices which determine the future of European welfare systems by examining the service areas where reform is most hotly debated in the contexts of specific countries which represent the range of European welfare states.

The rest of this chapter falls into three sections which will introduce the discussion of specific countries in Chapters 2 to 7 by reviewing the characteristics of European welfare systems as they affect restructuring, the challenges they face and the chief differences between policy-making frameworks.

The characteristics of welfare systems

European welfare systems have been understood in a number of ways (for reviews, see Bonoli et al., 2000: ch. 1; Kuhnle, 2000: 6–12). The dominant approach derives from the work of Esping-Andersen (1990, 1999) with variations designed mainly to extend the framework outside the north-west European welfare state heartland, and to acknowledge the importance of gender differences and household structure (see, for example, Abrahamson, 1999; Castles and Mitchell, 1990; Huber and Stephens, 2001; Orloff, 1993). It distinguishes Nordic universalist, Anglo-Saxon liberal, corporatist

Continental and Mediterranean regimes. The theory is based centrally on the concept of decommodification, intended 'to capture the degree to which welfare states weaken the cash nexus by granting entitlements independent of market participation' (Esping-Andersen, 1999: 43). To this is added 'de-familialization ... to capture policies that lessen individual reliance on the family' (1999: 45). From this perspective, the welfare state is about enhancing independence from market and family.

The notion of regime links a wide range of factors. It denotes 'the fact that in the relation between state and economy a complex of legal and organizational features are interwoven' (Esping-Andersen, 1990: 2). Since we do not wish to prejudge the relationship between political process and welfare outcomes, but rather to consider how welfare arrangements influence political responses to current pressures, we here use a fourfold descriptive categorization based simply on the characteristics of welfare provision (see Bonoli and Palier, 2000). This approach covers the chief aspects of welfare states which differ from one another: financing arrangements, mode of access, the nature and generosity of benefits and management of the system. We also add brief consideration of the context in which welfare policy operates, including the contribution of other systems for meeting needs (the private sector, the family and waged work), since these affect the impact of restructuring on outcomes, and of the role of underlying values in directing change, since these may influence the acceptability and direction of reform.

The finance of welfare

Welfare spending continues to increase across Europe, although the rate of growth had slowed in recent years. It is highest in the Nordic countries, and lowest in liberal-leaning UK and in Spain, although it is set on a trajectory of rapid growth in the Mediterranean countries (Morena, 2000). Figure 1.1 gives information on social expenditure in the seven countries of the study.

Two points should be noted. First, the statistics do not take account of the fact that in some countries – and particularly the higher spenders – governments tax welfare benefits. Net welfare spending would show less dispersion (Adema, 2000; CEC, 2000b: 70). Second, the graph does not include individual and employers' expenditure on compulsory private schemes. This makes little difference, except in the case of Switzerland, which has a substantial compulsory second-pillar occupational pension scheme covering almost all male and about 80 per cent of female workers. The inclusion of this aspect of spending raises the 1995 figure from 21 to 25.2 per cent of GDP – much closer to the European average. It is likely that inclusion of the Swiss semi-compulsory health insurance scheme and also of non-compulsory private welfare spending, which tends to be higher where state expenditure is lower (for example, the UK), would further narrow the range. The overall picture is thus one of real

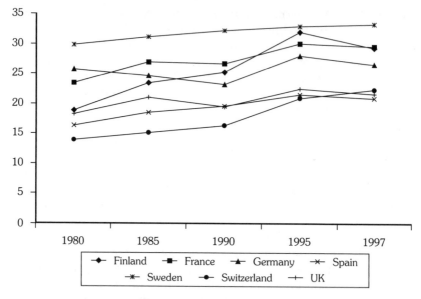

Figure 1.1 *Social expenditure as % GDP, 1980–1997*
Note: 1980–90 data for West Germany only
Source: OECD (2001): Social Expenditure Database

differences in welfare spending within a common trend to expansion, which slowed in the late 1980s. The fact that mandated and voluntary private welfare spending goes some way to bridge differences focuses attention on issues of access and level of provision, since private provision tends to be directed towards social groups who can pay for it.

Welfare states are financed in different ways. Table 1.1 gives information on the role played by social insurance. The first three columns, from OECD data, show how social insurance accounts for a much greater part of welfare state revenues in France, Germany and Spain than elsewhere. Inclusion of mandated private insurance contributions, for which detailed data are not available, would increase the Swiss statistic to approach the level in these countries. Social insurance in the continental corporatist countries also rests much more strongly on employee contributions, distinguishing them from the Nordic second-pillar pension schemes which have developed in recent years, and the Spanish system. Social insurance is notably less prominent in the UK.

The differences in patterns of financing have two main implications. First, insurance contributions are much more prominent in labour costs in the continental corporatist countries, a fact which has exerted a strong influence on public debate about welfare provision and competitiveness. This issue is particularly important in France, where contributions constitute over 40 per cent of labour costs against an EU average of 33 per cent (CEC, 1998: chart 25). Second, the experience of contributing directly

Table 1.1   *The finance of welfare*

	Social security contributions as % of tax receipts (1996)			as % of welfare state spending
	Employee	Employer	Total	
Finland	4	21	25	56
France	13	27	40	77
Germany	18	21	39	68
Spain	6	26	32	68
Sweden	5	25	30	47
Switzerland	12	11	23	n.a.
UK	7	10	17	40
EU 15	8	15	23	60

Source: Columns 1–3, OECD, 2000a: column 4, CEC, 2000b: Chart 35

to the finance of welfare has a powerful effect in establishing a sense of entitlement, which influences welfare debates about retrenchment, the legitimacy of state provision and the acceptability of taxes. The Nordic emphasis on tax finance fosters an understanding of social citizenship as universal, but requires strong collective support to endorse the tax increases necessary to meet rising costs. The continental work-based social insurance schemes may gain a buoyant income if employees believe that they are paying extra contributions to secure better welfare for themselves, but exclude those without access to secure employment. The UK model uses private contributions to compensate for a lower level of state provision, which skews entitlement towards those who can afford it and ensures that welfare follows the broad pattern of market allocation.

The mode of access

The differences in entitlement systems are based on the three principles of work, citizenship and need, and largely reflect the pattern of financing reviewed above. In the corporatist/social insurance systems, entitlement is by insurance record, with minor variations. The reforms of recent years designed to contain spending have linked benefits more closely to work record, by lengthening the qualifying period for benefits and the calculation period for pensions (Myles and Quadagno, 1997), while others, such as the inclusion of some of the years spent in child care in calculation of entitlement, expand the definition of useful work outside paid employment. In the more universal systems characterized by the Nordic countries, citizen entitlement is more prominent, although policy is oriented primarily to the needs of 'citizen-workers'. For example, entitlement to second-pillar pensions is linked to work-record. These countries have the largest and best-established activation programmes to involve unemployed people in training and other work-related activities. In the

Table 1.2   *Means-testing in European welfare systems – %
total spending means-tested*

	1990	1996
Finland	11	16
France	9	10
Germany	8	10
Spain	14	14
Sweden	6	7
Switzerland	n.a.	n.a.
UK	16	20
EU 15	9	10

Source: CEC, 2000b: 80, chart 29

more liberal systems state provision tends to be limited, with strong encouragement for private alternatives.

Reliance on proof of need through means-testing is often associated with liberalism, and is particularly prominent in The Republic of Ireland (34 per cent of spending by 1996) and the UK (20 per cent – CEC, 2000b: 80). However, the growing flexibility of labour markets and (in some countries) of patterns of family life has led to the expansion of means-tested systems throughout Europe for groups such as marginal workers, unemployed people and lone parents (see Table 1.2). This development opens up possibilities for structural divisions between the interests of those for whom entitlement is based simply on need and others, most marked in social insurance systems where contributions provide the standard means of legitimating benefit claims.

The generosity and effectiveness of benefits

The success of the welfare system can be measured along a number of dimensions. Here, we focus on benefit rates and on the success of welfare states in reducing poverty. The overall context is the reversal of the post-war trend towards greater equality. Inequality has increased most sharply in liberal countries and least in the Nordic group (see OECD, 1996b: 61). Good comparable data is scarce. Available studies indicate an increase in poverty in continental and (most sharply) in liberal countries, but not in all Nordic, nor under the expanding welfare systems of Mediterranean countries. Material from a study based on Luxembourg Income Study data and a recent EC analysis of the European Community Panel Study is included in Table 1.3. The broad findings are supported by other work using a variety of methodologies (Bradbury and Janatii, 1999; Bradshaw, 1999; Eurostat, 1997a; OECD, 1998c, Tables 3.1 and 3.2). However, the UK data on income ratios appears to exaggerate the impact of benefits in the

Table 1.3   *Poverty in Europe*

	% of population below 50% median household income		Ratio of share of total (equivalized) income received by top 20% to that of the bottom 20% of population (1996)	
			Disregarding social security benefits	Taking social security benefits into account
	1980s	1990s		
Finland	6.7c	2.4h		
France	8.1a	13.0d	7.4	4.4
Germany	4.5c, j	8.1g	6.8	4.5
Spain	13.5b	10.9e	9.2	5.7
Sweden	4.7c	5.2f		
Switzerland			not available	
UK	6.7a	17.3h	16.9	5.5/6.9

Note: a = 1979; b = 1980; c = 1981; d = 1989; e = 1990; f = 1992; g = 1994; h = 1995; j = West Germany
Sources: Columns 2 and 3, Makinen, 1999: Table 1; columns 4 and 5, Eurostat, 2000a

UK. UK government data show that benefits reduce the inter-quintile ratio to 6.9 rather than 5.5 per cent (CSO, 1999: Table 5.20).

Makinen's analysis indicates that state welfare has reduced poverty from the levels it would have attained without state provision every-where, most effectively in Nordic welfare states, and then in corporatist and finally liberal and Mediterranean systems (Makinen, 1999: 14–15). The more limited EC study paints a similar picture and also shows how the welfare state reduces inequalities (see also CEC, 1998: Chart 4). Similarly, persistent poverty (defined as poverty enduring for at least the previous three years) affected 7 per cent of the EU population in 1996, ranging from about 3 per cent in Denmark and the Netherlands to more than 10 per cent in Greece and Portugal (Eurostat, 2000b). Child poverty was higher than adult poverty – 21 as against 16 per cent on average – but lowest in both social democratic Denmark and Mediterranean Greece, and highest in the liberal UK and The Republic of Ireland. This indicates that the Mediterranean family system is able to mitigate some poverty effects (Eurostat, 2000c).

More detailed analysis which examines the impact of particular programmes shows how corporatist social insurance as well as Nordic citizenship welfare provides good quality benefits, although the poverty data indicates that the former is less successful at directing those benefits to the groups in the greatest need. For example, in the case of provision for unemployed people, Switzerland and Finland are rather more gener-ous in the case of married couples and Germany and Finland for single people (Table 1.4). The UK is markedly less generous overall, reflecting its

Table 1.4   *Net replacement rates^a for unemployed people, 1997*

	Single	Married couple, 2 children
Finland	60	83
France	72	72
Germany	60	72
Spain	75	73
Sweden	72	83
Switzerland	73	84
UK	50	62

^{a} Proportion of work income, net of tax and social insurance, replaced by unemployment, family and housing benefits in the initial phase.
Source: OECD, 1999c

liberal-leaning policies. However, these statistics do not tell us about other features of benefits. Entitlement periods differ – longer in the Nordic countries but limited to six months in the UK. The extent to which entitlement is conditional on approved behaviour – job-seeking, entering a training programme – varies.

Evidence on the difference that welfare systems make to the living standards of the poor in a context of increasing income inequality is incomplete but does indicate that welfare regimes have different impacts, and that the Nordic system is the most successful and the liberal least successful in reducing poverty, while corporatist systems have a specific work orientation. Mediterranean systems may have higher initial poverty levels, but family support plays a stronger role.

Management arrangements

The fourth key distinction between welfare systems concerns the extent to which consumers, employers, employees' representatives, professionals and other interests are involved in management. This affects the capacity of interest groups to resist change and also whether government is likely to be blamed directly by the electorate for unpopular reforms or can shelter behind a welfare system managed 'at arms length' which takes immediate responsibility for provision (Bonoli, 1997).

Differences in institutional structure affect both the speed of change and the stability of new systems once these are in place. On the one hand, the directly state-run, mainly tax-financed systems which predominate in the UK and Nordic countries may be able to introduce policy changes more rapidly than social insurance systems, especially where there is a high degree of involvement of employee representatives in welfare institutions, and where labour unions are closely identified with the defence of welfare as a working-class achievement, as in France. On the other

Table 1.5   *Private pension funds*

	Private pension fund assets as % GDP, 2000
Finland	40.8
France	5.6
Germany	5.8
Spain	5.7a
Sweden	32.6
Switzerland	117.1
UK	74.7

Note: a = 1999
Source: World Bank, 2000

hand, responsibility for policy change in the former group lies squarely with government. The capacity to initiate and pursue changes which are likely to be unpopular may then depend on the ability to obfuscate the new policies and avoid electoral punishment (Pierson, 1994: ch. 2). In schemes where responsibility lies with social insurance funds rather than government, it may be more difficult to initiate new policies, but change is likely to be achieved through negotiation and so be less politicized when it finally gets underway.

The context of state welfare: market provision and family care

Private market systems currently play a relatively minor role in most areas of provision. OECD analysis for a small group of countries designed to represent different welfare systems (including, in Europe, Finland, Germany, the Netherlands, Sweden and the UK) shows that only in the case of the Netherlands and the UK does private spending exceed 1.5 per cent of GDP. In both instances this is due to voluntary spending on private pensions of over 2 per cent of GDP (Adema, 2000: 194; OECD, 1998c: Table 2.7). There are large variations in the financial significance of private pension funds (Table 1.5). The assets of funds in Switzerland and the UK are not surprising given the importance of private schemes in social security in those countries, but the importance of the funds in Scandinavian countries indicates that policies involving the expansion of private pensions in Sweden will find substantial support.

The other main area of private spending is health care, where it accounts for about a fifth of the total in EU member countries – rather higher in Belgium and lower in Italy and Portugal (CEC, 1998: 132; OECD, 1998c: Table 2.5). The distinctive Swiss reliance on mandated private insurance has been discussed earlier. The development of the private sector figures prominently in debate about reform, but market provision does not at present provide a convenient and politically acceptable

Table 1.6　*Spending on social care (% GDP)*

	Services for elderly and disabled people, 1995	Child care support, 1995/6
Finland	1.7	2.9b
France	0.8	1.5c
Germany	0.6	1.7c
Spain	0.3	n.a.
Sweden	3.4	3.1b
Switzerland	0.5	n.a.
UK	0.7	0.4a,c

Notes: a = England only, b = 1996, c = 1995
Child care support includes all spending on parental leave, nursery, kindergarten and nursery education.
Sources: Column 1: OECD (1996) databank; column 2: Rostgaard and Ffridberg, 1998: Table A.7

substitute for retrenching state services in most countries, and this strategy has not, so far, been effectively pursued.

Families interact with state welfare through provision for dependent groups (particularly young children and frail older people) and through cultural assumptions about women's responsibilities for unwaged care and dependency on male earners discussed in relation to value-orientations below. Family provision has been central to the welfare system in the Mediterranean countries and assists in preserving a high degree of social cohesion.

There are clear variations in the level of state spending on social care (Table 1.6). In general, Nordic countries are most and Mediterranean least active in providing services which substitute for informal family provision. Although the data is imperfect, both OECD statistics and studies based on national data reinforce the point and indicate the distinctively high level of Swedish provision.

Social and child care provision may enable women to take up paid employment, although other factors, including cultural traditions, also influence such decisions (Table 1.7). Women's labour-market participation is high in the Nordic countries but also in Switzerland where state support for social care is weaker. It is the Nordic countries (and France) which have made the greatest progress towards equality in earnings, which further reinforces independence from the family.

Pressure on employment has also resulted in an increase in part-time working, especially in the case of women. Levels are highest in Switzerland, the UK and Germany (46, 41 and 32 per cent of women workers part-time against an EU average of 28 per cent – OECDa, 1999: Table E), reflecting assumptions about the role of mothers in the care of young children and the lack of a strong child-care policy in those countries. These factors are also reflected in the profile of employment among

Table 1.7 *Labour-market participation, 1998, and the wage gap –*
difference between female and male full-time earnings, 1997 (%)

	Men	Women	Wage Gap
Finland	75	70	20
France	74	61	15
Germany	79	61	24
Spain	78	49	29
Sweden	81	76	17
Switzerland	90	74	24
UK	84	68	25
EU	78	58	

Source: OECD, 1999a: Table B, OECD, 2000a: 83

single mothers, who are much less likely to be in paid work in these three countries than elsewhere (OECD 1998c: Table 4.1).

This brief review of the context in which welfare systems operate indicates the limited role of the private market sector in most European welfare states and the more extensive contribution of the family. The commitment of Nordic systems to provision for all citizens is underlined.

Policy-making frameworks: cultures of welfare

Policy-making structures operate within cultural frameworks which associate particular values with state, market, occupational and family welfare. Three core values have been important in Europe. First, a commitment to state universalism at a generous level, designed to promote an integrative social equality and summed up in the Swedish concept of state welfare as providing the 'people's home'. This approach is most clearly expressed in Nordic welfare states. It does not imply that generous support is available on demand, but is linked to the belief that social inclusion implies a contribution to society, typically through paid work, and that opportunities to work should also be made available. The 'work line' has become stronger in recent years (Eitrheim and Kuhnle, 2000; Kosonen, 2000).

The second approach is the contrary of this, the liberal market ideology of welfare state minimalism with the assumption that benefits will only be provided at subsistence level for those unable to survive in the market. The morality of independence from state welfare is strongly enforced. Such values are most clearly expressed in the Anglo-Saxon model, found in Europe in the Irish and UK systems. The approach reinforces a work ethic by a different route, since work and private property are more legitimate bases for a claim on resources than need, and welfare must be organized to reinforce work incentives.

The third value-orientation is associated with the Catholic/Christian democrat principle of 'subsidiarity' (Spicker, 1991). Needs should be met, but sources of support are conceived in a hierarchy of family, community, firm and state. The more distant institutions are only appropriate when those closest to the individual cannot meet needs. This principle influences the European Christian democrat approach which links welfare to family and occupational systems in Germany, Italy, Switzerland and to some extent France and Spain (van Kersbergen, 1995). In practice, social insurance has become the most important system for meeting welfare needs, so that work and welfare are linked, again by a different route, since it is work-based contribution record that guarantees entitlement.

To these three value-orientations, may be added recent moves towards gender equality. Traditional familialist assumptions about women's prime responsibility for the provision of social care outside the market as dependants on male bread-winners are challenged at the practical level by labour-market change and at the political level by the demands of feminism. Formal equality in relation to pay, conditions of employment and social security are required by EU directives and supported to a limited extent by national policy changes in relation to elder and child care and the extent to which unwaged work can earn entitlement to welfare benefits. Egalitarian values have had less impact in relation to race and ethnicity.

The expected contribution of 'worker-citizens' in Nordic countries, the limits on entitlement in Anglo-Saxon countries and the work-linked subsidiarity of corporatist welfare ensure that work legitimates entitlement everywhere. The importance of the family ethic varies, with corporatist Christian democrat and Mediterranean countries displaying more familism than universalist Nordic countries and with the Anglo-Saxon countries in an intermediate position.

European welfare systems: a summary

This brief review of the key characteristics of European welfare systems brings out three points in relation to welfare state restructuring. First, it supports a rough categorization on the lines of the dominant academic tradition into Nordic (high spending, high level of tax finance, citizenship access, generous and effective), continental social insurance (spending, generosity and effectiveness slightly lower, insurance finance and access), Mediterranean (lower spending, generosity and effectiveness, combination of access and finance mechanisms, rapidly developing) and liberal (lower spending, generosity and effectiveness, tax finance and need-based access).

Second, there is a measure of correspondence between the context in which state welfare operates and the overall orientation of services. The Nordic countries interpret universal provision for worker-citizens in terms of a limited role for the private sector and the assumption that everyone, including women, is involved in paid work. Continental systems also have relatively little private welfare but vary much more in their assumptions about gender roles and participation, often reflecting the interests of core and typically waged workers. In the Mediterranean systems the development of state welfare tends to supplant or incorporate private services, while still assuming a substantial input from the family.

Liberal systems permit and often actively support the expansion of private market provision and assume people work to gain an adequate standard of living, but do not accept a state responsibility to provide supportive services.

Third, both the structure of welfare provision and the values surrounding it are crucial to the capacity of government to carry through reforms. The chief directions of reform involve the activation of welfare to enhance economic performance and the containment of spending. The work line is supported by all three principal value-orientations. However, cost-containment is associated with different responses in the Nordic system, where it conflicts with citizenship entitlement to high-quality welfare, in the continental corporatist system, where core workers believe they have earned their benefits through contributions and in the liberal regime, where entitlements are less strongly entrenched. Welfare arrangements also influence the legitimacy of different agencies of reform. Corporatist regimes, in which contributors experience a sense of ownership of welfare, engender stronger resistance to government attempts to restructure welfare than either social democratic or liberal regimes, where the state takes direct responsibility for services.

The reform process faces different obstacles and opportunities in different welfare regimes. The fact that the re-orientation of welfare to serve economic performance can draw on all three value frameworks, while the value-basis of cost control is less clear, at least in social democratic, corporatist and Mediterranean regimes, may help to explain why it has been particularly difficult to resist pressures to increase the level of welfare spending (Figure 1.1). Nonetheless, while values support the work line, they do so in ways that have different implications for the direction of reform, which may help to explain the limited evidence of convergence.

Pressures on the welfare state

Welfare states deploy a substantial proportion of national resources to meet a range of needs for which market and family do not cater. Pressures for policy change come from three main directions:

- Factors which affect the capacity of government to finance and provide (including the impact of economic globalization and technological change on assumptions about how welfare influences competitiveness);
- New departures in the context of welfare policy-making (including the growing importance of the EU and new developments in welfare discourse which downplay state-centred solutions); and
- Factors which affect the demand for welfare provision (most importantly changes in patterns of employment and unemployment and in the population age structure).

The changing competence of government: globalization, technological change and the competitiveness imperative

Globalization refers to the move towards freer international commodity and fiscal markets following the dissolution of state socialism in East and Central Europe, progress towards removal of trade barriers through World Trade Organization agreements, the greater purchasing power of the rich world, improvements in transport technology and the availability of large amounts of footloose speculative investment currency. These changes effectively limit the range of instruments that governments can use to control their economies, since national taxation and regulation strategies must be designed within the constraints of more mobile capital and businesses and more open international competition. The restraints are intensified for EU members by the legal reinforcement of market freedom, the drastic limitations on permitted subsidy to industries, the fact that the Maastricht rules effectively prevent deficit-financing of state spending and the loss to national governments of control over monetary and exchange rate policies. Many of the instruments which governments used to meet critical pressures in the 1970s and early 1980s are now no longer available. The introduction of new technologies, particularly involving the use of microprocessors, coupled with new managerial techniques made possible through the application of information and communication technologies, has had an enormous effect on labour-markets. Productivity has been massively improved, particularly in relation to semi- and unskilled manual work and also in many routine clerical activities. Potential savings from new technologies demand heavy capital investment.

These processes can affect national welfare systems in three main ways. First, the openness of a national economy to overseas competition both in imports and exports can affect the balance and quality of employment in particular industries, a point which is discussed further below. This effect goes hand-in-hand with the introduction of new technology, and makes it particularly important to maintain high levels of investment to ensure that technology remains at the cutting edge.

Second, a more competitive environment can provoke concern about levels of taxation and particularly of social insurance contributions that bear directly on labour costs. This restrains government willingness to finance extensive welfare systems. The issue is lent added weight by the greater significance of cross-national investment. The growth of multinational corporations, which have a greater capacity to shift their activities between national or continental boundaries, strengthens the competitiveness imperative. The Maastricht criteria for monetary union in the EU limit the capacity of governments to deficit-finance welfare, redoubling the pressure from a tax squeeze on the capacity to pay for welfare services.

Third, the greater openness of fiscal markets increases the possibility that speculation may render a country's trading position and capacity to pursue a national interest or exchange-rate regime unstable, so that governments must promote confidence in their currency. The experience of forced devaluations consequent on attempts to deficit finance state investment-led expansion in France in the early 1980s and in Finland and Sweden in 1992, has compelled governments to abandon Keynesian approaches, a stance now embodied in the 'Stability and Growth Pact' that underpins fiscal convergence for monetary union, and which is the declared policy of the European Central Bank. Italy and the UK were also forced to leave EMS and effectively to devalue in 1992, a further illustration of the limited power of national government against global currency speculation.

The new international and technological context of production impacts on welfare policy-making by compelling governments to assign high priority to competitiveness and to a stable currency.

European countries differ very substantially in the size of their economies. All are heavily involved in international trade, mainly with each other; trade in manufactured goods makes up over three-quarters of both imports and exports in all cases; all are also locked into complex webs of inward and outward investment (OECD, 2000a). However, there are a number of important variations. The smaller economies among the seven reviewed (Finland, Sweden and Switzerland) rely more on exports than the other countries. Finland, Germany and Switzerland derive more from their manufacturing sectors. All countries are successful in attracting inward investment, and in all cases (except Spain) invest more themselves overseas than they receive. The countries with the highest state spending do not suffer obvious problems either in trade or in investment, although this observation does not in itself demonstrate a causal link, much less show the direction of causation. Nonetheless, competitiveness remains a strong theme in policy-making debate in all the countries and is particularly marked where international trade is especially important and where high social insurance contributions are seen to bear directly on labour costs (Pfaller et al., 1991; Scharpf, 1999). Scharpf demonstrates that, for the 18 OECD countries he examines, as a consequence of concerns about the impact of taxation on competitiveness and employment, 'average GDP shares of total taxation ... stagnated after the late 1980s and total government outlays ... sharply declined after the mid 1990s, even though average unemployment rates were still at a post-war high' (Scharpf, 2000: 15). Governments recognize limits to their freedom of action, but the practical imperative is that the welfare state should be more efficiently oriented to competitiveness, not that it should be abolished, as the studies reviewed at the beginning of the chapter show.

The changing context of welfare: 'Europeanization' and the EU

The EU is often understood as evolving a multi-level or multi-tiered political framework (Leibfried and Pierson, 1995: ch. 2). In relation to welfare, it has followed the principle of subsidiarity and developed few direct welfare policies, apart from those immediately relevant to employment conditions and opportunities. The principal interventions are concerned with: the equal treatment of women and men; the protection of workers and social security for migrant workers within the EU; establishing the European Social Fund; regulatory policies in the area of health and safety and more recently occupational pensions; and specific limited programmes such as the poverty programme.

'Soft law' (non-binding declarations or recommendations) covers a broader range of issues such as social assistance, public housing, provision for older people, education and public health. Legislation has been passed in member states based on agreements achieved through social dialogue, for example in relation to parental leave and part-time work (Cram, 1997). The Social Agreement attached to the Maastricht Treaty extended EU powers into public health, education and vocational training and also promoted the institutionalization of social dialogue in member states (see Leibfried and Pierson, 2000). This was incorporated into the Amsterdam Treaty, which also included non-discrimination legislation. The European Court of Justice has sought to expand its limited competence to regulate national law in ways that those who initially framed the legislation might not have anticipated. For example, the Barber case (C262/88) established that the EU's 1975 Equal Pay directive applied to occupational pensions on the grounds that these could be understood as deferred pay. A gender difference in pension age in the state but not the occupational sector then became untenable, with very substantial implications for costs, entitlements and working lives in the UK.

In addition, a number of EU policies have indirect impacts on welfare. The convergence criteria for EMU membership (low rates of inflation, low interest rates, the avoidance of large budgetary and national debt deficits and currency stability) and the macroeconomic requirements of the Stability and Growth Pact, which oblige members to pursue prudent fiscal policies and maintain broadly balanced budgets over the economic cycle, massively constrain national capacity in the finance of welfare and limits the possibility of borrowing to pay for extra spending (Nugent 1999: 331). The impact of the four economic freedoms (freedom of movement for people, services, goods and capital) from 1992 onwards intensifies the impact of economic globalization discussed earlier. The implications of planned EU expansion, with most of the current membership candidates (Bulgaria, Cyprus, Czech Republic, Estonia, Hungary, Latvia, Lithuania, Malta, Poland, Romania, Slovakia, Slovenia and Turkey) likely to join in the next decade and closer economic links with Iceland, Israel, Liechtenstein, Norway and Switzerland being developed, will ensure that competitive pressures operate more stringently across a larger free market with greater variations in labour costs.

The importance of indirect policies has been reinforced by recent European Court of Justice (ECJ) rulings. The Kohll (C158/96) and Decker

(C120/95) cases bring home the implications for national social insurance funds. Such funds can no longer impose territorial limits on the provision that they will reimburse. Tax harmonization with implications for social insurance finance and for levels of provision has been a focus of recent debate. The EU has signalled an increasingly strong concern with job creation and unemployment following the 1997 Amsterdam Treaty.

The Work Programme of the Commission includes 'a new economic and social agenda' as a strategic objective. The central thrust of this policy is economic: the 'promotion of strong and sustained growth', but the programme also includes recognition of the importance of policies aimed at full employment and at strengthening social cohesion (CEC, 2000a: 5). The strategy also informs the four priorities identified in the proposal that underlies it (CEC, 1999): to make work pay and provide secure income; to make pensions safe and sustainable; to promote social inclusion; and to ensure high quality and sustainability of health care. The first two reflect the dominant current directions in welfare reform identified at the beginning of this chapter (labour market activation and spending constraint). They are also, of course, national objectives, and the EU is unlikely to introduce radical new policy directions. However, both hard and soft law at the European level constitute an additional resource for national policymakers who seek to overcome internal obstacles, and the willingness of the Community to enforce policies through the ECJ may be of considerable significance in national reform in the future. Gradual progress on the extension of qualified majority voting (agreed for social protection and the modernization of welfare at the Nice conference in 2000) will increase EU influence. The shift to a European financial and fiscal system may also provide a bulwark against currency speculation and permit economic planning in a more stable environment.

The changing context of welfare: shifts in welfare state discourse

Shifts in external factors interact with new developments in the dominant pattern of ideas which frames discussion of state welfare. Three shifts are important: first, at the official level, Keynesianism (the view that state intervention is the best way to promote growth and employment) is quite simply dead, a result of the general acceptance that governmental capacity to manage investment within its borders is limited. Economic globalization has altered the fundamental assumptions behind welfare policymaking, which previously rested on the assumption that government was master in its own house. The acceptance by social democratic parties in a number of countries that the 'competitiveness imperative' must predominate over traditional concern with redistribution opens the possibility that an unarticulated broadly liberal consensus may underlie the overall direction of policy-making, and that party conflicts concern the detail of reform within this general model.

Second, new arguments about the role of government have joined the traditional right versus left debate, which set minimalist and market-based systems against substantive state-based models. The 'Third Way' (a term vigorously promoted by 'New Labour' in the UK and also referred to in policy statements in Germany and the Netherlands) is a centre-left variant of the traditional right stress on individual responsibility. It involves the linking of equality of opportunity rather than outcome with a strong work-ethic plus adequate welfare for those unable to work. National variants differ and place more or less emphasis on the role of state welfare in providing support (see Blair and Schröder, 1999; Giddens, 2000; Merkel, 1999; Taylor-Gooby, 2000; Van Den Broucke, 1999).

Third, the growing inequalities discussed earlier have generated fresh divisions between social classes, most noticeably in the UK and the Netherlands. Baldwin perceptively analysed the growth of welfare states in terms of the role of middle-class as well as working-class interests in a measure of collective provision (1990). New social divisions may fragment that interest: the middle-class may now feel sufficiently secure in access to private provision to withdraw support from state-based services that they believe will redistribute to others. This development is most likely to exert pressures in the more unequal countries which typically have the weakest state provision in the first place. It conflicts with the universalist and Christian democrat value-orientations identified earlier.

Discourse about the role of the state in welfare is moving in new directions. In general, the approaches to the role of government, welfare and social cohesion that supported the traditional interventionist welfare states, concerned to reinforce the interests of the male working-class within a political economy based on Fordist factory production are in decline, just at a time when welfare states face new challenges. The new discourses facilitate greater diversity of provision, a weaker role for government intervention and stronger emphasis on retrenchment and the targeting of welfare on support for economic competitiveness.

The shifting demand for welfare: employment, unemployment and the changing labour market

European countries are experiencing historically high levels of unemployment. Unemployment rose during the oil price crisis of the mid-1970s and, despite fluctuations linked to cyclical factors, has not returned to the low levels of the post-war boom years (Table 1.8). The UK (in common with the US) generally enjoyed substantially lower unemployment rates than continental European countries during the later 1990s, prompting debate about the dynamism of the liberal system as a 'job-creation machine'. However, unemployment in continental Europe is now falling and the argument that the labour-market requires a dilution of European standards of employment protection is less prominent. Unemployment is sharply higher among young people, except in Germany, putting labour-market entry high

Table 1.8   *Unemployment trends (%)*

	1970	1980	1990	1997	2000	Aged 15–24, 1999	Participation rate: men, 55–64
Finland	1.9	5.9	3.4	14.3	9.6	21.5	45
France	2.5	6.3	9.0	12.4	9.3	26.6	43
Germany	0.8a	2.9a	4.9a	9.8	8.2	8.5	55
Spain	2.4	11.1	15.9	20.6	13.6	28.5	58
Sweden	1.5	2.0	1.5	8.0	5.4	14.2	72
Switzerland	0.0b	0.2b	0.6b	4.2b	1.9b	5.6	81
UK	3.0	6.4	6.8	7.1	5.4	12.3	64
Eurozone	2.4c	6.4d	8.4d	10.6	8.9	17.2e	53e

Notes: a = West Germany only; b = National definition; c = EU9; d = EU12; e = EU14.
Source: Columns 2 and 3, OECD, 1996: Table R17; columns 4 and 5, OECD, 2000c; columns 6 and 7, OECD, 2000d: Table C

on the policy agenda. Early retirement has been significant in Finland, France and Germany.

The economic changes associated with technological innovation and globalization exert an additional pressures on jobs. One effect has been a general tendency for industrial employment to decline and service sector employment to expand. The proportion of the EU15 workforce employed in the industrial sector fell from 41 per cent in 1974 to 30 per cent by 1997, while service sector employment expanded from 48 to 65 per cent (OECD, 1998b: Table 7).

These changes are seen as posing two problems for traditional welfare states. First, the shift away from the industrial sector may lead to higher unemployment, or sub-employment in low-paid, insecure service sector 'junk jobs', expanding the need for welfare support (Mishra, 1999: ix; Strange, 1996). Second, the simultaneous pressures from globalization and technical change may imply transition to a 'Post-Fordist' political economy with accompanying changes in the gender balance of work and of domestic responsibilities (Jessop, 2000). One implication is that there is no longer a cohesive industrial working-class interest to press for state welfare on the traditional Beveridge/Keynes model. Another is that a greater diversity of interests and demands will emerge, so that existing welfare state systems find it increasingly difficult to cater for new needs, especially if existing patterns of provision are supported by entrenched interests.

The differential impact of these pressures in different national contexts can be highlighted by examining trends in sectors of the economy which are more and less exposed to international competition and vulnerable to innovation. The concern from the welfare perspective is that new technology reduces the number of jobs at the low-skill end of the market, while international competition also undermines employment in the exposed sector (for an authoritative review, see Scharpf and Schmidt, 2000).

European economies follow the familiar path towards the decline of manufacturing and the growth of service sector employment, but with

Table 1.9   *Employment shifts in sheltered and exposed sectors,*
1980 to 1997 – wage earners (%)

	Sheltered sector				Exposed sector			
	High-skill[1]		Low-skill[2]		High-skill[3]		Low-skill[4]	
	1980	% change 1980–1997	1980	% change 1980–1997	1980	% change 1980–1997	1980	% change 1980–1997
Finland	6	+67	23	−13	12	0	7	−57
France	8	+75	23	−4	18	−56	7	−43
Germany[a]	6	+50	22	+18	26	−31	6	−33
Spain	4	+75	24	+13	16	−37	10	−40
Sweden	7	+71	20	−5	15	−13	4	−50
Switzerland	10[c]	+50	30	+3	26[b]		−31	
UK	7	+100	23	+13	19	−63	6	−33

[a] Former West Germany only; [b] manufacturing total; [c] 1986
Note: 1 = finance, insurance, real estate and business services. 2 = construction;
wholesale and retail trade, restaurants and hotels. 3 = chemical, metal and machinery manufacturing. 4 = food, textile and clothing manufacturing.
Source: OECD, 1998b

important national differences. Table 1.9 contrasts employment patterns
in predominantly high-skill and low-skill work in sectors of the labour-
market that are more or less exposed to international competition. It shows
the very rapid decline of exposed manufacturing employment everywhere,
apart from Finland (which appears able to sustain its high-skill, high-
value-added sector), with the biggest losses in France and the UK.
Germany and Switzerland, followed by the Nordic countries, retain the
largest high-skill manufacturing sector, and this is reflected in the contribution of manufacturing to their GDPs which exceeds 23 per cent as
against 19 per cent elsewhere (OECD, 2000a). In line with the globalization
thesis, there has been a shift in employment to the sheltered sector of the
economy, and particularly towards banking and financial services.
Although the OECD statistics are limited, Switzerland appears distinctively able to combine both high-skill service and high-skill manufacturing
activity (see Chapter 6). The result is a tendency to labour-market polarization, most advanced in the UK, but also evident elsewhere, although
Nordic countries and Switzerland are successful at retaining exposed manufacturing jobs while expanding the more sheltered finance sector.
Experience of the post-Fordist economic transition broadly reflects the
other characteristics of welfare regimes (Scharpf and Schmidt, 2000: ch. 1).
    Welfare states increasingly emphasize the activation of the labour
market, including macroeconomic policies of deregulation and tax concessions or subsidized early retirement to promote jobs, more positive
activation involving training, specific public sector job creation and wage
subsidy, and negative policies, such as compulsory workfare and the direct
linkage of benefit entitlement to work-related activities. Such approaches

Table 1.10   *Population projections – over-65s as %*
of those in employment

	2000	2040
Finland	36	72
France	40	62
Germany	37	61
Spain	47	68
Sweden	28	60
Switzerland	26	52
UK	34	54

Source: OECD, 2000e

are particularly significant in Sweden, Finland and France, with over 10 per cent of the labour force entering active programmes in 1998 (OECD, 1999a: Table H), although all countries except Sweden spend more than half as much again on passive as on active measures. In countries where unemployment is high, longer spells of joblessness are more common (OECD, 1999a: Table E).

Labour-markets are changing in response to technical developments and globalization. However, it is not the case that high value-added employment is disappearing, either in the manufacturing or service sectors, although there are clear differences between national economies, generally corresponding to regime type (Nordic countries retaining high-skill, high-paid employment; corporatist balancing exposed sector losses against sheltered sector gains for the core working-class; liberal becoming more polarized). The expansion of the service sector does not necessarily produce a transition to insecure and low-paid work, but it does imply greater inequality and a fragmentation of interests. While labour-market changes produce common interest in broad policies of activation (in line with common work-ethic values), they do not generate pressures for convergence in other aspects of welfare.

The shifting demand for welfare: demography and household structure

The proportion of older people in the population of European countries is rising. The ratio of pensioners to people of working age is projected to increase rapidly everywhere during the next half-century (World Bank, 2000). Demographic ratios are only part of the story: the impact on the financing of pay-as-you-go pension schemes, in which the contributions paid by today's workers finance the pensions of those who are currently retired, will almost certainly be greater than shifts in the proportion of old to young imply, as people retire earlier and spend more of their lives in education. Table 1.10 shows sharp increases in the ratio of older people to those who are in employment (see also CEC, 2000b: 35). Schemes to promote early retirement as a way of resolving employment problems for younger workers have been cut back and governments are seeking to transfer some of the cost from pay-as-you-go to funded schemes, in which workers effectively save for their own future pension. The demographic shifts are also generating debate about the value of migration to replenish the workforce.

The reform of pension provision is one of the most controversial areas of welfare debate and one that exposes differences in policy-making structures. Pension entitlement has been restricted by increasing minimum contribution periods (France, Germany, Italy, Switzerland), levelling up retirement ages, cutting back on early retirement schemes (France, Germany, Sweden and, most notably, Italy) and adjusting the formula which determine final pension payments in almost all European countries (CEC, 1996; Hinrichs, 2000). Rates have also been cut by reducing the replacement percentage (Germany, Italy and Sweden) or revising the entitlement formula (for example, France and the UK). However, a number of countries have also recognized labour-market change by moderating the contributions required for years spent in childcare. The scale of reform is not commensurate with demographic change: the UK has responded to relatively weak pressures by the most thorough-going restructuring, effectively transferring the bulk of provision to the private sector.

Other aspects of household change impact on welfare in different ways in different national systems. Numbers of one-parent families, mainly female-headed, are rising in most countries to between 10 and 20 per cent of families with dependent children (OECD 1998c: Table 1.3). The increase is especially marked in France, Germany and Sweden and has been identified as a prominent policy-issue in the UK, where the limited availability of childcare and of opportunities for employment, coupled with widely held beliefs about the role of the mother as exclusive carer, have led to very high poverty rates for this group. The increase in numbers of single-person households among pensioners and never-married people is also sometimes seen as an issue, but one that again depends on the extent of other support mechanisms. Problems often relate to the adequacy of pensions, particularly for women, the implications for survivors and youth un- or sub-employment.

Policy-making frameworks

The discussion so far has analysed the range of welfare systems and the challenges they face. Recent research stresses the resilience and adaptation of welfare to a changing context. The question of how far adaptation can preserve the essential characteristics of a welfare state remains.

Welfare systems develop and are reformed within a larger policy-making framework. The key factors here are first, the constitutional structure, which determines opportunities for the various actors – voters, politicians, parties in and out of government, the executive, the civil service and the judiciary – to pursue their objectives, and for local and regional interests to influence policy, and second, the extra-parliamentary framework of organized interests – the various fractions of capital, employers, labour, religious organizations, the voluntary sector and others – within which formal politics takes place. In addition, the policy-making framework is set within a particular cultural tradition about the role of the state and civil society which may influence the response that policy-makers and the electorate will consider appropriate to particular issues.

Policy-making frameworks: executive authority, centralization and corporatism

In a path-breaking analysis of patterns of democracy, Lijphart distinguishes between majoritarian systems, in which policy primarily reflects the programme of the party supported by the largest group of electors, and consensus systems which seek to include a range of interests (Lijphart, 1999; Lijphart and Crepaz, 1991). He uses cluster analysis to produce a two-dimensional framework, identifying an 'executive-party dimension' concerned with constraints on the party of government in formulating and carrying through its policies, and a 'unitary-federal dimension', dealing with factors which might limit the autonomy of central government. The former includes the extent of coalition government, the relation between executive and legislature, the number of political parties, the role of proportional representation and the part played by corporatist interest groups. The latter comprises the role of second chambers and constitutional courts, the rigidity of the constitution, the independence of the central bank and the extent of federalism.

The UK (first-past-the-post voting, dominant executive, little consultation of social partners, limited autonomy of local government) and Switzerland (proportional representation, a tradition of over-sized coalitions, strong involvement of social partners, opportunities for dissatisfied groups to veto reform through referenda, the most highly federalized system in Europe) appear at opposite ends of both dimensions, as polar cases of 'majoritarian' and 'consensus' government. France (with its strong civil service and presidential system) is close to the UK in executive power, but rather more distant in the degree of devolution. Germany has an important regional tier of government, which elects a second chamber with the power to block legislation involving spending. It is sometimes described as a 'semi-sovereign state' (Katzenstein, 1987) and is close to Switzerland in terms of decentralization but has a stronger executive. Sweden and Finland resemble the UK in centralization of power, but include a much stronger formal and informal role for the social partners, particularly through close links with social democratic parties. Spain has substantial executive authority but a significant (and growing) local independence in the 17 regional and autonomous community governments which have acquired control over more than two-thirds of public spending.

The majoritarian/consensus framework requires modification for the specific field of social welfare policy, where the role of the social partners and the degree of decentralization are particularly important.

The part played by the social partners distinguishes the welfare systems of most European mainland countries, Nordic and corporatist, from those of the UK and The Republic of Ireland, where these groups are much weaker, leading to analyses of 'social corporatism' (Crouch, 1993; Teague and Grahl, 1998). This distinction is a central feature of the 'varieties of capitalism' approach of Soskice and colleagues (Hall and Soskice, 2000). In the corporatist systems (France, Germany and Switzerland in this book), with their heavy reliance on social insurance, the labour movement and employers are closely integrated into policy-making, and this extends in some cases to service delivery. Interestingly, France is characterized by strong executive authority in most policy areas, but the involvement of unions in welfare limits the dominance of the executive in this field, although recent reforms may weaken this. In the leading social democratic country, Sweden, there is close consultation between the government, which wields a good deal of centralized power, and social partners on policy issues, and the labour movement is particularly influential. Unions are slightly weaker in politics in Finland, where a broader range of political groupings influence policy-making. In Spain, social partners tend to be consulted on welfare policy, but are less closely integrated.

Federal and devolved systems can generate substantial policy differences between different parts of the country and can also influence welfare state development, by accelerating movement in a desired direction (social assistance in Spain, care insurance in Germany) or delaying change (the German 2000 tax reform). Swiss cantonal governments hold authority in all policy areas not explicitly identified in the constitution as the domain of central government, including education, social assistance and family benefits, leading to variations in provision. Thus, the more western French-speaking cantons tend to introduce minimum-income benefits on the lines of the French RMI or unemployment benefits additional to those provided federally.

Policy-making frameworks: current changes and contingent factors

Categorizations tend to present a static picture. Policy-making systems are currently subject to a number of pressures and are undergoing changes as a result. The most important shifts from the point of view of institutional and constitutional frameworks are the steps taken to dilute corporatism in welfare policy in France and the possible moves towards devolution in the UK. The competence of regional authorities in Spain continues to expand.

Some of the factors challenging the welfare settlement (globalization, shifts in family patterns and gender roles, shifts in the culture of citizenship) also demand change in policy-making systems.

Contingent issues may also affect policy-making at particular times. For example, the proximity of major elections or the extent to which a particular party has authority in both houses in a bicameral system (or provides both President and Prime Minister in the case of France) may be important, alongside such factors as the strength of welfare traditions (for example in the Nordic countries), the poll tax in the UK, reunification in Germany or the process of decentralization in Spain.

Policy-making frameworks: a summary

The relationship between frameworks, welfare regimes and possibilities for reform is not simple. On the one hand, formal constitutional arrangements give the party of government very different capacities to achieve its policy goals. On the other, extra-parliamentary factors – most importantly, the role of the social partners – exert a strong influence on policy-making and implementation. The mainstream of comparative work on how welfare states respond to current pressures has focused on the significance of differences in regime type. To this must be added the part played by the policy-making framework – both the constitutional factors that determine formal limits to executive authority and the context, including the role of social partners, in which the executive seeks to develop viable solutions – in order to understand the trajectory of development of European welfare states.

Conclusion

The European welfare system in all its variants clearly faces real pressures. Recent studies indicate that, thus far, it has responded by adaptation rather than retreat. The main themes in reform involve the activation of welfare to enhance economic competitiveness, and the containment of costs, particularly in relation to pensions and health care. The broad conclusion from the analysis of the values that surround welfare and the pressures for change is that both pressures and values run in the same direction in relation to the development of a competitiveness-oriented welfare system, involving labour-market activation, a strong work line and greater efficiency in the direction of welfare spending to sustain economic performance. This direction is also supported by new developments in welfare discourse.

In relation to cost containment, the picture is more complex. Both universalist and corporatist regimes require and legitimate, in their different ways, high spending levels, and their core values conflict directly with pressures to contain the cost of welfare. The former bases entitlement on citizenship and may enhance efficiency through a highly skilled and motivated workforce, mobilized to high levels of labour-market partici- pation. The latter justifies spending by entitlements won through work and may secure a strong economic contribution from the motivation of the core working-class, so long as the central economic role of that group can be maintained. The liberal regime, however, focuses entitlement directly on those in need and unable to work and is more open to retrenchment and privatization. Growing inequality intensifies the divi- sions between welfare benefit gainers and welfare state contributors. Thus, stronger conflicts may emerge over issues of cost containment than re-orientation to competitiveness, and these conflicts may be particularly severe in universalist systems, where citizens expect generous support as of right, and in corporatist systems, where workers believe that they have earned it. In short, current directions in welfare reform challenge under- lying values in these systems much more than in the liberal model.

The key questions concern future patterns of change, and, in particular, where the limits to the capacity of governments to maintain a successful process of adaptation lie. These can only be answered by reviewing the progress and vicissitudes of change processes in individual cases and attempting to understand the factors that influence policy development in particular national contexts. Chapters 2 to 7 of the book will discuss the process of welfare reform in the different countries chosen as examples of different European welfare systems. Chapter 8 will review the argument and seek to draw conclusions about the future trajectory of the distinctively European invention – the welfare state.

2 Earning Welfare Citizenship: Welfare State Reform in Finland and Sweden

Virpi Timonen

The Finnish and Swedish welfare states are famous for being universalistic and decommodifying. Citizenship-based and tax-financed flat-rate benefits, universally available social and health services, and earnings-related schemes that cover the entire working population are seen as the hallmarks of the model represented by Finland and Sweden. A number of recent analyses have demonstrated that the Nordic welfare states have in all essential respects survived the 1990s 'challenged, but viable' (Kautto et al., 1999; Kuhnle, 2000b). This chapter focuses on the changes that did take place, and shows that, while the above characteristics still apply to the Finnish and Swedish welfare states, they were weakened in many respects during the 1990s. In both countries, changes were introduced in the 1990s that made earnings-related benefits more tightly linked to contributions, diminished the role of universal benefits and made means-tested benefits more tightly conditional on participation in activation measures. These changes, although small, are significant because they reveal the weaknesses of social democratic welfare states and may change the future political dynamics of welfare state restructuring.

The main focus in the following analysis will be on pension and unemployment benefit reforms, as these were the most extensive and significant changes. However, means-tested social assistance is also discussed because its role expanded dramatically in Finland and Sweden in the 1990s. The increased emphasis on social assistance as a guarantor of minimum living standards was an in-built reaction in a welfare system that leaves many people dependent on means-tested benefits during periods of high and persistent unemployment. Indeed, most of the restructuring that took place in these welfare states was a direct result of high unemployment and fiscal crises: cutbacks were motivated by the perceived necessity to set certain key economic indicators right, not by neo-liberal ideology.

While the cuts and restructuring measures that are described in this chapter were not strictly speaking unavoidable, they were arguably necessary in order to preserve the overall characteristics of the Finnish and Swedish welfare states while stabilizing the economies. No social policy regime can survive a prolonged period of drastically increased demand for assistance and reduced ability to finance the system, and the generous Nordic welfare states are particularly vulnerable to such pressures. The fiscal crises that Finland and Sweden faced during the first half of the 1990s were extremely serious, and further exacerbated by the limits that open financial markets and the desire to qualify for EU (and later EMU) membership set to policy-making. However, economic crises, while giving the initial 'push' for cutbacks, cannot explain the pattern of restructuring: this is always the result of political choices. It is evident that Finnish and Swedish governments strove to distribute benefit cuts widely across different areas of social protection, but the pattern of cutbacks still bears evidence of the ability of some groups to shore up their benefits, as well as of the social policy preferences of the parties of government.

The policy-making framework: political actors and institutional structure

With the exception of two spells of centre-right rule, post-war Sweden has had single-party social democratic governments. Since 1970 these have been single-party *minority* governments. In Finland, no party has been in a position to form a government on its own and coalitions have therefore been the norm (coalitions with broad majorities were politically desirable and necessary until the early 1990s as voting rules in parliament required two-thirds majorities for key decisions to be passed). Minority governments in Sweden and coalition governments in Finland have necessitated compromises and consensus-building: a minority government is powerless without allies, and a coalition government unworkable without compromises (see Kuhnle, 2000a: 219). These governmental structures (to a large extent the result of electoral systems based on proportional representation) made cutbacks more difficult to push through than would have been the case with single-party majority governments. However, given that most social policies are very popular, single-party majority governments would not necessarily have been more willing and able to enact welfare reforms as the blame for them would have rested squarely on the governing party (Pierson, 1994).

Between 1991 and 1994 (the last three-year government before the introduction of four-year election periods) Sweden was governed by a centre-right coalition headed by Carl Bildt and consisting of the Moderate (conservative) party, the Centre (former agrarian) party, the Christian Democratic party and the Liberals. In 1994, a social democratic minority government was elected and headed first by Ingvar Carlsson and thereafter by Göran Persson (who continued as Prime Minister of a social democratic minority government after the 1998 election). In Finland, a centre-right government led by Esko Aho, comprising the Centre (former agrarian) party, the Coalition (conservative) party, the Swedish People's party and the Christian party, was elected in 1991. In 1995, this coalition was replaced by a 'rainbow' coalition that included the Social Democrats, the Left-wing alliance (former communist party), the Coalition party, the Greens and the Swedish People's party. This government stayed in power after the 1999 election and has been headed by Lipponen since 1995.

The parties that were most obviously associated with cutbacks (and left-wing parties in particular) had to pay for their policies through lost votes (although they did not necessarily lose their place in government). In both Finland and Sweden, electorates rejected centre-right governments after three (in Sweden) and four (in Finland) years of cutbacks and threats to reduce social expenditure further. Dissatisfaction with austerity brought into power left-wing parties that then resumed the cutbacks, often more effectively and in a more conciliatory manner than the preceding governments.

The Swedish social democratic minority government was severely punished for its determined deficit-elimination policies in the 1998 election (but in the absence of a viable right-wing or centrist alternative, remained in power) whereas the Finnish five-party 'rainbow' government performed sufficiently well at the polls and was able to stay in power after the 1999 election. Interestingly, the left-wing parties and the Greens suffered moderate losses (with the SDP losing 12 and the Left-wing alliance and the Greens two seats each in the *Eduskunta*), whereas the centrist Swedish People's party retained all its representatives and the conservative Coalition party gained seven MPs. It appears therefore that the right-wing electorate rewarded its representatives for austerity whereas the left-wing voters punished their representatives for doing the same.

Parties and governments in Finland

The centre-right government in Finland (1991–1995) tried to protect universal benefits, and in fact did not make any cuts in these benefits. It made several attempts to restructure earnings-related unemployment benefits but none of these were very successful (see below). The 'rainbow' coalition (1995–1999, and 1999–) was less concerned with basic security (universal benefits) and keen to appease the unions by avoiding cuts in earnings-related systems. Many universal benefits and perhaps more surprisingly, even some means-tested benefits, were cut or restructured in Finland from 1995 onwards.

As is evident from the Finnish case, rainbow coalitions can be especially effective at times when reforms need to be enacted; it is easier to spread the blame in a rainbow coalition that embraces both the Left and the Right than in a monochrome coalition that is easily branded as 'ruthless neoliberal Rightists' or Left parties that are either unable to take action or sell out their principles by making cutbacks. The Lipponen government had the advantage of embracing the entire political spectrum (the only major opposition party is the Centre party). The Finnish rainbow government's first period in office (1995–1999) was indeed a successful exercise in sharing blame between the five parties included in the coalition, and, as a result, no coalition parties suffered devastatingly heavy losses in the 1999 election. A steadily improving economy also made it possible for the five-party coalition to perform well in the election and to stay in office.

Parties and governments in Sweden

Party preferences are less evident in the cutbacks made by the Swedish governments. This is partly because the centre-right Bildt government (1991–1994) made many cutbacks with the help of the opposition social democrats and did not manage to put its own agenda (insofar as it had one) into practice due to disorganization and fear of an electoral backlash (which duly followed even in the absence of any radical cutbacks). As the social democratic leadership was committed to both eliminating the budget deficit and maintaining electoral, they spread cutbacks as widely as possible, and increased taxes on high-income earners after their return to power in 1995.

The social democrats had played such a central role in constructing the Swedish welfare state, and had been the hegemonic party for such a long time that, somewhat paradoxically, restructuring the Swedish welfare state was not possible, or at least extremely difficult, without them. Due to its minority status, the social democratic government needed support from non-governing parties. The Left party helped SAP to introduce tax increases for high-income earners and the Centre party lent a hand when cutbacks needed to be passed. Social democrats nevertheless shouldered most of the blame for cutbacks which in 1998 resulted in their worst election performance since the introduction of universal suffrage in 1921. Voters flocked to the Left party and to the Christian Democrats who were seen to represent softer, pro-welfare state values in contrast to the deficit-obsessed social democrats (Möller, 1999). The number of votes cast for SAP was 25 per cent lower than in 1994 which translates into 600,000 'lost' votes (LO, 1999: 3). As the centre-right parties were unable to form a coalition (not least due to memories of their poor performance in 1991–1994), SAP formed another minority government that has managed to guide Sweden into a new period of solid economic growth.

The social partners

Finland and Sweden have two of the most powerful and influential trade union movements in the world. While there are some indications that their power is gradually being undermined, there is no doubt that they continue to be important players in these countries' policy-making structures, and that they had an impact on some outcomes of welfare state restructuring in the 1990s.

The main sources of trade union power are the degree of unionization, the structure of unions and union confederations, the cohesion of left-wing parties and the extent of political support enjoyed by them, and the degree of co-operation between unions and the Left-wing party or parties (see Korpi, 1983: 39). The extent to which employers are willing to co-operate with unions has also become an important limitation on union influence and therefore an increasingly significant determinant of their power resources. For instance, the refusal of the largest employer organization (SAF) in Sweden to continue centralized wage negotiations at the peak organization level, led to the demise of that system some ten years ago. The consent or agreement of business interests has been important whenever major reforms have been implemented, and this is probably even truer today than in the past. Despite the end of centralized wage setting in Sweden, unions in both countries are involved in a network of political-economic practices and institutions that support the economic performance of these countries. Unions are integral to the bargaining model of economic adjustments (in wages, technology, training and so on) and are therefore in a position to put pressure on governments and employers. Last, but not least, welfare state structures themselves have an impact on the power resources of organized labour and other interest groups. In the case of Finland and Sweden, the fact that unions administer unemployment benefits is particularly significant, as entitlement to earnings-related benefits has traditionally been one of the most important reasons, if not *the* most important reason, for joining a union.

If the Finnish labour-market partners want to change parts of the social policy system, the unwritten rule is that they first negotiate between themselves, and only then turn to the government. For instance, employers and employees have a strong interest in making changes in the pensions system in order to secure its sustainability in the long run. Both employees and employers are liable to pay contributions to finance the pensions system and both therefore have an incentive to reform the system so that the contributions do not increase uncontrollably as the population ages and people live longer. In contrast to Sweden where the pension reform was negotiated between parties, the Finnish pension reform was for the most part the result of agreements concluded between the labour-market partners in the so-called Puro group (named after the chairman, a pensions expert, who also played an important role in designing the new system). Of course, this is not to say that the relations between unions and employers' organizations were always amicable, and some statements by the latter (often in conjunction with cutback proposals from the centre-right government) provoked strong reactions from the unions during the crisis years of the 1990s.

Since the unions are strong, employers cannot achieve all their goals in social policy, but they also know that the strength and organization of employees brings many benefits to them. For instance, employers benefit greatly from the stability and predictability that accompany wage negotiations and jointly negotiated reforms (such as the pension reform in Finland). While employers in principle would prefer to abolish the unemployment pension for instance, they are aware that certain benefits are 'holy cows' to the trade unions, and calling for cuts in them is likely to be counterproductive. Moreover, it is patently wrong to argue that employers are always opposed to social protection: unemployment benefits for instance have a strong skill-preserving role that benefits employers, and active labour-market policies serve to prevent hysteresis and thereby make the long-term unemployed more employable. Finnish employers are by and large satisfied with the existing social protection system and do not experience employer contributions as damaging to their competitiveness (interview with Markus Äimälä, Confederation of Finnish Industry and Employers, May 2000).

The language used in Swedish Employers' Confederation's publications and statements tends to be more aggressive than language used by its Finnish counterpart (see, for instance, SAF, 1994). This is probably due to fact that centralized negotiations have unravelled in Sweden, whereas they are still the norm in Finland. Finnish employers therefore have more to gain from maintaining a conciliatory atmosphere whereas Swedish employers have adopted a more confrontational stance as they do not wish to return to the old system of centralized negotiations between peak organizations. One of the most important reasons for SAF's withdrawal from centralized negotiations was the perception that the SAP/LO axis of co-operation had become too strong (SAF, 1994: 7; SAF, 1999).

The preservation of the institutional model in Finland and Sweden is arguably at least in part the function of continued employer support for the key parts of the social security systems. The support of business is not all-important, but in the absence of the broad approval of capital, the changes in Finnish and Swedish social security systems would probably have been more extensive and the restructuring process considerably more difficult.

The context of policy-making: globalization, Europeanization and societal change

Globalization

Both Finland and Sweden experienced severe recession and sharp increases in unemployment in the early 1990s (Table 2.1). Globalization was important in the Finnish and Swedish cases because it *coincided* with exceptionally serious macro-economic crises, largely brought about by unwise and unfortunately timed economic policies. Had there not been such a deep crisis and had economic policy-makers been shrewder, most of the social policy cutbacks and reforms that took place in the 1990s

Table 2.1   *GDP and unemployment rates (15–64 year olds) in Finland, Sweden and EU15, 1990–1995*

Year	GDP Finland	Unemployment Finland	GDP Sweden	Unemployment Sweden	GDP EU15	Unemployment EU15
1990	0.0	3.4	1.4	1.7	2.4	8.1
1991	−7.1	7.5	−1.1	2.9	1.1	8.5
1992	−3.6	13.0	−1.4	5.3	0.9	9.6
1993	−1.2	17.7	−2.2	8.2	−0.4	10.8
1994	4.4	18.2	3.3	8.0	2.9	11.2
1995	4.2	17.1	3.6	7.7	2.4	10.9

Source: OECD, 1997b

would not have been necessary. Equally, in the absence of globalization, Finnish and Swedish welfare policies would still have suffered some cuts in such heavily recessionary circumstances as prevailed during the first half of the 1990s. Nonetheless, we cannot ignore globalization, as it was an important link in the process of welfare state restructuring (Timonen, 1999).

The recession eroded the financial basis of the welfare state, necessitating reforms that would ensure the future viability of that basis. The changed rules of macroeconomic management, primarily the product of liberalized financial markets, rendered a number of economic and social policy responses to the economic crises redundant. Changes in Finnish and Swedish social policies in the 1990s were first and foremost due to the economic crisis and high unemployment in particular, that put great pressure on the ability of governments to finance social expenditure and to meet public expectations regarding social security. Globalization, which is here taken to mean the liberalization of credit and financial markets, was important because it effectively precluded the use of some traditional tools of economic management (devaluation, even more extensive deficit financing) that would have alleviated the crisis.

The European union and the economic and monetary union

Finland and Sweden joined the EU in 1995. In both countries, politicians justified many, if not most, of the social policy cutbacks as necessary measures for the economy if it was going to get into 'EU shape' (Timonen, 1999b). In contrast to Finland's decision, the Swedish government decided in 1997 against joining the Economic and Monetary Union in 1999. A Swedish economic commission had concluded in 1996 that early membership of EMU would pose considerable risks to the Swedish economic and social model due to persistent high unemployment and the weakness of the public finances. According to Professor Calmfors, head of the commission, Sweden needs to 'retain the freedom to use an independent monetary and currency policy as an "insurance" in case it is hit by another jump in joblessness'. Were production to fall and unemployment to increase again, it would be 'politically implausible that Sweden could control the resulting crisis through wage flexibility or cuts in employer contributions which would be the key adjustment mechanisms once monetary policy was fixed and strict EMU limits were imposed on the budget deficit' (*Financial Times*, 1996: 3). By 1999, however, Sweden's position had changed considerably and Prime Minister Persson stated that Sweden's entry was 'inevitable' (*Financial Times*, 1999: 8). This change of attitude is partly due to the recognition that EMU membership will not in itself pose a threat to the Swedish model of social policy.

Swedish policy-makers and the Swedish public were clearly more attached to, and trusted their 'traditional' model of macro-economic management more, than their Finnish counterparts, despite the essentially similar position of the two countries in the world economy. This is partly because the differences between the 'old' (pro-cyclical) Finnish model of economic policy and the regime imposed by EMU were smaller than the differences between the more counter-cyclical policies in Sweden and the demands for strict monetary and fiscal discipline in EMU (Andersson et al., 1993; speech by Sirkka Hämäläinen, Director of the Bank of Finland, June 6, 1986). Of course, this is not to say that Sweden did not adopt a strict monetary and fiscal regime in the 1990s, only that it was more reluctant to surrender the future use of certain central policy tools that had been used to shore up the welfare state.

Societal changes: the labour market and unemployment

It is not an exaggeration to say that the high levels of unemployment that came to dog the Finnish and Swedish economies in the 1990s were the root cause of most of the restructuring measures that were undertaken in these welfare states in the same decade. The institutional model has many strengths, but it is extremely vulnerable to high levels of unemployment as it is premised on the assumption that the vast majority of the population is in paid employment (and hence paying taxes to finance the welfare state).

Unemployment in Finland increased from a little over 3 per cent in 1990, to over 18 per cent in 1994 (OECD, 1997b: Table 1.8). Even more tellingly, the *employment* rate in Finland declined dramatically, from nearly 75 per cent in 1990, to a little over 60 per cent in 1993–1998 (OECD, 1999a). Unemployment in Sweden never rose as high as in Finland, and reached its peak later (1996–1997). However, since unemployment in 1990 stood at just over 2 per cent, a rise to over 9 per cent (total unemployment) in 1995 was a drastic increase and a great shock to Swedes who had not witnessed higher unemployment than the 'natural level' for decades. The level of employment decreased in Sweden from over 80 per cent in 1990 to a little over 70 per cent in 1993–1998 but has recently started to increase again (Ministry of Social Affairs, 1999; OECD, 1999a).

Societal changes: population shifts

In addition to the recessions, the Finnish and Swedish welfare systems had to respond to the longer-term challenges of ageing populations, falling birth rates and, in Sweden's case, a large immigrant community. Population ageing, and the resulting maturation of social policy commitments (first and foremost pensions) was perhaps the most important justification offered for pension reform. The number of Finns over 75 years old will triple between 1980 and 2030 (Ministry of Social Affairs and Health, 1996), a fact that helped to convince all parties that pension reform was inevitable.

Changes in family structures are also putting pressure on social policy systems, although this development started well before the 1990s. In both Finland and Sweden, marriage rates have been falling while divorce rates have crept up. However, since both welfare states are already designed to target benefits and services to individuals rather than families or breadwinners, and since the systems have for a long time coped with comparatively high divorce rates and offered extensive help to single parents, no major structural reforms in the social security programmes are necessary in order to cope with these developments.

From these demographic and social trends it follows that the welfare state will have to meet, on a very large scale, all the commitments that it has made in the past. However, these developments and their cost do not come as a surprise, nor are they something novel. Under favourable economic circumstances, these commitments are sustainable. A serious economic crisis would make the fulfilment of these commitments impossible. The possibility of such future economic downturns is the most serious threat to the sustainability of the Finnish and Swedish social policy systems.

The policy context: key features

While desired membership of the European 'clubs' (EU and EMU) and the forces of globalization in the form of aggressive currency markets and disabled macroeconomic policy tools did set some actual and perceived constraints on economic and social policy-making in the 1990s, there can be little doubt that the real threat to the Finnish and Swedish welfare states did not come from globalization or Europeanization, but rather from the economic crises. Population ageing and other structural changes put additional pressure on the financial basis of these welfare states, but recent reforms have secured pension and other transfer systems, at least in the absence of serious economic crises.

By and large, welfare state restructuring was politically easier and somewhat more extensive in Finland than in Sweden because both the Aho and the Lipponen governments were multi-party majority governments, and because the economic crisis was deeper. Minority governments are constrained by the necessity to strike (sometimes costly) compromises with opposition parties and often appear powerless, whereas multi-party governments tend to be more effective because blame for unpopular decisions can be apportioned between the coalition partners and because deals do not have to be struck with outside parties.

The finance of welfare

Until the first months of 1990, there were few signs that the Finnish and Swedish welfare states were under threat. Indeed, in both countries various plans were underway for expanding welfare entitlements, notably in the area of family benefits. During the first years of the 1990s, however, severe economic crises unfolded in both countries, caused first and foremost by imprudent policy-making that combined the liberalization of financial and currency markets with a commitment to strong currency. Social spending increased dramatically, and public debt and budget deficits reached record levels as the increased spending and reduced revenues necessitated recourse first to borrowing; soon, however, expenditure cuts and tax increases were deemed necessary as the levels of public debt became unsustainable.

Taxation and public spending

As soon as welfare spending started to increase dramatically, a clear policy stance was adopted by the centre-right governments in Finland and Sweden: the growth of public debt was to be stopped and borrowing curbed by cutting back on welfare spending. Achieving these aims proved extremely difficult, however. Alongside cuts in welfare entitlements, taxes were increased; cutting back the welfare state was so unpopular that governments preferred making smaller cutbacks and increasing taxes to making larger cuts. The only exception to this rule was the centre-right government in Sweden that opted to cut some taxes in the middle of the recession, a measure that to a large extent only served to deepen the crisis by necessitating increased borrowing. In contrast, the Swedish social democrats who returned to power in 1995 made it very clear that they would stabilize the state finances with the help of a combination of tax increases and spending cuts, as this was argued to be socially fairer than spending cuts alone ('the rich have to pay for the crisis, too').

In addition to borrowing and spending cuts, governments sought to stabilize state finances through reallocation of the financial burden of the welfare state. In both countries, the share of employees in financing their benefits was increased, albeit in most cases modestly and in the case of unemployment benefits in Sweden, only temporarily. Centre-right governments in both countries made some reductions in employers' social insurance contributions in the belief that this would improve the competitiveness of firms and contribute to reviving the economy. While employee contributions now play a larger role in financing the Finnish and Swedish welfare states, they are not as prominent as in countries of the conservative-corporatist model, and both services and transfers continue to be overwhelmingly tax- and/or employer-financed.

The impact on poverty and inequality

Despite the great economic difficulties and considerable pressure from international economic organizations to reverse the budgetary develop-ment through extensive cuts in social spending, both Finland and Sweden increased transfer spending drastically. Due to massive income transfers, primarily to the unemployed, poverty remained low and income inequal-ity virtually unchanged during the first half of the 1990s. Only during the latter half of the decade, when the split between labour-market insiders and outsiders became starker and more long-term, did inequality increase slightly (Aaberge et al., 1997; Ministry of Social Affairs and Health, 1995; SOU, 2000: 3).

Pensions

Before the 1990s, policy-makers and policy analysts in Finland and Sweden were aware of the risk that the pension systems of these countries might be difficult to sustain due to ageing populations and declining retirement age. It was only with the onset of the 1990s economic crisis, however, that widespread awareness of the vulnerability of the pension systems developed among politicians as well as among the population. The pension systems in both countries enjoyed a high degree of legitimacy and it was therefore not politically desirable to undermine them through radical systemic changes. Rather, the financing and incentive structures needed to be changed in order to secure the sustainability of the system.

Due to the popularity and importance of pensions, it was necessary to form broad reform coalitions. If all interests concerned are involved in a reform process, and if consensus can be reached, the sustainability of the reform is strengthened (Pierson, 1998). There is no scope for excluded par-ties and interests to damage the chances of success by criticizing the reform from the outside. The parties and interests involved also work to convince their members of the benefits of the reform, and in this way lessen popular dissent. In Sweden, the reform coalition included all the main parties, and in Finland the labour-market organizations were very closely involved in designing the reform. In Sweden, a representative of the largest pensioners' organization (PRO) was also included in the working group on pension reform.

In both countries, the cost of future pensions was reduced in two main ways. First, work incentives were improved with the aim of delaying retirement, and the link between pre-retirement earnings and pensions was made stronger. Second, a variety of more or less explicit cuts were introduced. In both countries, the universal national pensions were abolished, early retirement was made more difficult and employee contributions to earnings-related pensions were introduced. For the most part, pension reforms will have their full impact when the young workers of today retire. However, a number of changes affect all groups, even those who retired before the reforms came into force. While the structure of the pension systems changed fundamentally, the main aim remained the same: providing a high degree of economic security during retirement through a public system that redistributes income effectively between generations and income groups.

The Finnish and Swedish pension systems were under-funded as their design had not taken into account the growing old-age dependency ratio. In Finland, employment pension expenditure was projected to increase from 15 per cent of wages in the beginning of the 1990s to 40 per cent in 2030 (OECD, 1997a: 71). In the case of zero growth, pension levies in Sweden would have amounted to nearly 50 per cent of the total wage sum by 2025. The assumption of a 2 per cent growth rate, however, reduces the figure to 23.3 per cent (Ståhlberg, 1995).

In Finland, reductions in pension expenditure were achieved through five main reforms:

Ending public sector pension privileges

Under the old system, public sector employees in Finland were subject to more favourable pension rules than private sector workers. Public sector employees accumulated a pension which amounted to 66 per cent of the pensionable wage after 30 years, whereas in the private sector it was necessary to make contributions for 40 years in order to receive 60 per cent of the pensionable wage after retirement. Moreover, the official retirement age in the public sector was 63 years, in contrast to 65 years in the private sector (OECD, 1997a). Reforms in 1993 brought all these privileges to an end (HE 110, 1992, HE 242, 1992).

Work incentives

One of the most serious structural problems in the Finnish pension system was the effective retirement age. In 1995, for instance, the average retirement age in Finland was 58–59 years, and only 10 per cent of the workforce stayed in employment until the official retirement age of 65 (HE 118, 1995). A number of reforms were designed to reverse this trend, both by discouraging Finns from retiring early, and offering them incentives to retire later. The age limits in early retirement pensions were raised, and the accrual factors (the rate at which one's pension grows) were increased for older workers. Early retirement was discouraged by lowering the accrual factor for those who opted for early retirement or disability pension. The pension accrual factors of the unemployed were also reduced. In short, the income replacement rates of those who retired early were significantly cut, whereas those who remained active in the labour-market for longer could look forward to a better pension.

Indexation

Since 1996, 80 per cent of the indexation of employment pensions for over 65-year-olds has been based on changes in consumer prices, with the remaining 20 per cent being based on increases in earnings (HE 118, 1995). In the long run, this is likely to lead to a decrease in pensions relative to wages, and acts as a guarantee against pensions outstripping wage growth. The national pension will continue to be indexed solely on the basis of price increases; again, this will probably lead to a gradual erosion of the purchasing power of national pension recipients in relation to wage earners.

National pension offset against employment pension

The flat-rate component of the Finnish national pensions was gradually abandoned in the late 1990s, and national pensions are now fully offset against employment pensions with the result that most retired people will not receive national pensions. National pensions will therefore acquire a means-tested character and become akin to social assistance for the poorest pensioners. This was the most significant structural reform in the pension system, and was made possible by the universal coverage of employment pensions that will continue to guarantee high levels of retirement security for all who are able and willing to work full-time throughout their adult lives.

Employee contributions

Employees' pension contribution were initially set at 3 per cent of wages. An agreement in 1994 split any future increases equally between employers and employees (Työeläke, 1992: 38–9 [Finnish magazine about employment pensions]). This measure was justified by arguing that it strengthened the financial basis of the employment pension system and increased its credibility. It also gave unions a strong incentive to reform the system so that employee contributions would not have to be increased drastically.

The Swedish pension reform had three main aims. First, it was intended (like the reforms in Finland) to prepare the country for periods of slow or negative economic growth. Second, in order to maintain the dominance of the public sector, it was necessary to ensure that the public pension system continued to cater for high-income earners so that they are not encouraged to purchase private insurance. Third, the reformers also strove to make the system fairer and more redistributive.

From defined benefits to defined contributions

In the new system, every crown earned will contribute towards the earnings-related pension: the organizing principle of the Swedish pension system has shifted from 'defined benefits' to 'defined contributions' (Palme and Wennemo, 1997). Instead of predetermining the level of pensions as a certain percentage of wages earned during the highest-earning years, pensions are based on contributions made throughout a person's working life (Ds, 1992: 89). The level of pensions is therefore not fixed, and there is no guarantee that the pension will amount to a certain percentage of wages earned during active years. At the time of retirement, the pension accumulated by an individual is divided by a figure (*delningstal*) that is influenced by the average life expectancy of his or her cohort, the growth norm of 1.6 per cent and the person's age at the time of retirement: the later you retire, the lower the figure, and the lower the figure, the higher the pension (Ministry of Social Affairs, 1998: 10). The connection between the contributions paid and pensions received is thereby made stronger and more straightforward as those who elect to (or have to) work part-time or to withdraw from employment will no longer be subsidized by others (with the exception of those who stay at home to look after small children). The combination of the wage-indexing and the 'defined contributions' principles makes the Swedish pension system very similar to the German one.

From universalism to means-testing

Unlike the old national pension, the guarantee pension will be paid only to those with no, or a very low, earnings-related pension. This amounts to eliminating the universal element in the Swedish pension system.

Tying pensions to a wage index

This will result in pensions fluctuating to a greater extent in accordance with economic developments. The risk of pensions becoming an insupportable burden is thereby considerably lessened as the cost of pensions is automatically adapted to resources.

The income ceiling in pensions will be raised as the economy grows

This will effectively reduce the taxes of high-income earners as a larger share of their pension levies will become actual contributions that correspond to their pensions. As a result, the incentive for high-income earners to contract private insurance is decreased.

Funding

Although the pension system will continue to operate on a pay-as-you-go basis, 2 per cent of gross wages will go into funds. Individuals are free to decide where this contribution is placed and who manages it. The funded part of the pension system therefore represents a shift from public sector to private sector control (Palme and Wennemo, 1997).

Indexation

Both the centre-right coalition and the social democratic government manipulated pension indexing in order to reduce pension payments. In 1993, it was decided that the national pension was to be based on a reduced basic amount (*basbelopp*), namely, 98 per cent instead of 100 per cent. The social democratic government decided that pensions were not to be fully indexed as long as the budget deficit remained high (Prop. (1994/95): 150). Pension indexing was inversely related to the budget deficit so that the basic pension was indexed by only 60 per cent of price increases between 1995 and 1997. In 1999, the basic pension was based on 99 per cent of the basic amount, reverting to 100 per cent in 2000 (Kvist, 1999: 247–8).

Incentives for later retirement

Early retirement and part-time pensions were reduced particularly sharply. The national pension was reduced by 6 per cent for all those who retired before the official retirement age (Prop. (1994/95): 150). From 1995 onwards, it has no longer been possible to obtain an early retirement pension on 'labour-market grounds' i.e., due to unemployment. Work incapacity has to be more carefully medically documented and proved before an early retirement pension is granted (SOU, 1996: 113). Tightening the qualifying conditions for early retirement pensions has been politically remarkably uncontroversial (Palme and Wennemo, 1997). This is at least in part due to the perception that these pensions were too generous and too easily granted, and hence proving unnecessarily expensive.

The most striking aspect of pension reforms in Finland and Sweden was the ease of reforming universal national pensions. Although the coverage of these pensions was universal as they were paid to all residents regardless of contributions or working history, they were completely eliminated from the pension systems. National pension recipients were not organized and universal benefits therefore did not have any 'defenders'. Although the consequences of pension reforms will only be known in the long run and depend on economic and demographic developments, it is clear that the level of some pensions will in future be slightly lower, and people will tend to retire later due to the incentives built into the new systems. Trade unions were able to defend the pensions of those with working histories and indeed managed to secure good pension rights for those willing and able to work full-time until official retirement age. The residence requirement for guaranteed pensions is very tight, at 40 years. This means that many immigrants and those who reside abroad for part of their adult lives are only entitled to means-tested social assistance in old age. The pension rights of immigrants, those experiencing long spells of unemployment, and those who retire early are likely to continue to decline due to work/residence requirements, changes in indexation and tighter qualifying conditions.

Unemployment and the labour-market

Despite the comparatively universalistic character of their welfare states, there are no universal unemployment benefits in Finland and Sweden. Before the onset of the 1990s crisis, two forms of unemployment benefits were in existence. Both the basic and earnings-related benefits were (and still are) conditional on a minimum period of employment. While unemployment benefits have in both countries been comparatively generous, they have been strictly conditional on being 'at the disposal of the labour-market'. The system was designed to provide a high degree of economic security during brief periods of unemployment for a small share of the working-age population.

Expenditure on unemployment benefits increased dramatically in both countries during the first half of the 1990s. In Finland, the number of unemployed people in receipt of the earnings-related unemployment benefit increased from 171,000 in 1990 to 596,000 in 1993 (Statistics Finland, 1998). This, in addition to an increase in the number of recipients of the basic daily unemployment benefit, caused unemployment benefit expenditure to increase astronomically. Finland spent some FIM 7.7 billion on unemployment benefits in 1990 (5.9 per cent of total social expenditure). By 1994, this had risen to nearly FIM 27 billion (15.2 per cent of total social expenditure) (ibid.).

The structure of unemployment benefits caused a problem in Finland as more and more of the unemployed either lacked any work history, had been only temporarily employed, or lost their entitlement to benefits due to prolonged periods of unemployment. In order to cater for this growing group, a new system of unemployment security, Labour Market Support (LMS) was introduced in Finland in 1994. This benefit is available to all unemployed people who are at the disposal of the labour-market but lack entitlement to the basic and earnings-related benefits. As the cost of unemployment was skyrocketing at the time, LMS was designed to be as cheap as possible. Consequently, it is very low and means-tested for many groups. No such new benefit system came into existence in Sweden, partly because unemployment was not as high as in Finland, and partly because the Swedish active labour-market policies were more effective at involving the unemployed in activation measures and 'recycling' them between periods of unemployment and activation (the right to earnings-related benefits in Sweden is regained after six months' participation in an active labour-market policy).

Earnings-related unemployment benefits are administered by the trade unions in both Finland and Sweden (so-called Ghent system). The sense of entitlement attached to these benefits is very high despite the fact that employee contributions cover only a small share of the cost of benefits (this share has, however, grown notably in Finland since the 1990s). Unemployment benefit contributions paid by employers and employees are seen as deferred pay. Even more importantly, trade unions in both countries are ideologically committed to earnings-related benefits as they are both a symbol of their influence and a means of influencing the level of wages (low unemployment benefits tend to exert downward pressure on wages, especially at times of high unemployment).

Support for the unemployed in Finland

The introduction of labour-market support in 1994 was the most important change in the Finnish unemployment policy in the 1990s. The basic unemployment benefit was made conditional on minimum of six months' employment history, thus leaving out the young and the long-term unemployed (HE 235, 1993). The introduction of LMS was an attempt to control the costs of unemployment: in 1994, the average LMS payment was FIM 110.1 per day which was considerably less than the average earnings-related benefit and slightly less than the average basic daily benefit. The number of LMS recipients increased from less than 124,000 to nearly 315,000 between 1994 and 1996. The duration of the average period of benefit receipt increased from 96 to 149 days (Ministry of Social Affairs and Health, 1998). LMS was on average drawn for a longer time than earnings-related or basic benefits, indicating that LMS recipients experienced greater difficulties in finding work.

Unlike unemployment benefits (basic benefit and earnings-related benefit), LMS is for many recipients conditional on participation in training or government-subsidized work in the private or public sector. LMS aimed at re-integrating vulnerable groups of unemployed people into the labour-market but it also provides much lower and weaker benefits than the unemployment benefit system and in many cases the support is heavily means-tested (HE 235, 1993). For instance, long-term unemployed adults had their support reduced by 75 per cent and then to 50 per cent if their spouse's earnings exceeded a certain threshold.

The introduction of LMS and subsequent cuts in it were possible and fairly easy because of the weakness of the recipient group. The recipient group is unorganized and diffuse, comprising young, non-unionized people and the long-term unemployed, who in many cases saw retirement as a more realistic and desirable option than finding a new permanent job. The LMS has gradually been made more means-tested and more conditional on participation in work or training. The Lipponen government decided in 1995 to reduce unemployment benefit expenditure by FIM 300 million by removing the LMS from under 20-year-olds who were to be put 'back in education' instead. LMS is now paid only to those who participate in activating measures. The child supplement in LMS was cut by 40 per cent, whereas a similar supplement in basic and earnings-related unemployment benefits remained untouched. The waiting period for LMS was extended from three to four months, in addition to which five qualifying days were introduced (HE 172, 1995; *Helsingin Sanomat*

[Finnish daily newspaper] 1995a and 1995b). From 1996 onwards, the tighter qualifying conditions have applied to all under 25-year-olds. LMS is now conditional on participation in activating measures, and the waiting period for first-time labour-market entrants with no educational qualification was extended to five months (HE 75, 1996).

Some cuts in unemployment benefits were accomplished in Finland but they were less extensive and much more difficult than alterations in LMS, and both the centre-right government and the rainbow coalition experienced severe setbacks in trying to trim the benefits of organized workers. The Aho government was in fact confronted with the threat of a general strike or very extensive strikes on three separate occasions and even the Lipponen government had one serious confrontation with the trade unions over unemployment benefits. At the onset of the crisis in 1991, the Aho government proposed increasing employee contributions to unemployment benefit funds and freezing the unemployment benefit index (HE 143, 1991). Trade union protest resulted in the withdrawal of these proposals (State Council, 1991a, 1991b). The second clash between the Aho government and trade unions took place in autumn 1992, when the government proposed shortening the maximum benefit period from 500 to 400 days, cutting earnings-related benefits by 20 per cent after 130 days of unemployment and increasing the number of qualifying days from five to seven (HE 289, 1992). These proposals were withdrawn in the face of trade union protest.

While the centre-right government did not manage to make any substantial cuts in earnings-related or basic unemployment benefits, it did have some success in limiting the number of people eligible for unemployment benefits (HE 337, 1992, HE 338, 1992). The rules concerning the obligation to accept employment were also tightened (HE 359, 1992). Refusal to take up full-time employment on offer has since 1993 led to loss of benefit even when the wage offered is lower than the unemployment benefit (Kosunen, 1997: 58).

In order to avoid the confrontational atmosphere that prevailed during the centre-right government, the Lipponen government initiated tripartite negotiations over unemployment benefit restructuring in March 1996. After these negotiations failed to reach a compromise, the government had to take the responsibility for most restructuring measures. Although the Lipponen government did not manage to push through its entire agenda on unemployment benefits cuts, it managed to extend the qualifying working condition for unemployment benefit from six to ten months, to increase the qualifying days to seven and to increase the age limit for receiving earnings-related unemployment benefits until retirement from 55 to 57 years (HE 72, 1996). While the modifications in earnings-related benefits were very small, the Lipponen government managed to achieve more cuts in this area than its centre-right predecessor, which presented many plans for cutting back earnings-related benefits but was almost completely defeated every time by trade union protest.

Support for the unemployed in Sweden

In Sweden unemployment benefits are paid for 300 days (450 days for those over 55) (Olli, 1996: 56, 116). The income replacement level was decreased from 90 to 80 per cent in 1993. A five-day waiting period which had been abolished in the 1980s was also reintroduced. The social democratic government further reduced the income replacement level to 75 per cent between January 1996 and September 1997 (Prop. (1994/95): 150). This measure was heavily criticized by the unions, but they accepted it after the government promised that the cut was only temporary. Simultaneously with the reintroduction of the 80 per cent replacement level, employee contributions to union unemployment benefits were slightly increased, the employment condition was extended from five to six months, and those participating in certain active labour-market policies ceased to build up entitlement to unemployment benefits.

As in Finland, new benefits were introduced for the young unemployed in Sweden. The so-called development guarantee has been available for young persons between the ages of 20 and 24 from the beginning of 1998 (SAP, 1997c). If a young person has not managed to find employment within 90 days, municipal authorities can organize appropriate training or a work project for him or her. As with the Finnish LMS, the development guarantee is very small and frequently supplemented by social assistance (*Dagens Nyheter*, 1999).

The Persson government lost an important battle with the Swedish public and the LO in the winter of 1996/1997 (*Dagens Nyheter*, 1996c). The social democrats put forward a number of proposals regarding unemployment benefits which the unions and the unemployed considered unfair and inappropriate (SAP, 1996). For the first time ever, Swedish trade unions were openly and on a large scale protesting against a social democratic government. The proposals would have tightened the qualifying conditions for unemployment benefits considerably. They included extending the qualifying condition for basic benefits from five to nine months and for earnings-related benefits to one year, and increasing the number of waiting days from five to six. Instead of being based on income during the five highest earning months, they were to be based on earnings during the last 12 months in work (*Dagens Nyheter*, 1996b). There was to be an 'outer parenthesis' for unemployment benefits, a maximum duration of 600 days at a time, after which a working period of six months or longer was required to re-qualify for benefits (SAP, 1996). In combination with some changes in labour legislation which were intended to make temporary contracts easier, these proposals alarmed the unions and unemployed persons who staged mass protests in Stockholm and elsewhere in Sweden. In the face of this opposition the government gave in and abandoned the proposals.

Social assistance

Even in the absence of any cutbacks, high unemployment alters the character of institutional welfare states. The clearest example of this is the increased role of benefits of last resort, and social assistance in particular, in Finland and Sweden in the 1990s.

Means-tested benefits relate uneasily to the institutional welfare state model. These welfare states are supposed to, and strive to, secure everyone a comparatively high standard of living firstly through employment, and failing this, with the help of universal and earnings-related income transfers. Residual benefits are an admission of problems in this design. During periods of high unemployment some individuals are unable to reach a sufficiently high level of consumption with the help of the transfer system since, although there are some universal transfers, high benefit levels are closely linked to recent and regular employment history.

The importance of social assistance as minimum income guarantee increased markedly in both countries during the early and mid-1990s as the number of people receiving social assistance, total expenditure and the length of the period during which assistance was paid all increased. In Finland, expenditure on social assistance increased by 80 per cent from the beginning of the decade to the worst years of the recession (Ministry of Social Affairs and Health, 1996: 7). In 1996, when expenditure was at its highest, nearly 12 per cent of the Finnish population received social assistance (Ukkola, 1999: 2). Throughout the 1990s, on average 10 per cent of the Finnish population were receiving social assistance. The social assistance system had clearly not been designed to provide or to supplement the incomes of such a large proportion of the population.

While the explosion in the number of social assistance recipients was less dramatic in Sweden, the number of people receiving social assistance increased particularly among young people and the long-term unemployed, and the cost of social assistance increased from SEK 6 billion to SEK 12.4 billion between 1990 and 1997. The increase in Sweden was not as dramatic as in Finland because of lower unemployment and the efficiency of active labour-markets in transferring people from 'passive' benefit recipiency to periods of active education and training. The percentage of the Swedish population in receipt of social assistance increased from 5.9 per cent in 1989 to 8.1 per cent in 1994 (Statistics Sweden, 1996). The average length of the period during which social assistance was paid out increased from four months in 1990 to five and a half months in 1995–1998 (Socialstyrelsen, 1999).

Although expenditure on benefits of last resort increased dramatically, these schemes were not particularly good cut-back targets because they still absorbed a relatively small share of total social expenditure. Despite the dramatic growth in the number of social assistance recipients in Finland and despite the fact that social assistance expenditure tripled between 1989 and 1996, the share of social assistance expenditure of all public social expenditure was only 1.6 per cent in 1996 (HE 217, 1997). Its relatively low cost and the increased bureaucratization that would have resulted from more stringent means-testing served to discourage extensive cuts in social assistance. Social assistance was also a crucial policy tool in preventing a massive increase in poverty and an inequality. 'Taking from the poor' would have appeared particularly callous at a time of economic crisis.

As social assistance was already means-tested and paid out in small amounts, the cuts in it tended to be very marginal. Cuts through index-freezing are less visible than direct cuts in the amount of social assistance, and were a favoured method in the case of social assistance. While the level of social assistance payments was not significantly cut, a number of other measures made social assistance more tightly means-tested or otherwise more difficult to obtain. Simultaneously with the introduction of a national minimum payment in Sweden (Prop. (1996/97): 124), municipalities were given more freedom to decide the size of the non-predetermined components of social assistance which has in some cases led to great differences in social assistance payments between municipalities (SAP, 1997a). The right of social assistance applicants to appeal against decisions about eligibility for assistance has also been restricted in Sweden (SOU, 2000: 3). In March 1998, a number of changes were made in the Finnish social assistance system that were intended to make the recipients more 'cost conscious'. Children's personal allowances were cut, and instead of 100 per cent (as in the old system), 93 per cent of reasonable housing costs are now taken into account in calculating the amount of assistance (HE 217, 1997; *Helsingin Sanomat*, 1997). It also became possible to request applicants to present their bank statements; this discourages those with savings or income from the black market from applying for social assistance.

Elements of the work line were introduced in the social assistance systems of both countries in the 1990s (Politisk redovisning No. 6, February 1997). The National Board of Health and Welfare in Sweden ruled in 1992 that nobody should be punished for refusing to work for less than the wage agreed upon in incomes policy negotiations and without entitlement to social benefits. A stricter interpretation of the duty to be at the disposal of the labour-market emerged gradually in the 1990s (Socialstyrelsen, 1992). Municipalities were given more freedom to adapt the system to local circumstances and to tighten the work line through obliging benefit recipients to actively look for work or a training placement. If the social assistance recipient failed to participate in these activating measures, the municipal social welfare board was entitled to reduce the amount of social assistance or to deny it altogether (*Dagens Nyheter*, 1996a; SFS, 1997: 313). In Finland, refusal to take up work or training has led to a 20 per cent reduction in the basic amount of social assistance since 1996, and it is now possible to penalise 'work-shy' social assistance recipients by a 40 per cent cut (VNP, 1995).

While these sanctions are quite strong, they do not represent a completely novel feature in the Finnish and Swedish welfare states as the obligation to work has always been fairly strong, especially in Sweden. Sweden's active labour-market policies, one of the most striking examples of the extensive scope of the Swedish welfare state, have always embodied the idea that everyone has both a right and a duty to work and that only paid work will uphold the welfare state. In other words, increased emphasis on the duty to work does not in itself go against the grain of social democratic welfare states.

Conclusion

The main conclusions to be drawn from the above discussion are that changes in the Finnish and Swedish welfare states in the 1990s were for the most part limited in scope; that these changes were driven by determination to retain the key features of institutional welfare systems in the face of economic crisis rather than a political will to dismantle the welfare state; and that the Finnish and Swedish welfare states are strong because their structure is such that they enjoy solid popular support. Change in welfare state structures is not always system-threatening, indeed some degree of change is essential for the preservation of most complex systems, whether they be welfare states, political parties or private companies. In order to survive the challenges of economic crisis and increased internationalization, the Finnish and Swedish welfare states had to embrace a measure of change, but this did not alter their overall character fundamentally.

While the restructuring of institutional welfare states is evidently not impossible, the structure of these welfare states nonetheless protects them against retrenchment, even during economic crises. The fundamental reason for this resilience lies in the kind of politics that institutional welfare states produce: instead of creating divisions, they bring about unity, that is to say large constituencies in favour of social policies. As a consequence of the popularity of social policies in institutional welfare states, there is only a very small 'market' among the electorate for anti-welfare parties and ideas. When problems such as the difficulties in financing future pensions are recognized, appropriate policies are developed through negotiation and consensus-building. When government steps outside the consensus, as in the case of unemployment benefit cut-backs, it finds it difficult to sustain its reforms.

However, this chapter will not end with the pronouncement that 'all is and will be well' with the Finnish and Swedish welfare states. Rather, it is interesting to make some prognoses of future developments on the basis of the small changes that we have traced. There are indications that the role of universal income transfers will weaken as these benefits are not perceived to act as work incentives (being paid to all without any need to demonstrate merit) and as they no longer meet the income security needs of increasingly prosperous populations. There are pressures to bring taxes closer to the EU average, which would jeopardize the financing of universal benefits. As a result of these developments, the Nordic model may in future move increasingly towards a mixture of residual and earnings-related social security (as has already happened in the case of pensions). This in turn has implications for the future pattern of cut-backs: in most cases it is politically easier to reduce means-tested than earnings-related benefits. Also, the increased emphasis on earning benefits may bring about a more extreme insider–outsider problem that has existed in the Nordic countries until now, particularly during and as a result of periods of high unemployment.

The Finnish and Swedish welfare states are likely to remain highly distinctive and different from the other welfare state models: most importantly, the extensive public health and social service sector is likely to undergo only moderate privatization as demand for more personalized services increases, and the bulk of these services will be financed and provided by the public sector. In short, to finish with a bold prediction: in the long run the Finnish and Swedish welfare states are likely to become more 'central European' with the exception of the continued existence of an extensive public service sector.

3 Reshaping the Social Policy-Making Framework in France

Bruno Palier

Among the 'frozen' continental European welfare states (Esping-Andersen, 1996), the French social welfare system is often seen as one of the most 'immovable objects' (Pierson, 1998: 558, note 8). In France, social expenditure continued to increase rapidly throughout the 1980s, but no fundamental reform seems to have been implemented in health services or in old age pensions and attempts to introduce reforms have been fiercely opposed by strikes and demonstrations, especially in 1995. This gloomy picture must be modified. Reforms in unemployment and pension insurance for private sector workers were introduced under European pressure in the early 1990s. However, it remains true that, until recently, change has been difficult to implement in France as in other Bismarckian social insurance welfare systems.

Some of the peculiarities of the French social policy-making system help to explain the obstacles hindering major retrenchment: a highly popular but particularly fragmented social insurance system, financed mainly by social contributions; numerous divided trade unions, particularly keen to keep their position in the system since they are weak in industrial relations; a state relatively weak in this field and thus obliged to negotiate with the other social protection actors. However, French governments have adopted structural reforms in the early 1990s which imply the abandonment of some elements of the French welfare tradition and its progressive transformation: the development of means tested benefits, the growing importance of tax finance, and the empowerment of state representatives within the system at the expense of the social partners. Resistance to change may now be progressively overcome, leading to new patterns of social protection in France. This chapter describes the French social welfare system and policy-making framework and the challenges it faces, and then moves on to analyse how the institutional structure has delayed political reform but is itself now undergoing change.

The French social policy-making framework

The French welfare system

The current French social welfare system is mainly based on a specific set of institutions called *la Sécurité sociale*, built up from 1945 to the 1970s. *La Sécurité sociale* in France covers not only income maintenance, but also provision for health care and some aspects of personal social services. The main component is the social insurance system. There is also a non-contributory element, which caters for those who do not have access to insurance benefits. The most striking change of the last two decades is that this second component has grown considerably, leading almost to a two-tier system.

Social insurance clearly reflects the Bismarckian tradition: in France, most benefits are earnings-related: entitlement is conditional upon a contribution record and financing is provided mainly by employers' and employees' contributions. The system is divided into a number of different programmes (*branches*): health care, old age, family and unemployment insurance, and into different schemes (*régimes*) covering different occupational groups.

The social insurance system is highly fragmented. It consists of several *régimes*, a term that is applied to embrace both a specific organization and the people covered by it. There is a set of compulsory basic schemes, which all workers must join, and a further set of complementary schemes, improving the level of coverage, some compulsory some not. Each scheme insures groups of people working in a single economic sector. There are more than 500, including the *régime général* (employees in industry and trade, some 60 per cent of the population), hundreds of special schemes (*régimes spéciaux* and *régimes particuliers* nearly 20 per cent[1]), some 20 other schemes (*régimes autonomes*) for self-employed people (approximately 10 per cent) and the scheme for the agricultural sector (*Mutualité sociale agricole*, supervised by the Ministry of Agriculture).

The *régime général* is the most important scheme. It delivers health care, sickness, old age and family benefits, and is responsible for about 60 per cent of payments from all compulsory schemes. Other schemes cover only some of the risks, with various levels of contributions and benefits. Special and particular *régimes* tend to be more generous for health care and pensions. Autonomous and some agricultural schemes deliver less generous benefits, but require a lower level of contribution. Family benefits are the most unified area, nearly all falling under the responsibility of the *régime général*.

The different social security schemes are financially autonomous and have several sources of income, although the bulk of their funds comes from the contributions of those 'socially insured' (*cotisations sociales salariales et patronales*). Social insurance contributions play a greater role in the social security system in France than in any other European country (Table 1.2). Before 1997, they accounted for 80 per cent of the total revenue of the social protection system in France and about 90 per cent of the revenue of the *régime général*. Contributions are proportional to earnings, although in the case of pensions, there is an income threshold (called *plafond*, ceiling). The proportion paid for each risk is different. Taken together the contributions paid by employer and employee amount to half of each person's gross wage.

All the schemes are made up of different funds (*Caisses*) organized at national, regional and local levels. They are non-governmental agencies, except for the national ones. Their staff is neither paid by the state, nor under its authority. Each is headed by a governing board (*Conseil d'Administration*) comprising representatives of employers and employees, with a chairman elected from their ranks, and a director of the Fund, who is appointed by the governing board in consultation with the Ministry of Social Affairs. The schemes were originally intended to have some independence from the State, on the principle of *démocratie sociale* (management by the social partners). This means that the system should be managed by those who pay for and have an interest in it, subject to only limited supervision by the State, and decentralized, with small, local offices, easily accessible to the public.

The supervisory role of the state over *Sécurité sociale* is called *la tutelle* (tutelage). While the government's role is crucial, laying down the basic principles of the social security system, setting benefit and contribution levels, and attempting to ensure the system's financial stability, the lines of responsibility have never been entirely clear. Many decisions are taken through negotiation between trade unions and employers' representatives, with more or less visible pressure by the state. As a result, the problems faced by *la Sécurité sociale* were not seen as an institutional matter of government policy, its intervention being perceived as exceptional, even if the exception became the rule, implicitly in the 1980s and more explicitly by the late 1990s. This growing intervention by the state is resented by the social partners, thus structuring the politics of welfare around the opposition between governmental parties (left or right) on the one hand, and the social partners on the other.

The party system

France is a parliamentary democracy with a 'semi-Presidential' political regime. Political life in France is organized around two major elections: the election of members of Parliament, and the Presidential election, choosing the *President de la République*. Both elections use a two-stage ballot, the Parliamentary election being organized in 577 constituencies. The system produces majority governments, but the fact that the ballot is in two stages with some candidates eliminated after the first round leads to a fragmented party system with many political parties.

On the left, the most important party is the Socialist Party (PS), created in 1969. It has grown rapidly during the late 1970s on the basis of the *'Union de la gauche'* with the Communist Party and the affirmation of socialism *'à la française'*, which calls for rupture with capitalism and wants to 'change life'. After the victory of François Mitterrand in 1981, the socialist government, under Pierre Mauroy as Prime Minister, attempted a traditional Keynesian macroeconomic policy accompanied by nationalization of the main banks and industries. Economic problems (rising public deficit and debt, pressure on the franc, increasing unemployment) were so great by 1983, that the policy was changed, leading to a 'pause in the reforms', rigorous budgetary policies and wage restraint. The policies of 'modernization' introduced by the second socialist Prime Minister, Laurent Fabius (1984–1986) did not prevent defeat in 1986. After 1988, the new relative majority, still lead by the socialists under Michel Rocard as Prime Minister and Mitterrand as President (re-elected in May 1988), shifted the focus to the European integration process. However, the multiplication of financial scandals and the rise of political conflict within the PS damaged the party and led to defeat in 1993. Since 1995, under Lionel Jospin's leadership, the PS has started to restore its image under the slogan of 'realism from the left' . The strategy of alliance with the other main left parties (*'gauche plurielle'*) led to victory in 1997. Since then, the Jospin government has combined concessions to its left constituency (creation of public jobs for the young, imposition of the 35-hour week, tax cuts for the poorest) with adaptation to the new economic environment (more privatization than any right-wing government, tax reduction on stock option, the use of the 35-hour week to promote greater flexibility in work practices and encourage moderation in wage demands.

Relations between the Communist Party (Parti Communiste Français, PCF) and the PS are complicated. The PCF was created in 1920, and was the leading left party in all elections from 1945 to the late 1970s. In 1974, they allied with PS in the *'programme commun'*, which included nationalization. The PCF participated in the first socialist government (from 1981 to 1984) but quitted it in 1984, opposing the 'modernization line' but supporting the government in Parliament. During the 1980s, the PCF experienced internal conflicts and its electoral fortunes declined (from 16 per cent of the vote in 1981 to 11.2 per cent in 1992 and 9.2 per cent in 1993). Confronted with the fall of the soviet model and the necessity to develop an alternative political position to that of the PS, the PCF did not regain influence in the political arena until 1997, when the PS needed its support for parliamentary majority.

New left political parties have emerged since the mid-1980s, following the relative decline of the PS and PCF: the ecologist (*les Verts*), the *Mouvement des Citoyens*, the *Radicaux de Gauche*, which all constitute elements of the current 'plural majority' (*majorité plurielle*). In the extreme left, two movements are gaining influence (*Lutte Ouvrière* and *Ligue Communiste*

Révolutionnaire) with more than 5 per cent in the 1995 Presidential election and MPs elected at the last European election.

The leading party on the right during the 1980s and the 1990s is the RPR (*Rassemblement pour la République*), created by Jacques Chirac in 1976. It is the heir of Gaullism but tends to ideological inconsistency. For example, Chirac claimed to represent French Labour (*travaillisme à la française*) when Prime Minister from 1974 to 1976. From 1981 to 1998, he claimed that France needed to pursue neo-liberal policies, although he had not implemented this as Prime Minister from 1986 to 1988, except through some minor privatizations of the formerly nationalized firms. Internal divisions within the RPR have created further complications since Edouard Balladur, Prime Minister from 1993 to 1995, and candidate in the Presidential election in 1995, tried to implement a 'sensible liberal policy'. Jacques Chirac, also candidate in 1995, organized a populist campaign against the *'fracture sociale'*, denying that wage increases threatened economic growth. After six months in power, he reversed policies yet again, on the grounds that austerity was essential to meet the Maastricht criteria. This in turn lead to the Juppé plan in 1995, analysed below. The multiplication of political mistakes lead to the defeat in 1997.

RPR can only form a majority in alliance with other right-wing parties. The other main right-wing party is UDF (*Union pour la Démocratie Française*), founded in 1978 by former President Giscard d'Estaing, which includes Christian democrats, centrists and liberals. Its influence has always been second to that of the RPR, but its support is absolutely necessary to form a majority. After the defeat in the regional election in 1997, the liberals left UDF to create DL (*Démocratie Libérale*). Meanwhile, some important members of the RPR left to create the RPF (*Rassemblement pour la France*), committed to the defence of 'souverainism' (or euro-scepticism). Since 1983, the *Front National* (FN) has become an extreme right party of growing importance (from 10 per cent of the vote in the late 1980s to about 15 per cent in 1995 and 1997). The traditional right has never pursued coalition with FN at the national level. In 1998, FN split in two. The deputy leader left to create another extreme right-wing movement: MNR (*Mouvement National Républicain*). Both parties failed to achieve significant support in the last European election, and their influence seems to have decreased since. Their performance in the 2002 national election will confirm their status.

The political system

In the immediate post-war period, the French political system suffered from instability. The Constitution of the fifth Republic, adopted in 1958, was designed to give more power to the executive branch. The President can 'dissolve' the Parliament but the Parliament cannot dismiss the President. The Parliament can only dismiss the Prime Minister and his government, an event which has occurred only once in 42 years. Moreover, the executive can initiate legislation and can force the Parliament to vote

Table 3.1   *French Presidents and Prime Ministers, 1981–2000 and Parliamentary Election Results*

	1981– 1984	1984– 1986	1986– 1988	1988– 1991	1991– 1992	1992– 1993	1993– 1995	1995– 1997	1997...
President	François Mitterrand			François Mitterrand				Jacques Chirac	
Prime Minister	Pierre Mauroy	Laurent Fabius	Jacques Chirac	Michel Rocard	Edith Cresson	Pierre Bérégovoy	Edouard Balladur	Alain Juppé	Lionel Jospin

Parliamentary Election Results (percentage)

	1981	1986	1988	1993	1997
Communist (PCF)	16.2	9.8	11.3	9.2	9.9
Socialist (PS)	37.5	31.2	37.0	17.6	23.5
Centre (UDF)	21.7	15.5	18.5	19.1	14.2
Gaullist (RPR)	21.2	27.0	19.2	20.4	15.7
National Front (FN)	0.2	9.9	9.8	12.4	14.9
Green (VERTS + GE)	1.1	1.2	0.4	7.6	6.8
Other*	2.1	5.4	3.8	13.7	15.0

on the laws it initiates. Since 1962, the head of the executive, the President, has been elected by the whole population for seven years (to be reduced to five in 2002), with no limit to the number of terms. However, there is also a second chief executive in France, the Prime Minister, nominated by the President and responsible to Parliament. This system is supposed to allow the government to act decisively in implementing reform. Why then was the French government unable to impose major reforms on the welfare state?

Part of the answer is to be found in the actual functioning of this political system. During the 1980s and 1990s, France has moved between two kinds of political regime: a semi-Presidential one, when the President and the Parliament (and therefore the Prime Minister) belong to the same political party (Table 3.1). During these phases (1981–1986, 1988–1993, 1995–1997), the President leads on policy, the Prime Minister managing implementation with the passive support of the Parliament. However, the majority was only relative from 1998 to 1993, limiting the room for manoeuvre of the different left-wing governments. When the President and the Parliamentary majority (and therefore the Prime Minister) differ, the political regime becomes more parliamentary; the Prime Minister is supposed to take the lead with the support of the Parliament, and the President acts as arbitrator. However, competition between the two heads of the executive may obstruct government action. Since 1986, France has known three periods of 'cohabitation': 1986–1988, 1993–1995 and from 1997 onwards.

In relation to the government's capacity to introduce substantial changes, one should differentiate between the periods when the same hand holds all the power and is free to impose reforms (1981–1986, 1988–1993 and 1995–1997) and the periods of cohabitation, where governments may be impeded. One would expect to see more important reforms imposed during the periods when one camp holds all the trumps, and relative inactivity at other times. However, the facts do not confirm this hypothesis. A relatively important pension reform was implemented in 1993 (under cohabitation) whereas the Juppé attempt to reform pension in 1995 (when the right held the reins of power) failed.

It may be that the rapid succession of changes in majority affects the political capacity of government. Since the presidential term is seven years and the parliamentary one five, changes in the majority can occur frequently. Since 1981 every election produced a change. There has been no substantial period of domination by one political camp, in contrast to the period from 1958 to 1981, when only the right-wing parties were in power in France, or as with the period of conservative domination in the UK from 1979 to 1997. This may weaken the capacity of one camp to impose major reform.

The rapid succession of changes in majority may have undermined the capacity of parties to pursue welfare state reforms that reflected their ideology. In any case, the approach of both sides to welfare issues converged during the 1980s and 1990s.

The social policy-making system

Historically, the French social insurance system is identified with the values of solidarity, collective effort and social justice derived from the French resistance during the Second World War, which decided a *'plan français de Sécurité sociale'*. It is also associated with the strength of social movements (Communist Party and trade union) in the immediate post-war period and presented as the result of social struggles (an *acquis social*). Since the mid 1970s, each citizen is supposed to be covered by one social insurance fund and to receive quite generous benefits from it. Meanwhile, the fragmented corporatist organization guarantees to each social group that its specific interests are addressed. As a result of the combination of all these elements, the system has created a large constituency among salaried workers. In the UK or the USA, the interest groups associated with social policies (retired people, patients, doctors, social workers) are more limited and different from the traditional political and social forces supporting welfare (Pierson, 1994). The French salaried workers' constituency is represented by the trade unions, who are legitimate participants in debate about welfare reform since the system is financed by social contribution paid on labour and since they participate in management. This particular institutional setting generates tension between governments (regardless of political persuasion) and the trade unions. The politics of welfare are not so new in France, since trade unions play a leading role in the debate and constitute a major force in deciding whether the welfare state will be an 'immovable' or a 'movable object'.

Giuliano Bonoli and I (Palier and Bonoli, 1995; Bonoli and Palier, 1996) showed that the political debate on the future of social protection in France in the mid-1990s was characterized by the opposition of two different and incompatible conceptions of what the French social protection system should look like. These two visions were not held by opposing left and right parties, but by the main political parties, right or left, on the one hand, and the social partners (the main trade unions involved in the management of the social insurance funds, sometimes joined by the employers' representatives) on the other. Governmental, political and administrative actors would like to implement major retrenchments. They also support a shift from the original structure towards a system in which the state plays a much larger role. However, a vociferous section of the labour movement opposes retrenchment, displays strong attachment to the original structure of French welfare and demands an even stricter division between the insurance and tax financed systems (mainly CGT and FO). In their view, the social insurance system should continue to cover employees only, be financed through contributions and be managed by representatives of trade unions and employers. The state tax-financed sector should continue to fulfil its function of a last resort safety net for those who do not have access to social insurance. The state should finance the latter, whereas social contributions should be confined to the finance of social insurance benefits.

The 1990s have been characterized by the alternation in government of left and right. Despite these changes in the country's leadership, the direction of reform in social policy has remained more or less constant. In fact, the right-wing government adopted pension reforms in 1993 which were prepared by their socialist predecessors and the new socialist government adopted measures in 1997 that had been planned by their right-wing predecessors. Detailed analysis of the numerous administrative reports of the 1980s and the early 1990s shows that most of the reforms implemented by either left- or right-wing governments had been planned by experts in special commissions. Accounts of French welfare politics must include more actors than the political parties. Since the French social protection system consists mainly of social insurance funds, the representatives of trade unions and of employers (*Mouvement des Entreprises de France*, MEDEF, former CNPF) are legitimate actors in the policy-making process.

In France, trade unions are weak and divided, with the rate of unionization the lowest among OECD countries. The French labour movement is highly fragmented. There are five main confederations of trade unions with different ideological orientations: CGT (*Confédération Générale du Travail*, Communist orientation); FO (*Force Ouvrière*, Socialist and Trotskyist orientation); CFDT (*Confédération Française*

Démocratique du Travail, Socialist and pragmatic orientation): CFTC (*Confédération Française des Travailleurs Chrétiens*, Catholic), and *Confédération Générale des Cadres* (white collar union). The proportion of unionized employees lies somewhere between 8 and 10 per cent (Labbé, 1996). Unions have a limited degree of influence on government policy, except in the area of social protection (Jobert, 1991). Their managerial role in social insurance is a source of legitimacy in the eyes of public opinion. In particular, the unions are often regarded as the 'defenders' of the social protection system, who oppose government attempts to retrench provision. If they are weak within French firms or in collective bargaining, French unions partly derive their importance through their mobilizing capacities where social protection reforms are concerned. No important welfare reforms could be achieved without either formal or informal agreement from at least one of the most important French trade unions.

Globalization, Europeanization and societal change in France

Within the general literature on welfare state crisis and reforms, globalization and European integration are often seen as creating specific pressures for changes. However, it is difficult to see how globalization or European integration has a direct effect on state welfare. In order to understand their possible impact, one has to examine the way the new policy environment creates pressure at particular points through specific welfare institutions. The same global forces create different problems depending on the kind of welfare institutions they affect (Sykes et al., 2001).

Globalization

The internationalization of the French economy confronted the welfare state with two major challenges. First, the greater openness of French economy from the late 1970s meant the end of traditional Keynesian reflation measures. Jacques Chirac (1974–1976) and Pierre Mauroy (1981–1982) sought to boost private consumption and thus economic activity by increasing social benefits. Both ended with a major public deficit, negative trade balance and increase in interest rates. Their failure discredited the Keynesian approach to social expenditure. Economic policy was reversed. Social expenditure was now treated as a cost and an unproductive source of public deficit rather than an investment.

Second, the internationalization of the French economy meant that it was necessary to improve the competitiveness of French firms. Contribution financing plays a bigger role in France than in any other EU country. This issue – the impact of social charges – became central to the French debate, since the high level of contributions has been understood to damage competitiveness by increasing labour costs. This claim is supported by international comparisons, which highlight the poor performance of the French economy in job creation. Between 1983 and 1991, total employment increased on average by 0.5 per cent in France, but by 1.7 per cent in the EU as a whole, 1.3 per cent in Japan and 1.9 per cent in the US (OECD, 1994: 5). After 1982, French employers started a campaign on social charges (*La bataille des charges sociales*), which led to a trend to reduce contributions on low salaries after 1993.

Europeanization

From the mid-1980s onwards, European integration meant mainly the integration of European economies into a single market. The progress towards this free open market put French firms in competition with other European companies, reinforcing the necessity to reduce non-wage costs.

After the early 1990s, European integration also included the adoption of the single currency and imposition of the Maastricht criteria. During the 1980s, one solution to the problem of financing the social security deficit was to increase the level of social contribution paid by employees rather than cut back on social spending. After Maastricht, French governments were obliged to reduce the public deficit (including the social security deficit) as well as the inflation rate, and therefore to control the growth of social expenditure. After 1992–1993, retrenching social expenditure had be included in the strategy of reducing public expenditure and public deficits in order to meet the Maastricht criteria. Commitment to the single currency lead to the imposition of sectoral reforms (especially in unemployment benefits and in pensions) and put these reforms on the political agenda in a way which had previously seemed impossible.

The main reasons for reform were, first, the increasing number of unemployed and socially excluded people, and second, the fact that population ageing put at risk the finance of social insurance pensions.

Unemployment and social exclusion

In 1974, the unemployment rate was 4.1 per cent of the active population (900,000 people). It rose to 6.4 per cent in 1980 and the symbolic threshold of 2 million was passed in 1983. The rate reached 10.1 per cent in 1985 and 10.5 per cent by 1987. It fell slightly to 8.9 per cent in 1990, but rose after 1991 to 11.6 per cent in 1995 and 12.5 per cent in 1997. Since then, unemployment has diminished steadily and fell below 10 per cent in 2000 (L'état de la France, 2000). After 1974, long-term unemployment also started to increase. In 1974, 16.9 per cent of the unemployed were jobless for more than one year, 2.5 per cent for more than two years. These proportions reached 42.7 and 21.0 per cent by 1985. The average length of unemployment was 7.6 months in 1974, 15 months in 1985, 16 months in 1998 and 14.8 months in 1999 (L'état de la France, 2000).

Mass unemployment and social exclusion revealed specific problems of the predominantly contributory social insurance system. It is unable to meet the needs of those who have never worked or have exhausted their entitlement, and reinforces social exclusion, particularly among young people and the long-term unemployed.

Population ageing

In France, the 1980s have seen a growing concern over the issue of financing the pay-as-you-go pension system. Between 1985 and 1993 a series of government reports were published.[2] All take a pessimistic view of the future of French pensions, and call for savings. In 1999, another report (Charpin, 1999) showed that population ageing will accelerate after 2006 in France, when the baby boom generation will reach the retirement age of sixty. If current trends continue (low fertility, low immigration and a falling mortality rate) one French person in three will be over 60 by 2040. The dependency ratio of retired to active people will rise from 4:10 to 7:10. The decrease in the number of both children and unemployed people should release resources for pensions, but the financial viability of the pension system after 2010 is called into question.

Social exclusion and ageing were identified as important problems by experts and government reports in the early 1980s. However, no major reforms were implemented, for two reasons: first, the strength of the status quo prevented government from cutting unemployment insurance or old age pensions; second, governments could pursue another solution which was more attractive politically but more damaging from an economic perspective: increasing social contributions to pay for higher spending.

Before retrenchment

The increase of social contributions

For a considerable period, the most politically feasible policy was to increase social contributions instead of trying to cut social spending. France, like other European countries, encountered severe economic problems after the first oil shock. However, the impact of these difficulties on welfare was mediated by the distinctive institutional structure of the system. As the social insurance system is not formally part of the state in France, its budget is presented separately from the state budget. A 'Social security deficit' (or *trou de la Sécurité sociale*), appeared in 1974. It was treated differently from the state deficit. After years of positive balances, the deficit of the main social insurance scheme (*régime général*) was 2.8 per cent of its resources in 1974, 4 per cent in 1978, around 2 per cent from 1981 to 1987, between 0.9 per cent and 1.8 per cent from 1988 to 1992, and around 5 per cent from 1993 to 1996. It has since diminished to 0.3 per cent in 1999 (reports of SESI (service des statistiques, des Etudes et des systèmes d'information)).

During the 1970s and the 1980s, this deficit was understood in two different ways. Governments, experts and economists analysed it as a consequence of decreasing resources (lower growth rates leading to smaller wage increases and a rise in the number of inactive or unemployed people who pay no contributions) and rising expenses (more unemployed people, higher demand for health and old age provision). For them, the solution was either to increase the resources (social contributions) or cut expenses. However, trade unions had a different interpretation. They claimed that the deficit resulted from the state's use of social insurance funds to pay for non-contributory benefits (such as social minima for poor elderly people or lone parents). For the defenders of the social insurance systems, the 'undue charges' (*les charges indues*) explained the deficit, which could be removed if the state paid for its own welfare policies (national solidarity benefits implying vertical redistribution). The deficit did not justify reduction in the level of the contributory benefits for which workers had paid in their contributions.

For at least 15 years, governments have avoided major retrenchment and have preferred to increase social contributions (Table 3.2). Instead of developing an accusatory rhetoric against the welfare state which would have provoked the whole population and the trade unions, they recognized the importance of the *Sécurité sociale*, but underlined the dangers of its current situation and presented measures which were aimed not at reforming the system but only at restoring its viability. Until the early 1990s, no French government, left or right, even the most neo-liberal (under Jacques Chirac as Prime Minister, from 1986 to 1988) attempted to dismantle the system, or even to change it.

From 1975 to 1993, unless an election was imminent, every announcement of a *Sécurité sociale* deficit was followed by the presentation of a *plan de redressement des comptes de la Sécurité sociale* (programme for balancing the social insurance system's budget). The plans consisted typically of contribution increases for employees and limited economizing measures, mainly in health. Between 1975 and 1992 the plans resulted in higher user

Table 3.2   *The transformation of tax structures in France (%)*

	Average 1970–1975	Average 1981–1985	Average 1988–1992	1992	1995
State taxation (VAT, income tax, corporation tax, capital tax, oil tax)	59.2	53.4	51.4	50.1	51.5
Social contributions	39.0	44.8	46.1	47.4	46.2
European tax	1.8	1.8	2.5	2.5	2.3

Source: INSEE, *Tableaux de l'économie française 1996–1997*, Palier, 2000

charges and a gradual reduction in the level of reimbursement of health care charges, from 76.5 per cent in 1980 to 73.9 per cent by 1995. During the same period, all contributory benefits such as sickness pay, old age pensions and unemployment insurance benefits increased or were at best stabilized. Consequently, social expenditure continued to increase rapidly until the mid-1980s, and more slowly ever since from 19.4 per cent of GDP in 1974 to 27.3 per cent in 1985 and 27.75 per cent in 1992 (Palier, 2000; SESI, various years).

Increasing costs have always been compensated by extra resources. During the 1980s, while they were decreasing the level of direct income taxation, French governments also increased the level of employees' contributions. The share of contributions in taxation has increased sharply as well as their proportion of GDP: social contributions amounted to less than 20 per cent of French GDP in 1978 and almost 23 per cent by 1985. It has stabilized at this level ever since (Palier, 2000).

Until the early 1990s, there was no real incentive in France to reform social spending, since its growth was financed through contribution increases. It was only when the social security deficit became too large to be financed through another rise in contributions (after 1992) in a context of economic recession (especially in 1993), and when the economic constraints of the European single market and single currency became stronger, that French government changed their strategy and started to implement limited retrenchments.

Retrenchment strategies for unemployment and old age pensions

Government retrenchment strategies for unemployment and pensions were based on a distinction between the appropriate areas of responsibility of social insurance (to be financed by social contributions) and national solidarity (where tax finance is appropriate). Unions accepted retrenchment measures in exchange for tax-financed benefits for those who did not contribute and a shift in the financing of some non-contributory benefits from contribution to taxation.

Policies for unemployed people: from 'traitement social' to activation

Policy for unemployed people developed in three distinct phases. During the 1980s, the main themes are the stabilization of relatively generous unemployment insurance benefits and the implementation of the 'social treatment' (early retirement) of unemployment. In the early 1990s, some structural changes were introduced, with the removal of early retirement measures, the new role of the *Revenue Minimum d'Insertion* (RMI) and the unemployment insurance reform of 1992. The late 1990s were characterized by the development of active policies.

The 1980s

Unemployment insurance, independent from state provision, was created in 1958, through agreement between the 'social partners' (representatives of employers and employees). The system provided various different benefits, which were periodically increased from 1974 to the early 1980s. From 1982 to 1992 there were several attempts to rationalize the system and to stabilize benefit levels, which remained very generous compared to those in the UK. In 1982, half of those unemployed received benefits equivalent to 80 per cent of their previous salary for the first year. Benefits were then reduced to 75 per cent for the next nine months (Join-Lambert, 1997: 575). This first (minor) reduction in benefit was implemented in 1984, when two non-contributory tax-financed benefits (*Allocation d'Insertion* and *Allocation de Solidarité Spécifiaue*) were created. During the 1980s, the main issue was not benefit levels, but problems in rationalizing the development of the system, which the state was unable to control and which the social partners found difficult to manage through negotiation.

The second development has been called *le traitement social du chômage* (social treatment of unemployment). These policies are designed to remove older workers from the labour-market by lowering the retirement age from 65 to 60 in 1981 and encouraging early retirement: (840,000 people retired early in 1975, 159,000 in 1979, 317,000 in 1981 and 705,000 in 1983; Bichot, 1997: 132). The programme also creates 'subsidized jobs' (*emplois aidés*) for the young and the long-term unemployed. This role of the state as employer of second resort can be illustrated by the numerous contracts offered to the unemployed through the different insertion policies (for example the *Stages de réinsertion en alternance, Action de réinsertion et de formation, contrats de retour à l'emploi*; Outin,

1997). The re-insertion dimension of the RMI played an important role in these policies.

RMI guarantees a minimum level of resources to anyone aged 25 or over, which takes the form of a means-tested differential benefit. The basic rates in January 2000 were slightly above FF 2,500 for a single person, and FF 3,800 for a couple. In addition, the RMI has a re-insertion dimension, in the form of a contract between the recipient and 'society'. Recipients must commit themselves to take part in re-insertion programmes, as stated in a contract signed by the recipient and a social worker. Such programmes can be either job-seeking, vocational training or activities designed to enhance the recipient's independence.

The early 1990s

Retrenchment in welfare for the unemployed did not arrive on the political agenda until the early 1990s. Since the late 1980s, early retirement has been cut back, to 433,000 by 1988 (Bichot, 1997: 132). The unemployment insurance system was reformed in 1992 through an agreement between the social partners following a change in the alliance between employers and some employees' representatives. The reform meant that all unemployment insurance benefits were replaced by the *Allocation Unique Dégressive* (AUD). The new unemployment insurance benefit is payable only for a limited period of time, depending on contribution record. The amount of the benefit decreases with time and entitlement expires after 30 months. Afterwards, unemployed people must rely on tax-financed means-tested benefits.

The level and the volume of unemployment benefits started to fall after 1992, more rapidly for means-tested than for insurance benefits (Bonoli and Palier, 2000). As AUD was delivering smaller benefits for a shorter period, RMI increasingly functioned as a safety net for the long-term unemployed (Outin, 1997). In January 1999, 1,112,108 households, or 3 per cent of the population, were receiving RMI.

Insurance benefits in the area of unemployment compensation seem to have suffered less in France than in other countries (especially the UK) until the late 1990s. The French benefit, with replacement rates of between 75 per cent and 57.4 per cent of salary for the first six months is obviously very significant to a middle-class person, and sharp cuts in benefit levels would be unacceptable. The involvement of the trade unions as representatives of claimants in the management of the French scheme may also account for its resistance to change, as is indicated by the difficulties experienced in the 1980s and the fact that the 1992 reform required agreement between the social partners. Comparison between insurance and means-tested benefits in France shows that spending on the former (run by employers and trade unions) is still rising while the latter (ASS and RMI, financed and controlled by the state) did not increase between the late 1980s and 1995. When the state directly controls the volume and the level of benefits (as for ASS and RMI), retrenchment through gradual erosion is easier to implement than in social insurance.

The late 1990s

The main activation strategy in France is based on reducing the level of social contributions which is believe to damage competitiveness and create unemployment by increasing labour costs. Since 1993, a strategy of reducing labour costs by cutting contribution levels for lower-paid workers and subsidizing part-time and casual employment has been pursued. This strategy was strengthened in 1997. Since then, subsidized public employment for young people (under 26) has been introduced and the working week cut to 35-hours. Meanwhile, the employers' representatives have initiated a process of social negotiation to reform the employment and social protection system. This recently produced an agreement on a further unemployment insurance reform.

Since 1997, about 230,000 *emplois jeunes* have been created in the public sector (education, police, local government) and the voluntary sector. These jobs are paid at the minimum wage level, with the state paying 80 per cent of the cost. They are intended to respond to new local needs (assistance to teachers, neighbourhood security, environmental work) and to last for five years, after which the private sector would take responsibility. As a result, the rate of youth unemployment, previously high in France, is falling. However, there is little private support and the government is preparing a programme to extend publicly subsidized work. This programme has succeeded in reducing the level of youth unemployment while subsidizing (and developing) low-paid work in the public sector.

The second major social programme of the Jospin government was the reduction of working time. The supposedly 'dirigist' laws 'imposing' the 35-hour week are in reality intended to invigorate social dialogue within firms, encourage more flexible work organization, reduce wage costs and promote work sharing. The two laws (1998 and 2000) required the social partners to negotiate the application of the 35-hour week in re-organizing work within firms. While the head of the employers' organization (MEDEF) protested against these 'dirigist' laws, many agreements have been signed by the employers at branch and firm level. They saw an opportunity to freeze wage increase for a while (against a working time reduction which could be compensated by job creation but supported by the growth of productivity obtained through the re-organization of work), to re-negotiate social advantages included in former social agreements (parental leave, days off) as well as implementing a standard working year. In addition, the second 35-hours law raises the threshold for reduced social contributions from 1 to 1.8 times the minimum wage.

If there has been no national social pact in France, the 35-hour week seems to be playing an equivalent role, since the content of the collective agreements includes the key components of national pacts in other European countries: work-sharing, flexibility and wage moderation (Rhodes, 2000).

Moreover, the employers' organization has recently initiated a movement to re-negotiate the 'social constitution' (*refondation sociale*). These medium term negotiations put the revision of collective agreements on unemployment insurance, complementary pension schemes, labour-market organization and the role of the social partners within the social protection system on the agenda. The content of the measures proposed by the employers seems quite neo-liberal: they propose the extension of private pension funds, and a new five-year private employment contract to replace the current indeterminate duration contract (*contrat à durée indéterminée*). Within this framework, MEDEF, CFDT and CFTC have recently signed an agreement on the reform of the unemployment insurance system to reduce the unemployment contributions paid by both employers and employees. In exchange for the removal of the tapering of the unemployment allowance (AUD) over time, they agreed allowances should be suspended for all job seekers who refuse three job offers at a level appropriate to their ability. The state intervened to smooth the passage of the agreement and ensure that the personal evaluation and support planned in the agreement were offered to all unemployed people. However, there is an ongoing process of negotiation between certain social partners (MEDEF, CFDT, CFTC) which may be understood as developing a concerted strategy to adapt and modernize the French economy and social relations. Such a social dialogue has not yet emerged in relation to pensions.

The shift to a three-pillar pension system

The development of policies in relation to pensions can also be divided into three phases. During the 1980s, governments requested reports on future problems, but only increased contributions to deal with immediate problems. The 1990s were characterized by two linked processes: the attempt to cut the level of public pensions, successful in 1993 but not in 1995; and the probable development of voluntary privately funded pensions schemes.

The 1980s

Pension reform is widely perceived as a politically sensitive issue, so that throughout the 1980s, governments of the left and right were inclined to procrastinate. Instead of taking difficult decisions which would mean future pension cuts, governments preferred to do nothing or simply to increase the level of social contribution paid to pension schemes to meet existing deficits. Employees' pension contributions were increased in 1977, 1978, 1987 and 1989.

The delay in reform again shows the importance of the institutional design of the social protection system. The pension schemes have faced serious difficulties since the 1980s, but a (still incomplete) programme of reform was not started until 1993. In France, government has to negotiate with the trade unions for each different professional scheme before implementing any reform. Proposals for retrenchment are likely to face strong popular opposition.

The 1990s

The newly elected right-wing government succeeded in implementing reform only of the main basic pension scheme, covering private sector employees, in 1993. This was made possible by a package which traded benefit cuts against the tax financing of non-contributory benefits and by the fact that the reform was limited to the private sector general scheme (Bonoli, 1997). The indexation of benefits was based on prices, as against earnings, initially for a five-year period, and since extended indefinitely. The qualifying period for a full pension was extended from 37.5 to 40 years, and the period over which the reference salary is calculated, from the best ten years to the best 25. These reforms are being introduced gradually over a ten-year transition period. Finally, a '*Fonds de solidarité vieillesse*' has been created to fund non-contributory benefits.

The impact of the reform on long-term pension expenditure is substantial. Projections by the administration of the old age insurance scheme (CNAV) indicate that, without the 1993 reform, contribution rates in 2010 would have had to be increased by around 10 percentage points. With the reform, if indexation by prices is maintained, the figure falls to between 2.73 and 7.26 percentage points. The 1993 reform will also have an impact on pension levels and retirement ages, since some employees will delay retirement in order to qualify for a full pension. The extension of the period over which the reference salary is calculated will reduce benefits by 7 to 8 per cent for high salaries, but does not affect those on the minimum wage, who continue to receive the minimum pension (*minimum vieillesse*), which remains unchanged (Ruellan, 1993: 922).

In 1995, the Juppé government attempted to extend these measures to the pension schemes of public sector employees. Since Alain Juppé thought he held all the political trump cards (the presidency and a huge parliamentary majority), he was unwilling to negotiate his plan or to include concessions to unions in it. The reform was kept secret until the last moment. The result was a massive protest movement, led by a rail workers' strike, which forced the government to abandon its plans (Bonoli, 1997).

French experience in the area of pensions shows strong resistance to reform of the (non-state) contributory pensions schemes and stabilization of the (state-controlled) minimum pension. The French resistance to change is certainly not due to good financial prospects. The delays in reform and the relative weakness of the cuts can only be explained by the strong public support for the social insurance system and the involvement of the social partners in the management and defence of the schemes.

Towards the development of private pension funds?

In spring 1997, a new law was passed by the right-wing government to encourage the introduction of pension funds at the company level through fiscal incentives, but implementation was blocked by Jospin immediately after he took office. Since 1997, Jospin has sought to negoti-ate another general pension reform, including the public sector, with the agreement of the social partners. He has appointed several commissions, which have produced numerous (sometimes contradictory) reports (Charpin, 1999), without reaching a consensus. The reform will now probably be postponed until after the next important (parliamentary and presidential) elections of 2002. However, in the autumn of 2000, the new Finance Minister, Laurent Fabius, proposed the creation of *Plan partenari-aux d'épargne salariale*. These are not described as pension funds, but offer workers the opportunity of saving money with the support of their employers and the state (through tax exemptions) for a ten-year period. The accumulated assets can be received either as capital, or 'fragmented' (as an equity). Behind the semantic euphemisms (the schemes are not called pension funds but the investment is repaid as income, not as a lump-sum equity), the funds are intended to complement contributory benefits which have been cut back by the 1993 reforms and are likely to be retrenched further in the light of gloomy demographic prospects (Palier and Bonoli, 2000).

Since the cut-backs are limited, are often hindered by veto players (mainly the trade unions) and are inadequate for a return to financial sta-bility and economic competitiveness, governments have also decided to implement more structural reforms aimed at rendering the French welfare system more 'movable'. These changes have been further assisted by a shift in the position of one of the major trade unions (CFDT).

Beyond retrenchment: structural reforms in finance and management

The shift to tax finance

An important debate on the financing of social protection has developed in France since the mid 1970s. This debate is mainly nourished by experts through reports. There are three main phases in the debate. From 1945 to 1974 the main issue was the role that the state budget should play within the financing of social protection. Two main objectives were proposed: to increase resources and to improve the redistributive consistency of financing and spending. Although the unions claimed that the state should pay for non-contributory welfare, they did not want the system to become mainly tax-financed, since they would then lose their role within it. Therefore, no substantial changes occurred during this period and social contributions continued to play a major role in the financing of the French social protection system.

From 1974 to 1981, the debate changed and became more oriented towards economic efficiency than towards redistributive consistency. Seventeen reports were published on financing between 1974 and 1982 (Dupuis, 1989). They all emphasized the negative impact of contributions on employment. Before 1981, various reports favoured a new 'social' indirect tax (VAT). After 1982, however, all the main reports suggested that the new forms of finance should affect households rather than firms. A new tax which would be earmarked for social spending and proportional on all income was proposed (Dupuis, 1989: 29). Different arguments were put forward to justify this new tax: it would permit a more equitable distribution of taxation than social contributions which are only levied on wages; it would cover everyone, compared to income tax which in France affects only about half of all households; it would cover all personal revenues and not firms; and it would finance the non-contributory part of the welfare system.

However, the majority of trade unions opposed this innovation since it would mean a reduction of their role within the system. Progress towards the reform has been slow. In 1983, a tax of 1 per cent on all revenue was introduced as a temporary measure, to deal with a particularly large social security deficit. It was withdrawn in 1985 before the 1986 general election, but re-established in 1986, at only 0.4 per cent on wages.

After two years of a positive balance in the social security account in 1988 and 1989, the deficit reappeared in 1990. The project of a new tax for all revenue was reintroduced by the Rocard government. The new tax was adopted in November 1990, but the government almost failed to pass the reform because of the opposition of both the right-wing and Communist parties. Following the usual strategy of distinguishing between insurance and national solidarity, this *Contribution Sociale Généralisée* (CSG) was originally aimed at replacing the social contribution financing non-contributory benefits. Unlike insurance contributions (called *cotisations* in French, and not *contributions*), it is levied on all types of personal incomes: wages (even the lowest ones), but also capital revenues and welfare benefits. Unlike income tax in France, CSG is strictly proportional and designated for non-contributory welfare programmes. Finally, the tax is deducted at source (household income tax returns in France are made three times a year).

In the early 1990s, the CSG appeared to play a marginal role in the system, but its place has become increasingly important. When it was introduced, the CSG was levied at 1.1 per cent; in 1993, the Balladur government increased it to 2.4 per cent; in 1995, the Juppé plan set it at 3.4 per cent, and the rate increased to 7.5 per cent in 1998, replacing most of the health care contribution paid by employees. In 1999, CSG provided more than one-fifth of all social protection resources and paid for more than one-third of the health care system.

The introduction of this tax has enabled a shift in the financing structure of the welfare system towards state taxation. There are two main consequences: first, since financing does not come only from the working population, the CSG breaks the link between employment and entitlement. Access to CSG-financed benefits cannot legitimately be limited to any particular section of society. The continuing shift in social security finance from employment-related contributions to the CSG thus creates the conditions for the establishment of citizenship-based social rights, especially in health care; it also weakens the legitimacy of the financing mechanism, as well as the costs associated with it. This reform may increase pressures to contain spending and cut costs. Significantly, the issue of reducing taxes, including CSG, entered the debate in 1999, after the rapid economic growth of the preceding years. The second, main consequence is that, the shift reduces the legitimacy of participation by the social partners in the decision-making and management of provision which is now financed through general taxation. The shift in financing is likely to increase government influence over the system (Palier, 2000). This development corresponds to more important political changes in the distribution of power within the system which have occurred since the mid-1990s.

These 'institutional' reforms (Visser and Hemerijck, 1997: 77) were mainly implemented after the Juppé plan of 1995 in order to modify the organizational structure of the social insurance system. New institutions have been created, especially in the health care system, where the state representatives are playing a major role. These changes do not mean that the system has gone from a corporatist to a statist one, but that the state has more effective instruments for controlling costs (Palier, 2000). The most important reform of this kind is the constitutional amendment of February 1996, which gives parliament power to vote on the annual social security budget (*loi de financement de la Sécurité sociale*). This new parliamentary competence helps the government to control the social policy agenda. Instead of having to legitimize their intervention in a field originally belonging to the realm of labour and employers, they are now able to plan adaptation measures, especially cost-containment, and have done so in 1997, 1998 and 1999. This new ability also introduces a new logic of intervention. Instead of trying to find resources to finance a level of social expenditure that is driven simply by the demands of insured people, the vote of a *loi de financement* implies a limited budget. As most of the social benefits are still contributory, it is impossible to set absolute limits to the budget a priori, but parliament can now adopt new strategies intended to achieve this aim, for example, cash-limited budgets for hospitals and overall ceilings and growth-rates for social spending (Palier, 2000).

Conclusion

I have argued that the reasons why the French government has been so slow-moving and so limited in reducing social expenditure are mainly linked with the institutional structure of social protection in the country (earnings-related benefits delivered to workers, financed by social contributions and managed by the social partners). Aware of these structural difficulties by the late 1980s, French governments have decided to act indirectly in reforming the institutional causes of the blockages instead of directly cutting social benefits.

However, these important changes would not have been possible if trade unions had maintained their defensive position during the 1990s. An important political shift has facilitated sectoral and structural reforms. The more pragmatic left union, CFDT, which had not been involved in the management of social insurance funds since 1967, revised its economic and social stance in the mid-1980s. It has been one of the most active proponents of re-insertion policies (RMI), CSG and the 35-hour week. FO and CGT, however, retain their traditional defensive position, opposing all reform proposals. The new political balance among unions has produced a shift of responsibilities within the system. In the re-appointment of the heads of the social insurance funds after 1995, FO lost all its important positions (especially at the head of the National Health Care Insurance Fund) to the benefit of CFDT, who then allied with the employers' representatives.

A shift in the position of at least one major employees' representative is a precondition for policy change in a 'corporatist-conservative' social insurance system. The combination of such a change with a set of carefully designed reforms aimed at differentiating social insurance and national solidarity (assistance), both in specific areas and in basic institutional features of the system (such as financing and management), have restructured the framework in which French social security policy is made, leading the country away from the 'frozen landscape' in which it is typically situated. The generous and highly popular social insurance system managed by social partners at arms' length from the state proved resistant to change. Reforms in the financing of welfare, a stricter division between the state's role in assistance and the sphere of social insurance and realignments between the social partners may produce much more rapid reform in the near future, leading to retrenchment, a diminished role for social insurance and an expansion of the private sector and of provision directly controlled by government.

Notes

1 *Régimes spéciaux* protect the staff of the *SNCF* (National Railway Company), of the *RATP* (Parisian Underground), of the *Banque de France*, of the *Chambres de Commerce*, the military, notary, clerks, miners and others. *Régimes particuliers* cover civil servants, local civil servants, employees of public firms, war widows, orphans.

2 *Vieillir solidaires*, 1986, Rapport du Commissariat Général au Plan; INSEE, 1990, *L'avenir des retraites*; *Livre blanc sur les retraites*, *Garantir dans l'équité les retraites de demain*, 1991, Rapport au Premier Ministre, Paris, La documentation française; COTTAVE, *Rapport de la mission Retraites*, 1991; Bruhnes, B., 1992, *Rapport sur les retraites*.

4 Stumbling towards Reform: The German Welfare State in the 1990s

Frank Bönker and Hellmut Wollmann

In the second half of the 1990s, Germany was widely perceived as a laggard in welfare state reform. Foreign and domestic observers alike voiced concerns about 'deep-seated structural problems' (IMF, 1999a: 3) and a 'blocked society' (Heinze, 1998; own translation). Analyses that contrasted German immobilism with successful reforms in the Netherlands and other countries abounded. 'Reformstau' (reform gridlock) became one of the most quoted political slogans. It became the 'word of the year' in 1997 and was taken up by then-president Roman Herzog in a famous speech in which he lamented the political stagnation in Germany and ended with a dramatic call for change. Since then, the situation has changed. The 2000 tax reform and the 2001 pension reform have been praised as major breakthroughs and have attracted massive international attention. Part of the broad interest in recent reforms stems from the fact that they were adopted by a 'red-green' government made up of the same parties which had strongly rejected similar reforms in the past.

This chapter deals with welfare state reform in Germany in the 1990s in the fields of pensions, policies for the unemployed and taxation. In line with the other contributions to this volume, it reconstructs policy developments and asks how they have been shaped by the prevailing policy-making framework. The chapter comes in six parts. The first section sketches the policy-making framework that prevailed in the 1990s. It shows that most of the 1990s were characterized by a combination of strong constraints on executive authority, a weak consensus on welfare state reform and a high level of political confrontation. The second section summarizes the various challenges which the German welfare state faced in the 1990s. It documents how traditional arrangements came under considerable stress, not least because of German unification. The next three sections then give details of reform in the three fields under analysis. Each section identifies major trends in policies and reconstructs how the policy-making framework has impacted upon the initiation and consolidation of reforms. The final section puts the different threads together by comparing the trajectories in the three fields and by drawing some more general conclusions.

Weak consensus, strong constraints:
the policy-making framework in the 1990s

The 1990s saw a far-reaching renegotiation of the German welfare state. Fierce controversies over welfare state reform contributed to a high level of political confrontation during most of the decade. Controversies took place in a context of strong constraints on executive authority.

Renegotiating the German welfare state

In the early 1990s, there was a relatively strong consensus on economic and social policy. Major reform projects such as the 1989 pension reform, the 1992 health care reform and the introduction of the new care insurance scheme in 1993 were drawn up in a consensual fashion and were backed by the Social Democrats in opposition. When the German political economy came under stress in the mid-1990s, however, a renegotiation of the 'German model' set in. Unlike in other European countries, no coherent and consented reform discourse emerged (Cox, 1999; Schmidt, 2000). Key actors did not agree on the major problems, let alone on solutions. Instead, they took opposite positions.

On the one-side, in line with internationally rampant neo-liberal positions, business, the FDP and growing parts of the CDU/CSU called for tax cuts, reductions in benefits and a greater privatization of social risks. Within the CDU/CSU, the labourist wing, represented by Norbert Blüm, Minister of Labour and Social Affairs from 1982 to 1998, lost ground.

However, the great majority of the SPD and the trade unions rejected neo-liberal recipes. Under Oskar Lafontaine, who became Chairman of the SPD in 1995, the SPD moved to the left and subscribed to a more explicitly Keynesian position. The 'traditionalists' in the SPD were challenged by a 'modernist' wing that flirted with 'Blairism' and was represented by Gerhard Schröder. However, modernists remained in a minority position for most of the 1990s. After the 1998 change in government, the struggle between traditionalists and modernists continued. Lafontaine became Finance Minister in the Schröder government and sought to commit the government to the party line.

The situation changed in February 1999 when Lafontaine resigned and the Schröder government turned towards a more neo-liberal policy. Hans Eichel, the new finance minister, stressed the need for fiscal consolidation and argued for comprehensive tax cuts. Chancellor Schröder fashioned himself as a pragmatic modernizer with an open ear to the sorrows of business. Some grumbling notwithstanding, the new course was supported by the SPD. The 'relaunching' of the government has made controversies over economic and social policy less fundamental.

Political confrontation

The controversies on welfare state reform from 1993 onwards contributed to the high degree of political confrontation that characterized most of the 1990s. Between 1993 and 1998, neither the Kohl government nor the opposition behaved in a very co-operative manner. The conservative-liberal government pushed through controversial welfare state reforms against the opposition. The SPD in turn refused compromise solutions and sought to block legislation in the upper house. This confrontation was partly grounded in different views on the need for and the direction of reform which made compromises difficult. In addition, both camps were guided by tactical motives. The SPD tried to improve its rating in the polls by rejecting unpopular cuts in social benefits and by demonstrating the government's lack of strategic capacity. Conversely, the government took an assertive stance because it did not want to be perceived as 'weak'.

The confrontation between the two party camps was accompanied by tenuous relations between trade unions and employers and between trade unions and the government. In 1996, the government provoked the end of the short-lived 'Alliance for Jobs', an attempt at tripartite concertation that had been initiated by the Metal Workers' Union in 1995. In late 1996, relations turned even more sour when government and business tried to change the rules on wage payments in the case of illness. As the existing rules had been the result of a severe strike in the past and were thus seen as an important achievement of the labour movement, unions interpreted this move as a major attack on the welfare state and mobilized strikes and demonstrations.

When the red-green coalition took over in 1998, the political confrontation continued, as the incoming government was quick to undo some of the policy decisions into which its predecessor had invested much political zeal. Finance Minister Lafontaine cultivated a confrontational policy style. The CDU/CSU in turn was driven by feelings of revenge. Moreover, it scented the chance to bring down the government whose public reputation suffered from internal struggles and unpopular and half-baked reforms.

After the Schröder government's neo-liberal turn and its move towards a more inclusive policy style, political confrontation did not fade away. The CDU has continued to campaign aggressively against the government and has desperately tried to block major legislation in the upper house. Unlike the situation in the mid-1990s, however, confrontation is now primarily motivated by tactical considerations rather than by unbridgeable ideological differences.

Constraints on executive authority

The renegotiation of the German welfare state has taken place in a politico-institutional setting characterized by strong constraints on executive authority. These constraints have been rooted in a number of features of the German polity which have led a perceptive observer to call the Federal Republic a 'semi-sovereign state' (Katzenstein, 1987).

German electoral law on both the federal and the state level is based on proportional representation. As a consequence, coalition governments are the rule. Only once in the history of the Federal Republic (1958) has a single party (the Christian Democrats under Chancellor Konrad Adenauer) gained an absolute majority of seats in the Federal Parliament. This predominance of coalition governments means that German governments are typically forced to accommodate a broad range of interests. As a result, abstaining from even minor policy changes can easily turn out to be the least common denominator.

Germany is characterized by a peculiar type of federalism that does not vest the states (*Länder*) with much autonomy, but gives them a strong role in deciding upon and in implementing federal legislation. The states exercise their power through the upper house (*Bundesrat*), a second chamber which is made up of representatives of the state governments and can veto a broad range of legislation. The power of the upper house limits the federal government's executive authority. For one thing, it forces the federal government to accommodate state interests. For another, it gives the opposition in the lower house (*Bundestag*) the opportunity to block federal legislation if it commands a majority of votes in the upper house.

Parliamentary elections on the federal level and in the states are not synchronized. This makes for frequent elections. Given the crucial role of the upper house in the legislative process and the leading role of state politicians in the two major parties, the CDU/CSU and the SPD, this high frequency of elections forces the federal government to take short-term electoral consequences into account.

Germany has a number of powerful 'non-majoritarian institutions' (Majone, 1996), most notably the Federal Constitutional Court and – with a diminishing salience since the creation of the European Central Bank – the Bundesbank. Benefiting from far-reaching legal competencies and strong popular support, both institutions have enjoyed a high degree of independence and have shown little 'self-restraint' in their decisions.

Germany shows a high density of well-organized interest groups. These groups are not only consulted extensively in the process of legislation, but also benefit from an extensive delegation of competencies. Collective bargaining between unions and employers' associations covers a wide range of social issues. The 'social partners' are also heavily involved in the self-government of the social insurance funds. Non-profit organizations (*Wohlfahrtsverbände*) still run the large majority of personal social services (from kindergartens to drug counselling and hospitals).

The particular strength of these constraints has differed at different stages in the history of the Federal Republic. In the 1990s, constraints were strongly felt.

All governments in the 1990s were coalition governments. Chancellor Helmut Kohl relied on a coalition of CDU/CSU and FDP; Chancellor Gerhard Schröder has headed a government made up of SPD and the Greens. Under both governments, the need for intra-coalition compromise has complicated decision-making within government.

The 1990s were a period of 'divided government' or 'cohabitation'. As a rule, the parties forming the federal government did not command a majority of votes in the upper house. The Kohl government lost its majority in the Federal Council in 1991 and became dependent upon support by state governments run or co-governed by the SPD. In 1996, SPD-led state governments even gained a majority of seats, thus being able to block part of the legislation promoted by the federal government.[1] However, the red-green majority in the upper house did not hold for long and disappeared soon after the 1998 change in government.

1992 was the only year in the 1990s in which no elections to the federal, the European or a state parliament were held. In all the other years, elections took place. As each of the state elections was seen as a test election and influenced the majorities in the upper house, this steady flow of elections added up to an almost permanent electoral pressure.

In the 1990s, the Federal Constitutional Court adopted an activist stance towards tax and social policy reform. In a number of rulings, the court urged the federal government to overhaul the tax system and to reform policies towards families (Gerlach, 2000; Köppe, 1999).

The German welfare state under stress: the policy-making context

Since the early 1990s, the German welfare state has come under heavy stress (Carlin and Soskice, 1997; Bönker and Wollmann, 2000: 516–20). Some of the challenges have been similar to those in other OECD and EU countries. This applies to 'mega-trends' such as economic globalization, European integration, socio-demographic change or the de-standardization of employment. In the German case, these challenges have been aggravated by the effects of German unification (Czada, 1998).

Globalization

As in other countries, globalization has become a major issue in debates on welfare state reform. In line with employers' associations and many economists, the conservative-liberal government invoked globalization as an argument for wage restraint, tax cuts for corporations and cuts in social spending. Germany's disappointing economic performance and the fall of the iron curtain fuelled the looming worries about Germany's declining attractiveness as a location of investment (*Standortdebatte*). However, it remains controversial as to whether the German economy has really suffered from a lack of competitiveness (Carlin and Soskice, 1997; Lindlar and Scheremet, 1998).

European integration

European integration has shown a double impact on welfare state reform in Germany. By imposing ambitious fiscal targets, the Maastricht Treaty put fiscal consolidation high on the agenda. Moreover, German social policy increasingly has been confronted with harmonization and 'portability' requirements formulated by the EU. Compared to other countries, European integration has been a politically uncontested issue. All major parties have subscribed to supranationalism and international co-operation which are widely regarded as a lesson learned from the Nazi period and the Second World War. In the aftermath of German unification, the commitment to a deepening of European integration was also seen as a means to reduce concerns about the power of a united Germany. Moreover, the peculiar structures and processes of policy-making in the EU are highly compatible with German federalism and corporatism, so that the increasing role of the EU has posed less severe problems of legitimation and institutional adjustment than in countries with more unitary and statist polities (Schmidt, 1999).

Socio-demographic change

Germany has not been exempt from a number of socio-economic trends that challenge the traditional welfare state arrangements. These trends include the ageing of the population, shifting female life patterns and a transformation of family structures. Germany is among those OECD and EU countries that are hit most strongly by the greying of the population. Frequently cited OECD estimates put the ratio of people aged over 65 to people of working age at 49.2 per cent in 2030. This percentage compares to a mere 21.7 per cent in 1990 and exceeds the OECD average by more than 30 per cent (Börsch-Supan, 2000: F35.).

German unification

A unique challenge has stemmed from German unification (Czada, 1998). Unification has been associated with the large-scale public transfers to the East. Ever since 1991, net transfers to East Germany have amounted to DM 100–150 billion or 4–6 per cent of West German GDP annually and have thus put a heavy burden on the budget (Boss, 1998). A significant part of this burden has fallen on the social insurance funds which finance about two thirds of all German social spending. The transfer of West German institutions that has characterized German unification has also meant that, with some delay, West German benefit schemes were extended

Table 4.1   *Unemployment in Germany, 1990–1998*
(standardized rates)

	1990	1991	1992	1993	1994	1995	1996	1997	1998	1999
Germany				7.9	8.4	8.2	8.9	9.9	9.4	8.8
West Germany	4.8	4.2	4.5							
Other EU countries (average)	7.2	7.9	9.1	10.3	10.5	10.0	9.8	9.1	8.3	7.4
Other 'traditional' OECD countries (average)	6.8	7.5	8.4	9.3	9.2	8.6	8.5	8.0	7.6	6.8

Note: EU figures exclude Greece and, from 1990 to 1992, Austria. Other 'traditional' EU countries comprise the EU countries plus Australia, Canada, Japan, New Zealand, Norway, Switzerland (1991–1998) and the US.
Source: OECD, 2000b, Annex, Table 22

to East Germany and that East Germans joined the pension and unemployment insurance funds.[2] Given the massive decline in employment in East Germany, this transfer of the West German welfare state implied massive extra spending for the social insurance funds. Ten years into unification, annual transfers to the East within the framework of the pension and unemployment insurance schemes still amount to about DM 40 billion. Only part of the resulting financial burden has been covered by federal grants; the rest has been financed directly by the insured. As a consequence, unification has brought a strong upward pressure on social insurance contribution rates and downward pressure on benefits.

Labour-market changes

In the 1990s, the German labour-market experienced substantial changes. Germany has suffered from a lagging employment performance and a continuing de-standardization of employment. The figures in Table 4.1 highlight Germany's 'unemployment crisis' (Lindlar and Scheremet, 1998). In the course of the 1990s, unemployment almost doubled. After the end of the unification boom, the unemployment rate steadily increased until 1997. This contrasts with the development in the other EU and OECD countries in which average unemployment has fallen since 1994. As a consequence, the German unemployment rate, well below average in 1990/1991, surpassed EU and OECD averages in 1996/1997. This can only be partly explained by German unification. While it is true that the unemployment catastrophe in the East has pushed the German unemployment rate upwards, West German unemployment also more than doubled between 1991 and 1997.

The high unemployment has gone hand in hand with other symptoms of lagging employment performance (OECD, 1997d): structural unemployment, as measured by the non-accelerating wage rate of unemployment (NAWRU), went up in the first half of the 1990s; both the share of long-term unemployed and the low-skilled unemployment rate have been high from an international perspective; and finally, Germany's already low employment ratio further declined in the 1990s (Siegel and Jochem, 2000: 543–5).

Parallel to these changes in the level of employment and unemployment, Germany has also experienced a continuing de-standardization of employment. According to some estimates, the share of permanent full-time work for an employer in overall employment fell by about 5 percentage points between 1985 and 1995 and is now down to about 50 per cent (Becker and Falk, 1999: 273–6). This reflects both an increase in part-time employment and a growing number of self-employed. In German debates, two forms of atypical employment have attracted particular attention, namely the so-called 630 DM jobs (*geringfügige Beschäftigung*) and dependent self-employment (*Scheinselbständigkeit*) (Buch and Rühmann, 1999).

Until recently, the so-called 630 DM jobs were defined by a working time of less than 15 hours per week and earnings below a threshold of one-sixth of the average monthly gross wage.[3] Prior to April 1999, these jobs were exempt from social insurance contributions and subject to a flat-rate income tax to be paid by the employer. The exemption from social insurance and the greater flexibility rendered the 630 DM jobs attractive for many employers and employees and made them the most dynamic segment of the German labour-market. Whereas overall employment declined, the number of 630 DM jobs soared. In the late 1990s, the number of employees with one or more of these jobs was estimated at between five and six million, up from four million at the beginning of the decade. According to estimates, about a fourth of these employees have a 'regular' first job. Despite the welcome boost in employment, the rise of the 630 DM jobs has been highly controversial. While their advocates have praised their contribution to labour-market flexibility and lower labour costs, critics have voiced concerns about gaps in social protection, a loss of social security contributions and a violation of equity norms. Finally, the privileged treatment of the 630 DM jobs has been associated with a bias towards part-time employment.

A second development that stirred considerable attention has been the increase in the numbers of formally self-employed workers who are in fact wholly dependent on one employer. In the mid-1990s, the number of those who were self-employed on paper, but otherwise subject to working conditions similar to employees, had increased to between 500,000 and 1.4 million people (Becker and Falk, 1999: 280–2). The rise in dependent self-employment has been favoured by high and increasing social insurance contributions. Similar to the increase in 630 DM jobs, it has raised concerns about gaps in social protection and an erosion of social insurance contributions.

Fiscal problems

In Germany, the combination of unification and high unemployment made the 1990s a period of fiscal stress. An increase in government expenditure

Table 4.2 *Government fiscal performance, 1990–2000 (% GDP)*

	1990	1991	1992	1993	1994	1995	1996	1997	1998	1999	2000
Outlays	43.8	44.2	45.0	46.2	45.9	46.3	47.3	46.4	45.8	45.9	43.0
Balance	−2.0	−3.0	−2.5	−3.1	−2.4	−3.3	−3.4	−2.7	−2.1	−1.4	1.4
Gross finan-cial liabilities	42.0	38.8	41.8	47.4	47.9	57.1	60.3	61.7	63.0	60.6	59.6
Net debt interest payments	1.9	2.2	2.6	2.7	2.7	3.1	3.1	3.1	3.1	3.0	2.9

Note: Figures for 2000 are estimates. Gross financial liabilities and net debt interest payments include the Inherited Debt Fund from 1995 onwards. In 2000, the substantial one-off revenues from the sale of mobile telephone licences are recorded as negative capital outlays.
Sources: OECD, 2000b, Annex, Tables 28, 30, 33, 34

and a weak tax performance translated into relatively high fiscal deficits. In addition German unification implied a non-deficit related increase in the public debt because the West German government had to shoulder the explicit and implicit fiscal liabilities accumulated in the former GDR. As a consequence, Germany, traditionally the preacher of fiscal conservatism, faced serious problems in meeting the fiscal criteria enshrined in the Maastricht Treaty. In 1993, 1995 and 1996, general government fiscal deficits exceeded the magic 3 per cent ceiling (Table 4.2). It took various short-term measures and an acceleration of privatization to eventually qualify for EMU (Zohlnhöfer, 2000).

Fiscal pressures were felt particularly strongly in the budgets of the social insurance funds. The increase in federal grants did not suffice to finance the costs of German unification and high unemployment. This led to a strong increase in social insurance contribution rates from 35.6 per cent of gross wages in 1990 to a peak of 42.1 per cent by 1998, falling back to 40.9 per cent by 2001. The unemployment insurance contribution rate was raised by more than 2 per cent in 1991 (from 4.3 to 6.8 per cent) and has remained almost unchanged ever since. The pension insurance contribution rates were initially reduced to 17.7 per cent, but rose by more than two percentage points between 1993 and 1997. In addition, the average sickness insurance contribution rate increased slightly to 13.6 per cent, and a contribution to the new care insurance scheme of 1.7 per cent was introduced in 1995.

Stop-and-go: pension reform in the 1990s

The German system of old-age protection traditionally has been dominated by a large public pension pillar. The statutory pension scheme was established by Bismarck in 1889 as the first formal pension system in the world. Originally confined to a small group of blue-collar workers, the scheme was gradually transformed into a comprehensive scheme that provides disability, retirement and survivor benefits for virtually all workers (Börsch-Supan, 2000: F25–7; Schmähl, 1999: 92–100).[4] According to estimates, public pensions account for more than 80 per cent of overall retirement income. Compared to other countries, both occupational pensions and private savings thus play a relatively small role in old-age protection.

The statutory pension scheme has traditionally been financed by a combination of social security contributions and a small federal grant. Since 1967, the scheme has been a purely pay-as-you-go system. Net retirement incomes for a worker with a 45-year earnings history and average lifetime earnings increased from about 60 per cent of average earnings of all dependently employed workers in the early 1960s to about 70 per cent in the 1980s and 1990s. A system of generous survivors' benefits has provided additional entitlements. As a consequence, poverty rates among older people have sharply fallen over time and are low from an international perspective. A recent analysis suggests that, in 1998, average (weighted) household incomes of pensioners were a mere 3 per cent below those of employees (Bedau, 1999).

At the outset of the 1990s, the German pension system found itself in an apparently favourable shape. The short-term fiscal situation was good. Favoured by the unification boom, the pension scheme ran huge surpluses which made it possible to reduce the contribution rate in 1991. Moreover, a comprehensive pension reform that promised to address the medium-term challenges became effective in January 1992 (Nullmeier and Rüb, 1993; Schmähl, 1999: 100–5). Adopted by parliament on November 9, 1989, the very day the wall came down, the '1992 Pension Reform' concluded more than 15 years of minor adjustments and represented the first major pension reform since 1972. Measures included: the move from an indexation of pensions to gross earnings, to an indexation to average net earnings; a gradual re-increase in the retirement age and higher deductions in the case of early retirement; an extension of credits for child rearing; and a one-time increase in the federal grant.

The '1992 Pension Reform' substantially reduced future pension claims. It was expected to bring about a decline in the projected contribution rate by 1.7 percentage points in 2000 and by almost 10 percentage points in 2030 (see Table 4.3). The reform could build on a far-reaching consensus. Save for the Greens, all parties in parliament, including the SPD in opposition, supported it. Moreover, it was backed by business and trade unions.

The re-opening of the reform debate

At the time of its adoption, the '1992 Pension Reform' was praised as a 'centenary reform' and thought of as a fix for at least a decade. Contrary

Table 4.3 *Projected pension insurance contribution rates*[a]

	2000	2010	2020	2030
1989 (without '1992 Reform')	22.0	24.5	28.1	36.4
1989 (with '1992 Reform')	20.3	21.4	22.8	26.9
1994	19.7	21.5	23.1	27.0
1996	20.4	21.6	23.2	26.2
1996 (with February measures)	20.1	20.6	22.6	25.5
1996 (with '1999 Reform')	19.7	19.1	20.0	22.4
2000		19.6	20.5	23.6
2000 (with 'Reform 2000')		18.7	19.7	21.9

[a] Contribution rates required to balance the budget and to meet reserve requirements. 1989: West Germany only.
Sources: Schmähl, 1999: 107, Table 2; press releases

to expectations, however, a new reform debate was already underway in the mid-1990s. This re-opening of the debate was triggered by a combination of short-term fiscal pressures and a re-assessment of medium- and long-term prospects. For one thing, the high unemployment and the heavy use of early retirement schemes in East and West Germany led to an increase in contribution rates. Total social insurance contribution exceeded 40 per cent in 1996; the contribution to the pension scheme passed the 20 per cent threshold in 1997. Parallel to these short-term developments, the medium- and long-term perspectives of the pension scheme increasingly drew criticism. The main problem was not that projections had changed. In 1994 and 1996, the contribution rates projected for the years after 2010 did not differ very much from the ones taken for granted in 1989. In the light of the dire economic situation and a growing concern with 'generational equity', however, these rates were no longer regarded as economically and politically acceptable.

Pension reform in the mid-1990s

While the need for a new round of reforms was broadly accepted, positions on the design of reforms differed (Hinrichs, 1998; Meyer, 1998; Nullmeier, 1996). Unlike in the late 1980s, no agreement could be forged. The lack of consensus on the direction of reforms and the party strategies in the run-up to the 1998 elections prevented an agreement. What was most controversial was the need for a further slowing of pension growth. Whereas the government insisted on a decline in the pension level in order to constrain the rise of contributions and to spread the burden of adjustment more equally, the SPD questioned the need for cuts. It argued that such cuts would increase poverty among pensioners and undermine popular support for a contribution-based pension scheme by bringing average pensions close to social assistance. The SPD also claimed that the fiscal problems of the pension scheme could be solved by increasing federal grants, by streamlining survivors' pension, by making self-employed people, civil servants and housewives subject to social insurance and by adopting a better overall economic policy. However, most of these proposals were strongly opposed by the FDP and by business.

As positions diverged strongly and as government and opposition remained intransigent, it was not possible to arrive at a consensus. Instead, the Kohl government pushed through various reform measures unilaterally. In February 1996, the phasing in of the early retirement deductions agreed upon in 1989 was accelerated. In addition, the government reduced the maximum number of years of schooling credited without paying contributions. In summer 1997, parliament adopted more far-reaching reforms. The '1999 Pension Reform', as it was called, consisted of the following main elements (IMF, 1997: ch. v; Schmähl, 1999: 109–14):

- In addition to the already adopted changes for old-age pensions, deductions were introduced for disability pensions.
- Crediting for child rearing was further extended by raising the value of credits and by allowing to add credits to other entitlements from the period of child rearing.
- In order to limit future pension growth, a so-called 'demographic factor' was introduced into the pension formula. Accounting for increases in the (further) life expectancy of people aged 65, this factor was to produce a gradual decline in the standard pension level from 70 per cent of average net earnings today to 64 per cent in 2030.
- The federal grant was raised once more. This increase was financed by raising the standard VAT rate by 1 per cent in April 1998.

Together, these measures added up to a substantial further reduction in future contribution rates. Compared to the projections on the basis of the measures adopted in February 1996, the contribution rate in 2030 was set to fall by another 3.1 percentage points. At the same time, the '1999 Pension Reform' was an 'immanent' reform. Reforms were confined to changes within the existing pay-as-you-go system. In 1996/97, calls for a move to a multi-pillar system remained weak.

The '1999 Pension Reform' was the first major pension reform in the history of the Federal Republic that was adopted against the parliamentary opposition. What made this possible was the fact that the only component reform that required the approval by the Federal Council – an increase in the standard VAT rate in order to finance a federal grant to the pension scheme – was uncontroversial.

Pension reform under the Schröder government

In the run-up to the 1998 parliamentary elections, the SPD had campaigned massively against the '1999 Pension Reform'. The incoming red-green government stuck to campaign promises and suspended the introduction of the demographic factor and the reform of invalidity pensions. This suspension was as unprecedented in post-war history as the prior passage of reforms without the votes of the opposition.

The new government quickly implemented various measures aimed at improving the short-term fiscal situation of the pension scheme. It tightened the rules on dependent self-employment and on the 630 DM jobs. Moreover, it raised the federal grant to the pension scheme. Part of the increase was financed by the newly introduced ecotax, a number of taxes on energy consumption. These measures helped to achieve a step-wise reduction in the pension contribution rate from 20.3 per cent in April 1999 to 19.1 per cent in January 2001. With these reforms, however, the government all but exhausted the possibilities to boost the federal grant within the logic of the existing system. It is widely agreed that the federal grant now exceeds those pension expenditures that represent non-contributory benefits.

These early moves were accompanied by the vague announcement of additional 'structural' reforms to be effective from early 2001. A first outline was presented by Minister of Labour Walter Riester in June 1999. The presentation coincided with the government's spectacular turn-around in fiscal policy after the resignation of Finance Minister Lafontaine. Like Hans Eichel's move towards a more restrictive fiscal policy, Riester's proposals marked a considerable change in the government's position and took most observers by surprise. The most controversial of these measures was the proposal to abandon the indexation of pensions to net earnings for two years and to index pensions on prices in 2000 and 2001. A second proposal that drew much attention was the introduction of a mandatory private pension pillar to be financed by employee contributions increasing from 0.5 per cent of gross earnings in 2003 to a total of 2.5 per cent by 2007. In addition, Riester announced the introduction of a minimum pension and an overhaul of survivors' pensions.

These proposals represented a substantial departure from the SPD's previous reform plans. The idea of making new groups subject to social insurance was dropped. The change in the indexation of pensions also meant a much steeper initial decline in the pension level than would have resulted from the plans of the Kohl government which had been fiercely rejected by the SPD opposition. Similarly, the introduction of a private pension pillar implied a new public-private mix in old-age protection and a departure from the traditional proportional financing of social security contributions by employees and employers. What made Riester's proposals even more remarkable was the fact that the idea of a supplementary private pension pillar hitherto had not featured very prominently in German debates on pension reform.

It goes without saying that Riester's plans were highly controversial both outside and within the governing coalition. The obligatory character of the private pillar was attacked as illegitimate compulsion. The trade unions and the traditionalist wing within the SPD criticized the cuts in pensions and insisted that the private pillar should not 'replace', but only 'top up' public pensions. In addition, the unions argued that the private pillar should take the form of occupational pensions subject to collective agreements between the social partners. The CDU/CSU seized the opportunity to capitalize on popular dissatisfaction with the government's pension plans. It criticized the temporary indexation on prices for its discretionary character and for imposing an unjust burden on current pensioners. It also strongly opposed the idea of a minimum pension as a departure from the traditional contribution-related pension system and a blurring of the differences between pensions and social assistance. At the same time, the CDU/CSU quickly embraced the idea of a supplementary private pillar, yet called for making state subsidies more generous and dependent upon the number of children. Pension reform also featured prominently in a number of state elections that went badly for the government as a result of the opposition's attempts to benefit from popular discontent with the Riester plans. The government stressed its interest in a consensual solution and agreed upon a series of talks with the opposition parties. These talks took place in the first half of 2000. They were complicated by the fact that the CDU/CSU lacked a clear reform concept and was absorbed by the fall-out from the scandal about its illegal financing practices.

At the end of May 2000, Riester presented a new and more detailed version of his plans. The new draft included a number of concessions. In particular, the government refrained from introducing a minimum pension and from making the private pension pillar obligatory. However, incentives to take out a private pension were strengthened. Riester renewed his commitment to indexing pensions on prices in 2001 and to the creation of a supplementary private pillar. In one important respect, Riester's new plans were even bolder than his original announcements. The new pension formula he eventually presented provided for a decline in the public pension level down to 61 per cent of net earnings in 2030. According to Riester, these measures would make it possible to keep pension contribution rates at 22 per cent in 2030.

Riester's proposals did not put an end to controversies. Both the trade unions and the CDU/CSU continued to attack Riester's plans. This critique and a number of internal inconsistencies led to a further round of amendments. In December 2000, the trade unions eventually endorsed Riester's plans when the government, on the initiative of its parliamentary factions, modified the pension formula so as to keep pensions in 2030 at a level of 67 per cent of net earnings.[5] But the CDU/CSU voted against the government when the pension reform was passed in January 2001. The opposition also announced that it will veto those parts of the legislation that require approval by the upper house in the Federal Council.[6] The rejection of the government's pension reform plans by the CDU/CSU cannot hide the fact that government and opposition now basically agree on the direction of pension reform. This applies to the goal of confining the increase in social insurance contributions and the resulting need for cuts in the pension level as well as to the move to a multi-pillar system. Underneath the surface of political confrontation, an implicit pension consensus has emerged.

The pension reform in the form it was eventually adopted suffers from a number of weaknesses. The new pension formula is arbitrary. The provisions for the new private pillar strongly restrict the range of assets and are difficult and expensive to administer. The government's targets for contribution rates and pension levels are based on unrealistic economic assumptions and do not add up. Hence, it is a safe guess that the 'biggest social reform in the post-war period' (Riester) will not hold for very long.

Despite these problems, however, the recent pension reform marks a major change which will transform old-age protection in Germany and will also influence other fields of social policy (IMF, 2000: ch. v). This is largely due to the introduction of the private pension pillar. The bringing in of a state-backed privately funded scheme means a first step towards a new public-private mix in old-age protection; it weakens the traditional proportional financing of social security contribution and provides new instruments and parameters for pension reform. Finally, the new private pillar will also transform the policy arena by bringing in new actors and interests (from banks and insurance companies to the Ministry of Finance and the Federal Council).

Gradual change: policies for the unemployed

German policies for the unemployed traditionally have been characterized by institutional fragmentation, strong negative rights and little emphasis on the 'activation' of the unemployed (Hagen and Steiner, 2000). Germany has a three-tier system of transfer payments to the unemployed. The Federal Labour Office (*Bundesanstalt für Arbeit*) provides two kinds of benefits: unemployment insurance benefits (*Arbeitslosengeld*) are financed from contributions to the unemployment insurance scheme and are limited in duration. When the unemployment insurance benefit is exhausted, people can claim unemployment assistance (*Arbeitslosenhilfe*), a lower, means-tested benefit. Until recently, unemployment assistance was also granted to part of the unemployed who did not qualify for the unemployment insurance benefit (so-called 'primary unemployment assistance'). If unemployed people are not eligible to unemployment assistance or if unemployment assistance is inadequate, they can receive social assistance (about one-third of those on unemployment assistance do). The German social assistance scheme is regulated by Federal law, yet financed and administered by local government. Like unemployment assistance, social assistance is means-tested.

In the past, the unemployed had strong negative rights. They had to honour few obligations, were not obliged to engage in community-related work and enjoyed far-reaching rights to decline job offers at a lower level of income and qualification than they formerly earned. Moreover, the jobs created by means of active labour-market policy were paid in line with the regular public sector pay. The strong negative rights of the unemployed have coincided with scant emphasis on the 'activation' of the unemployed. While the Federal Labour Office has administered a plethora of measures of active labour-market policy, both the rights and the duties to participate in such programmes have been limited. In addition, recipients of social assistance and unemployment assistance have traditionally enjoyed little scope for topping up benefits with additional earnings.

Changes under the Kohl government

In the 1990s, discontent with the received policies intensified. As elsewhere, critics lamented about overly generous benefits, weak work incentives, a lack of 'activation' and ineffective active labour-market programmes. Further problems stemmed from the prevailing institutional fragmentation. Owing to the separation of unemployment assistance and social assistance, the huge number of those who simultaneously receive both benefits have to deal with two different bureaucracies and have to conform to different – sometimes even contradictory – provisions. Moreover, institutional fragmentation has distorted bureaucracies' incentives. In particular, the fact that the unemployed are eligible for unemployment insurance benefits after a year of gainful employment has given municipalities an incentive to shift the fiscal burden of unemployment by paying social assistance recipients a temporary wage income. From a political point of view, fragmentation has complicated reforms by provoking conflicts between local governments and the federal government over the responsibility for the unemployed and the costs of unemployment.

Starting in 1993, the Kohl government began to reform policies for the unemployed. In line with the neo-liberal creed, the new policy direction called for cuts in benefits and a weakening of the rights of the unemployed. In addition, it launched a number of initiatives aimed at inducing local governments to provide work opportunities for social assistance recipients and at 'activating' transfer recipients by allowing them to keep a greater share of their addition earnings. These initiatives were accompanied by cuts in spending on active labour-market policy and an attempt to target labour-market programmes on the long-term unemployed (Bieback, 1997; Heinelt and Weck, 1998; Schmid, 1996; Sell, 1998).

Most of the Kohl government's plans were rejected by the opposition and by local governments. Resistance was driven by different motives. Local governments first of all feared negative repercussions on their budgets. They were anxious that cuts in unemployment assistance might make more people dependent upon social assistance, that work requirements might oblige them to provide jobs and that more generous provisions on additional earnings might make low-income earners eligible for social assistance. In contrast, the SPD and the trade unions attacked the government's initiatives as an assault on the welfare state and criticized cuts in benefits as a disguised attempt to keep down wages. As part of the legislation on policies for the unemployed required the approval of the Federal Council, Social Democrats and local governments managed to block part of the government's plans and to force the government to make concessions. Nevertheless, the Kohl government succeeded in passing a number of reforms:

- Benefits were subject to cuts. In 1993, the government reduced unemployment insurance benefits for unemployed people without children from 63 to 60 per cent and unemployment assistance benefits from 56 to 53 per cent of previous net earnings. The maximum payment of primary unemployment assistance was limited to one year. In 1996, unemployment assistance was made digressive, so that the rate fell over time. In 1997, age limits for the extended duration of unemployment insurance benefits were raised. Various laws limited the annual uprating of social assistance benefits.
- The 1997 Employment Promotion Reform Act (*Arbeitsförderungsreformgesetz*) restricted the rights of the unemployed to decline job offers in other places and at a lower level of qualifications or income. The Kohl government also imposed more stringent controls on the availability of work and tightened the sanctions for refusing job offers.
- Pay rates for jobs created by means of active labour-market policy were progressively lowered, so that these jobs were no longer paid in line with public sector pay-scales.
- From 1993 onwards, the requirements for recipients of unemployment assistance benefits to improve their employability and to carry out community-related work were tightened.

These changes substantially worsened the legal and material situation of the unemployed. Unlike in other countries, measures were largely 'negative' and not balanced by increased job-search assistance or by new entitlements such as a right to participate in training measures (Rabe and Schmid, 1999). 'Activation' remained limited in another respect, too. Owing to opposition by local government, the rules on additional earnings for benefit recipients were largely unchanged. In December 1997, the Federal Council rejected the government's long-delayed initiative to give social assistance recipients better opportunities to top up social assistance by additional earnings.

The changes in policy brought about by the federal government were complemented by initiatives at the local level. Confronted with a growing number of long-term unemployed and looming fiscal pressures, local governments have intensified their attempts to put social assistance recipients into work. According to estimates, the number of recipients engaged in some kind of organized work increased from 120,000 in 1993 to about 300,000 in 1998, about a third of those able to work. The quality of employment has taken different forms. In some cases, recipients of social assistance have to do some work on an *ad hoc* basis and receive a small allowance. In other cases, municipalities offer temporary employment in municipality-owned job-creation companies (*Beschäftigungsgesellschaften*) which pay a regular wage income. This move towards 'workfare' has partly been driven by fiscal considerations: estimates suggest that up to a quarter of all prior social assistance recipients give up their claims when being obliged to work. Moreover, paying social assistance recipients a wage income has allowed municipalities to shift the fiscal burden of unemployment to the federal level (Feist and Schöb, 1999).

Under the Kohl government, unemployment assistance and social assistance remained separated. While calls for the integration of the two systems grew louder and were taken up by the government's parliamentary party groups in the mid-1990s, policy change was limited, largely confined to the extension of local government access to the programmes and funds of the labour offices. The integration of unemployment assistance and social assistance is a sensitive issue, since it touches on the division of labour between the federal and local government. The elimination of unemployment assistance, as has been suggested, would put a heavy fiscal burden on local governments and would force them to engage in job placement.

Policies for the unemployed under the Schröder government

Policies for the unemployed have not featured prominently on the agenda of the Schröder government. In July 1999, the new government undid some of the restrictive measures taken by the Kohl government.[7] Unemployed people are no longer obliged to show up at the labour office four times a year and to accept job offers that imply up to three hours of commuting. The Schröder government has also pumped more money into active labour-market policy and has relaxed the targeting of these programmes on the long-term unemployed. Finally, it has supported local attempts at improving co-operation between local governments and labour offices by increasing the scope for experiments and by subsidizing model projects at the local level.

The Schröder government has kept a low profile in the field of policies for the unemployed for various reasons. The close involvement of local governments and trade unions has made reform a minefield. The energies of the Federal Ministry of Labour and Social Affairs have been absorbed in pension reform. Finally, the government has lacked a clear reform concept.

From stalemate to reform: tax reform in the 1990s

The German tax system traditionally has been characterized by the following features (Leibfritz et al., 1998; see also Table 4.4):

Table 4.4   *The German tax system from a comparative perspective (1996)*

	Total tax receipts	Revenues from various taxes as % of total tax receipts				
	% of GDP	Personal income tax	Corporate income tax	Social security contributions	Taxes on goods and services	Other taxes
Germany	38.1	24.7	3.8	38.1	27.9	5.5
Other EU countries (average)	42.7	26.1	7.8	25.6	31.4	9.1
Other traditional OECD countries (average)[a]	41.7	30.2	9.2	24.0	30.8	11.0

[a] In addition to the EU countries, this includes Australia, Canada, Japan, New Zealand, Norway and the US.
Source: OECD (1997b and 1999g), own calculations

- Since pensions, health care, unemployment benefits and the benefits of the care insurance scheme are largely financed by earmarked social security contributions, both the contribution rates and the share of contributions in overall tax revenues are high.
- In contrast, the share of indirect taxes in revenues is relatively small. The standard VAT rate is the lowest in the European Union. It stood at 14 per cent in 1990 and was raised to 15 per cent in 1993 and 16 per cent in 1998.
- The taxation of personal income has suffered from a combination of high rates and a relatively narrow tax base. Personal income tax revenues declined substantially during the 1990s as a proportion of GDP, partly due to generous tax incentives for housing investments in Eastern Germany. In the mid 1990s, the share of personal income taxes in GDP was below the EU and OECD average.
- Corporate income taxation similarly combines high rates with a narrow base and accounts for a relatively small proportion of overall revenues. In addition to generous depreciation rules and accounting standards, this reflects the fact that the large majority of German enterprises are not incorporated and are thus subject to personal income taxation.

Tax reform until the 1998 elections

The situation in the 1990s was not very favourable to the initiation of tax reform: German unification and the fiscal requirements of the Maastricht Treaty reduced the scope for tax cuts. In addition, fiscal pressures limited the readiness of the states to agree on tax cuts and intensified conflict over the distribution of revenues. Finally, the government and the opposition disagreed for a long time on the direction of tax reform. Whereas the governing parties increasingly subscribed to comprehensive tax cuts, the SPD argued for revenue-neutral tax reforms and criticized cuts in the top personal income tax rate.

Tax reform in the first half of the 1990s was largely reactive. First, the Kohl government had to deal with the unexpectedly high fiscal burden of German unification. Although the government relied heavily on borrowing and higher social security contributions, it was eventually forced to break its initial promise not to raise taxes (Zohlnhöfer, 2000). Measures included the introduction of a temporary income tax surcharge ('solidarity surcharge') in July 1991, an increase in the standard VAT rate from 14 to 15 per cent in January 1993 and several increases in excise duties. Further reforms were triggered by the Federal Constitutional Court. A number of rulings forced the government to overhaul the taxation of interest income, to reform the Asset Tax and to almost double personal tax allowances and child allowances.

Starting in 1993, the government began to emphasize the need for tax reform in the corporate sector. In 1994, it reduced corporate income tax rates and limited the personal income tax rate on income from business activities. Owing to the precarious fiscal situation, these cuts were compensated by less generous depreciation allowances. In addition, the government gradually reduced local business taxation.

In the mid-1990s, calls for a more comprehensive tax reform grew louder in the governing coalition. In 1996, the government drew up a large reform package which included substantial changes in the taxation of personal and corporate income and promised an overall tax relief of DM 30–40 billion. In addition to these measures, the government's plans included a reduction in the 'solidarity surcharge' and a further increase in the standard VAT rate (IMF, 1997: ch. iv).

The government's plan met resistance from state governments and the opposition. The state governments complained that the government had departed from previous practice by not compensating the states for the tax reform-induced revenue losses. The SPD criticized reforms for distributional reasons claiming that they were biased towards the better-off. Moreover, it argued that the bad shape of the public finances did not allow for as strong a net tax relief. The government's tax reform plans led to a show-down in the Federal Council. For tactical reasons, both camps remained intransigent. At the end, the SPD-leadership managed to keep the prime ministers of SPD-led states in line and to block the lion's share of the government's package (Zohlnhöfer, 1999).

Tax reform under the Schröder government

In line with the positions taken in opposition times, the initial tax reform plans of the red-green government concentrated on tax cuts for lower income strata and a reduction in social security contributions to be financed by a new ecotax (IMF, 1999b: 41–3; OECD, 1999g). A first income tax reform was legislated in March 1999 and covered the period from 1999 to 2002. Measures included a gradual increase in child allowances and in the basic personal income tax allowance, as well as reductions in personal income tax rates and in the corporate income tax rate on retained earnings. The bulk of these cuts was financed by base broadening measures. Net tax relief was confined to about DM 12 million and was to materialize largely in 2002, the year of the next elections. In April 1999, these measures were complemented by the introduction of various ecotaxes and a concomitant reduction in social insurance contribution rates.

In addition to these measures, the government announced a comprehensive reform of business taxation which aimed at stimulating investment by privileging retained over-distributed earnings. In December 1998, a reform commission in charge of drafting a new system of business taxation was installed. The commission's suggestions were presented in April 1999 and endorsed by the government in June 1999.

Tax reform gained further momentum in the second half of the year. Hans Eichel, the new finance minister after the resignation of Lafontaine, prepared a comprehensive reform package which combined the reform of business taxation with further reforms of personal income tax and changes in the taxation of capital gains. Approved by the cabinet in February 2000, the full package implied an overall tax relief of DM 44 billion and included the following measures:

- A phasing in of the tax cuts for households planned for 2002 to begin in 2001, followed by a reduction in the lowest income tax rate to 15 per cent and the top rate to 45 per cent by 2005 and a progressive increase in the basic personal income tax allowance.
- A reduction of the corporate income tax to a uniform 25 per cent from 2001 onwards, accompanied by the replacement of the full imputation of corporate income tax by the half-income method, by which half of the dividends are subject to personal income tax.
- The exemption of capital gains on inter-corporate shareholdings from corporate income tax from 2002 onwards.
- The introduction of a new model for corporate taxation allowing unincorporated companies to opt to be taxed as incorporated companies.

Eichel's tax reform package marked a clear departure from the SPD's previous positions on tax reform: it included significant cuts in the top personal income tax rate and envisaged a substantial net tax relief for both households and enterprises. Moreover, the exemption of capital gains on corporate shareholdings implied substantial tax savings for corporations, especially big banks and insurance companies. Not surprisingly, critics from within the SPD and the trade unions complained about 'tax gifts for corporations and the better-off' and a 'justice gap'. Despite these complaints, however, Schröder and Eichel managed to commit the SPD and its parliamentary group to Eichel's plans.

The government's tax reform plans were well-received by business. This applied particularly to big business, which was to benefit most strongly from the envisaged reforms. The opposition criticized the plans for various reasons: it argued for further cuts in personal income tax rates and a bigger net tax relief; it pointed to the high administrative costs of the 'option model' and the favouring of big business; finally, it criticized the bias towards retention as a distortion of incentives. The last line of criticism in particular was echoed by many academic economists.

The passage of tax reform was complicated by the government's lack of a majority in the Federal Council. The newly installed CDU/CSU leadership provoked a show-down in the Federal Council and tried to block tax reform. Unlike the SPD in 1997, however, the opposition did not succeed. By accommodating some of the demands of the opposition and by 'bribing' some of the 'neutral' states through the promise of additional federal spending, the government eventually forged a majority for its plans. This was facilitated by the favourable short-term fiscal situation which made concessions to the states easier. Compared to the original draft, the final version of the tax reform provided a further cut in the top personal income tax rate to 42 per cent in 2005 as well additional tax relief to by small and medium-sized companies. At the same time, the originally proposed 'option model' was dropped.

Along with the moves towards fiscal consolidation and pension reform, the 2000 Tax Reform became a symbol for the Schröder government's new economic policy and the end of the reform gridlock (IMF, 2000: ch. iv). Reforms have widely been seen as boosting Germany's attractiveness to investment. The top personal income tax rate and the headline corporate income tax rate are now low by international standards and well below the current EU average. Inclusive of 'solidarity surcharge' and local taxes, the tax burden on corporations is now at about EU average. The exemption of capital gains on inter-corporate shareholdings represents a major stimulus for the unfreezing of corporate cross-holdings and the restructuring and international opening of the German economy.

At other fronts, tax reform progressed more slowly. In particular, the government has failed to bring overall social security contribution rates down to a level below 40 per cent, as it had promised in the coalition treaty. Despite an improving financial situation the government has refrained from reducing the contribution rate for the unemployment insurance scheme. Instead, it has assigned priority to the consolidation of the federal budget and has seized the opportunity to reduce federal grants to the scheme.

Conclusions

This chapter has surveyed German welfare state reform in the 1990s in the fields of pensions, policies for the unemployed and taxation. The analysis has confirmed the received view that welfare state reform has been a protracted process. At the same time, it has identified quite different patterns of change in the three fields:

- Pension reform has been characterized by a lack of consolidation. Favoured by the limited role of the upper house, the Kohl government managed to pass a major pension reform against the SPD in opposition. However, key reform elements were suspended by the new red-green government. After some haggling, the Schröder government adopted a new pension reform in 2001.
- Policies for the unemployed have seen more gradual changes. While the Kohl government was forced into concessions by the Federal Council, it succeeded in pushing through some benefit cuts and a substantial reduction in the negative rights of the unemployed. The Schröder government has refrained so far from major reform initiatives.
- Tax reform suffered from stalemate in the mid-1990s. The Kohl government drew up a major reform package in 1996 which was blocked by the majority of the SPD-led states in the Federal Council. The Schröder government initiated a comprehensive tax reform package in 1999/2000. Despite the lack of a majority in the Federal Council, the government managed to shepherd the package through the upper house.

As has been shown, the policy-making framework was unfavourable to welfare state reform during most of the 1990s. The combination of strong constraints on executive authority and a high level of political confrontation has complicated the initiation and consolidation of reform:

- The fierce political confrontation has made it more difficult for governments to share the blame for unpopular measures and to sell them to the public. This problem has been aggravated by the fact that both SPD and CDU/CSU traditionally have been attached to the welfare state. As a consequence, the rejection of reform plans by one of these parties has nourished doubts about the need for and quality of reforms (Kitschelt, 2001).
- The strong constraints on executive authority, most notably the veto power of the Federal Council, have given the opposition the chance to block reforms and to force government into concessions. From this perspective, the combination of a highly constrained executive

authority and fierce party competition has raised the danger of deadlock (Lehmbruch, 1998).

* The lack of consensus and the high level of political confrontation have weakened the consolidation of reforms. The 1998 change in government allowed (and, in a way, forced) the SPD to undo some of the reforms undertaken by the Kohl government.

These mechanisms help us to understand why welfare state reform in Germany has been such a protracted process. However, the analysis has also made clear that these constraints on the initiation and consolidation of reform have lost importance after the 'neo-liberal turn' of the SPD. Although it is true that the Schröder government's lack of majority in the Federal Council and the confrontational strategy adopted by the CDU/CSU have complicated the passage of reforms, obstacles to reform have weakened. As party positions on both problems and solutions are now rather similar, conflicts over pension and tax reform have become of a more tactical nature. This makes it more difficult for the opposition to justify the blocking of reforms. Moreover, it means that controversies in the Federal Council are less likely to derail reforms. In the case of the 2000 tax reform, a failure of the government to forge a majority in the upper house would have marked an embarrassing political defeat for Schröder and Eichel and would have made additional concessions necessary. However, it would have resulted neither in a medium-term blockage of tax reform nor in a basic change in policy. The same will be true if the opposition succeeds in vetoing those parts of the Schröder government's pension reform legislation that require the approval of the Federal Council. These observations help explain why welfare state reform in Germany is now well under way, even though constraints on executive authority and political confrontation are still strong.

Notes

1 As Wolfgang Gerhardt, the chairman of the FDP, complained in the mid-1990s: 'We hold the government, but we don't hold power.'

2 Health care is somewhat different. In Germany, the sickness insurance scheme is traditionally administered by a plethora of different funds. Thus the majority of East Germans are members of East German funds and the direct transfer from the West to the East within the framework of the scheme has been limited.

3 Strictly speaking, the 630 DM jobs were thus in fact 610 DM jobs in 1997 and 590 DM jobs in 1996. Moreover, the threshold differed between East and West Germany. In April 1999, it was made uniform and frozen at 630 DM.

4 Formally, the German pension system consists of several branches. Blue-collar workers, white-collar workers and miners have their own systems, yet are subject to more or less the same rules. With some qualifications, this also applies to civil servants whose pensions are financed directly via the government budget.

5 Owing to a change in methodology, the pension level in 2030 roughly corresponds to the one envisaged by the '1999 Pension Reform'.

6 Two elements of the government's reform legislation bring the Federal Council in because they have a fiscal dimension: first, the provisions on state subsidies and fiscal incentives for the private pension pillar. Second, the creation of a special social assistance regime for pensioners.

7 In other areas, the government introduced measures that it had opposed in the past. The most prominent is the eventual abolition of primary unemployment assistance in 1999.

5 Spain, a *Via Media* of Welfare Development

Luis Moreno

The Spanish welfare state incorporates elements of both Bismarckian and Beveridgean traditions, and can be labelled as a *via media* with respect to other regimes of social protection. It combines universal and targeted access to services and benefits. The most relevant factor conditioning welfare development in Spain is the importance of decentralization both at the level of planning and policy implementation. Decentralization of social services has had a much greater impact than privatization.

After a long hyper-centralist dictatorship (1939–1975), a peaceful transition to democracy (1975–1979), and an active involvement in the process of Europeanization after its accession to the EEC (1986), Spain has undergone deep and far-reaching social transformations. In economic terms, Spanish development has been outstanding: in 1959 the Spanish GDP per head was 58.3 per cent of the EU average; in 1985, 70.6 per cent and, by 1998, 81.5 per cent. Spain would match the EU mean by the year 2025 if the annual 'catching-up' rate of 0.8 per cent were maintained. No other country in the group of the advanced industrial democracies has achieved a comparable rate of economic growth. However, economic problems, high levels of unemployment, a severe demographic imbalance and the abrupt decline of the traditional system of domestic care are now threatening the stability of the welfare settlement.

This chapter analyses developments in social policy and welfare in Spain during the second half of the 20th century and examines current reforms and policy changes for the near future. In particular, it focuses on the process of devolution of powers to the regions (*Comunidades Autónomas*). It also examines changes in the areas of unemployment, pensions and the financing of social policies, which are regarded as having particular relevance to Spain's welfare future. The development of the Spanish welfare system is a story of relatively successful expansion. It shows how subnational government can play a leading role in welfare innovation.

Political and social actors

The development of welfare in Spain can only be understood in the context of the historical background prior to the transition from Francoism to democracy (1975–1978). The peaceful reformist democratic transition was made possible by the deployment of consensual politics among representatives, parties and social actors, who accepted the fact that the reform process had to take into account the previous institutional framework. Thus, the consolidation of Spain's welfare state had to evolve from the institutions and social protection policies developed during Franco's dictatorship.

The legacy of Francoism

After the Spanish Civil War (1936–1939), the Francoist regime brought together a heterogeneous alliance of conservative and fascist groups, whose paramount concern was law and order. Their legitimacy was founded on the support of both the Army and the Catholic Church. This loose coalition enjoyed a certain degree of autonomy, in comparison to the type of state that developed in France, Germany, and Italy after the Second World War. The social losers of the Spanish Civil War were mainly the working class, the peasantry in the south of Spain, the republican and liberal middle-class factions, and some important political and cultural groups in Madrid as well as among the peripheral nationalities (mainly Catalonia, the Basque Country, and Galicia).

Francoism was above all representative of a reactionary despotism which aimed to accelerate and guarantee a rapid process of capitalist accumulation. In order to achieve this goal Francoism deployed political repression and violence in a selective manner (Flaquer et al., 1990). The long duration of Franco's regime allowed for the slow coalescence of several ruling classes of Spain. This coalescing ruling class was essentially a 'distributional coalition', engaging in rent-seeking rather than in the general well-being of society and in the increase of collective welfare and prosperity. Having said that, Francoism manufactured a demagogic façade concerned with the social well-being of Spaniards: the so-called *obras sociales* (social works).

In general terms, social policy in Spain under Francoism can be divided into three periods:

From 1940 until the late 1950s

This period was characterized by an attempt to achieve total autarchy with no foreign interference. Social policy was largely neglected and oriented towards both charity and beneficence.

'Our State must be Catholic in the social', declared Franco in 1937. The *obra social* was set up in order to 'bring joy and bread to the Spanish families'. The worker was regarded as a unit of economic production and, accordingly, was entitled to receive social protection against unexpected risks. In turn, he or she should be obedient and diligent. This kind of Catholic paternalism had been elaborated by the most reactionary sector of Spanish Catholicism, which advocated that income should correspond to social status.

A peculiar aspect incorporated in the *Fuero del Trabajo*, a constitutional Labour Act implemented by Franco's Government in 1938, concerned the social status of women. The Francoist State pursued the 'return' of women from the factory to the household. To this end a family subsidy was introduced within social security to encourage women to remain at home 'taking care of their husband and children'.

In 1939 the SOVI (*Seguro Obligatorio de Vejez e Invalidez*, Compulsory Insurance for Retirement and Invalidity) was introduced to provide benefits for low-waged employees. Public insurance was initially combined with a voluntary system of mutual benefit societies, which collapsed. In 1942, statutory sickness insurance was implemented. Its duration was limited in time regardless of the health condition of the claimant, and its implicit aim was to 'encourage' the employee to go back to work as soon as possible. Health services were delivered by both public and private institutions in agreement with the social security system. This latter arrangement secured the incomes of medical doctors, who in most cases also worked in the private sector. The pharmaceutical industry profited abundantly as well. In turn, the quality of the public health service was very poor.

The years from 1959 to 1967

These years marked *desarrollismo* (economic 'developmentalism'). The Stabilization Plan of 1959 marked the turning point for the progressive liberalization of the Spanish economy. Technocrats of the *Opus Dei* held the key posts in Franco's government and imported models of 'indicative planning' from France.[1] Some steps were taken to implement a system of labour regulation that moderated somewhat its *dirigiste* nature. In 1958, for example, a Collective Agreements Act allowed employers and employees to negotiate wages (which had previously been regulated by the Ministry of Labour) at the factory level.

Catholics aimed to develop their own trade union movement, intended to support a dominant Christian Democratic party after the demise of General Franco. Paradoxically, during the 1960s, some youth organizations became radical Catholic institutions that collaborated with Marxist organizations opposed to the Franco regime. The Social Doctrine of the Roman Catholic Church was 're-interpreted' by radical Catholics according to more egalitarian principles. They advocated the disappearance of the huge disparities between classes. In fact, many of the early Catholic activists during the 1960s took a leading role in the subsequent articulation of the Communist-controlled CCOO (Workers' Commissions). They also participated actively in the opposition to the Franco regime as members of clandestine left-wing parties.

In 1967 the Basic Law of social security (*Ley de Bases de la Seguridad Social*) was put into effect. It had a universalistic vocation and went hand in hand with a timid fiscal reform. A peculiar model of economic development – vocationally neo-Keynesian but constrained by the rigidities of an authoritarian regime – attempted the transition from an agrarian society to a fully industrialized polity with some degree of success, modifying in this process the occupational structure of the country.

From the late 1960s until the transition to democracy (1975–1978)

During this period the opposition movement against Francoism became very active. These were the years of political and social turmoil that constituted the prelude to the transition to democracy after the death of Franco in November 1975. In 1969, Don Juan Carlos had been appointed future head of state and, in 1970, a preferential treaty had been signed between Spain and the European Economic Community (EEC).

With the implementation of the General Education Law (*Ley General de Educación*) in 1970 and the General Law of social security Law (*Ley General de la Seguridad Social*) in 1974, the level of public spending rose very significantly. Considerable wage increases also took place between 1974 and 1976. These factors set the basis for the subsequent climate of social consensus that contributed to making the peaceful transition to democracy possible. From the 1970s onwards the bulk of social spending has been devoted to retirement pensions and unemployment benefits.

Governmental policy in democratic Spain

With the transition to democracy in Spain (1975–1978), a series of agreements among the main social and economic actors inaugurated a mode of democratic neo-corporatism as opposed to the non-democratic and despotic corporatism characteristic of Francoism. Early negotiations were geared at controlling inflation by means of wage restraint. In 1977, after the first democratic elections held in Spain since the II Republic (1931–1939), the *Pactos de la Moncloa* were signed by all main Spanish political parties. These Pacts established a policy of mutual restraint between government, employers and trade unions, and were signed with the explicit intention of consolidating democracy. The avoidance of strikes and lockouts and the introduction of wage restraints were also accepted by all concerned in order to allay the fears of a military *coup d'état*.[2] The Moncloa Pacts, as well as the other social peace and wage restraint agreements that followed, were crucial for securing the consolidation of democracy in post-Franco Spain.

The first democratic Government of the post-Franco era established the General Directorate for Social Action and Social Services (*Dirección General de Acción Social y Servicios Sociales*) within the Ministry of Health and Social Security. This governmental body took over the responsibilities of social assistance and public charities, which had previously been attached to various departments of the central government (principally, the Home Ministry). It ran programmes such as those related to the Social Assistance Fund (*Fondo de Asistencia Social*), whose non-contributory benefits covered old-age and disability pensions. This constituted the principal instrument of social assistance at that time.

The contributory sector of the social security system provided services for employees and their dependents. In 1978, social security was restructured with the grouping of old-age and disabled services into the Institute for Social Services (INSERSO – *Instituto de Servicios Sociales*), a quasi-autonomous public agency within the framework of the Ministry of Labour.

In parallel, local authorities (municipalities and provincial authorities) continued to run various programmes of social assistance, which were in many cases the inheritors of traditional public charities and beneficence. Private institutions also continued to provide charitable donations and some services, particularly those offered by Roman Catholic Church organizations. During the transition to democracy renewed demands for the implementation of new social services were coupled with an active mobilization of social workers to develop a new framework of service provision (Casado et al., 1994; Sarasa, 1993).

Between 1980–1982, the centre-right government of the UCD (*Unión de Centro Democrático*) initiated a process of economic rationalization. This meant a moderation in wage increases, as well as the beginning of a process of restructuring 'unproductive' industries. These policies were coupled with containment in the level of social spending (Rodríguez-Cabrero, 1989).

The *Partido Socialista Obrero Español* (PSOE) (Spanish Socialist Workers' Party) formed the government from 1982 to 1996. Policies carried out by the PSOE governments were mainly aimed at the economic moderniza-tion of Spain and the expansion of welfare. The 1982 electoral programme of the Spanish Socialists was phrased along 'orthodox' social-democratic lines. It advocated neo-Keynesian measures to strengthen internal demand by means of increasing public and social expenditure. However, the 'social liberals', whose policies diverged from the dogma of the tradi-tional social-democratic left, took the initiative in economic policy-making. They recognized the shortcomings of the Socialist government in neigh-bouring France (see Chapter 3), which had implemented demand-side policies unsuccessfully. They argued that large 'unproductive' industries had been kept alive artificially during late Francoism and should be 'restructured'.

The tough economic policy of adjustment carried out by the first Socialist governments pumped resources into industrial restructuring and liberalization policies to the detriment of other public spending. Macroeconomic reforms concerned large 'lame-duck' economic sectors (shipbuilding, iron or steel industries), and were implemented in a favourable international situation. This conjuncture allowed the govern-ment to carry out unpopular policies that would not jeopardize the politi-cal stability of the country.

1988 marked the beginning of a cycle of expansion of social spending and of major developments in social services. The Ministry of Social Affairs[3] was established, intended to develop social policies and public welfare intervention, which had been 'hidden' within the organizational structure of the Ministry of Labour. However, central intervention was conditioned by the consolidation of the regional systems promoted by the Spanish *Comunidades Autónomas*. Some argued against the establishment of a Ministry which would lack many powers already decentralized to the meso-government (Beltrán, 1992).

The newly created Ministry pursued co-ordination with the meso-governments in the development of general plans such as those concerning old age, drug addiction, equal opportunities, or young people. These plans did not pass into law, but were agreements intended to improve the working of systems of welfare provision throughout Spain. In particular, they paved the way for the future transfer of the social services of INSERSO to the regional level. The PSOE Government had previously failed in attempts to pass a National Social Services Act, designed to integrate all the social provisions of the contributory system of social security into one centrally managed institutional framework, in 1983 and 1984. The Spanish regions were reluctant to lose their role as the main protagonists in the structuring of welfare provision.

The most important agreement between the three layers of government took place in 1987, with the approval of the 'Concerted Plan for the Development of the Basic Provision of Social Services by the Local Authorities' (*Plan Concertado para el Desarrollo de Prestaciones Básicas de Servicios Sociales de las Corporaciones Locales*). This intergovernmental agreement has resulted in administrative co-operation between central, regional and local governments. The aim is to provide services at the municipal level for: information and counselling; social and day care services for the disabled and elderly; refuges for abused women, single mothers, orphans or mistreated minors; sheltered housing for the homeless; and services to prevent unemployment and aid labour-market re-entry.

This network of centres constitutes the basic level of primary provision in Spain, and was supported by all nationalities and regions except the Basque Country. The annual financing of this plan is met on equitable terms by the three layers of government. This agreement was the first in a model of intergovernmental relations characteristic of the process of the federalization of politics in Spain. It has had substantial implications for other policy areas (Agranoff, 1993).

During this period the major reform carried out by the central government was the generalization of means-tested old-age and disability pensions. In 1990, legislation on non-contributory pensions provided means-tested benefits for old-age and disabled citizens and their dependents, outside the social insurance system.

After the 1996 general elections, the centre-right *Partido Popular* (PP) (Popular Party) secured sufficient parliamentary support for its minority government. This was provided by the Basque Nationalists of PNV (Christian Democrats), the Catalan Nationalists of CiU (*Convergència i Unió*) (Liberals and Christian Democrats), and the nationalists of the Canary Islands (*Coalición Canaria*) (wide ideological spectrum).

In the period 1996–2000, and as a result of this wide parliamentary coalition of interests, the attempts to cut social expenditure advocated by neo-liberals within the PP were neutralized. An 'expenditure competition' between the governmental party and its parliamentary allies took place. Further to this, the more centrist members of the PP cabinet managed to gain control in those ministries related to social policy and welfare development, and maintained an attitude of negotiation with the social partners (trade unions and employers' associations). The *diálogo social* (social dialogue) among government and social partners led to several agreements, and was maintained with the objective of preserving the *paz social* ('social peace').

The PP renewed its mandate in the 2000 General Election with an absolute majority of parliamentary seats. The newly formed Cabinet was more inclined to the political centre and declared its commitment to some of the 'Third Way' proposals related to the 'new economy', and to continue the practices of pact building and politics by consent. This latter approach has been an important feature of political conduct in democratic Spain since 1975, and is now succinctly analysed.

European convergence and the 'Toledo Pact' on social protection

In 1986 the country joined the European Economic Community. Spain has become an important political partner in the process of further Europeanization. Since its accession to the EEC/EU the country has followed a path of growing convergence in economic policy output along the lines of some other European Continental countries. Similarly, the government has pursued neo-liberal responses to economic pressure and globalization. Nevertheless, trade union pressure for more welfare spending brought about neo-corporatist practices. This course of action, in response to neo-liberalism, reinforced the mode of consensual politics inaugurated in the period of transition to democracy, which has maintained negotiation as the cornerstone of welfare development in Spain.

The Social and Economic Agreement (AES: *Acuerdo Económico y Social*) was signed in 1984, and extended until 1986, by the government, employers' associations and the trade union UGT (CCOO declined to support the pact). Some of the predictions included in the agreement were later realized: inflation came down in 1984 from 12 to 8 per cent. However, unemployment increased and the employees' income share of the national total also diminished.

The confrontation between government and trade unions characterized the second term of the Socialists in power (1986–1989). This period was one of greater governmental concern for social policy and expenditure. Percentage coverage of the unemployed increased up to nearly 50 per cent of the total. A general improvement of retirement pensions was also implemented, as well as the public universalization of basic education (primary and secondary). These measures completed what some authors have labelled the 'social transition' of Spanish democracy (Estefanía and Serrano, 1987). The trade unions began to give priority to social policy in their programmes of action.

In the aftermath of the 1992 financial crisis of the European Monetary System and its knock-on effects on the Spanish economy, the trade unions revised all attempts at economic pacts with both government and employers. The year 1993 witnessed a deep economic crisis with a high level of unemployment, hardly any job creation and an acute ageing of the working population. The following year the main parliamentary political parties (PSOE, PP, IU and CiU) worked out a crucial inter-party pact on social security which was signed in the city of Toledo at the beginning of 1995. The Toledo Pact was ratified by the Spanish Parliament on April 6, 1995, and was the origin of subsequent reforms of the system of social protection (Cabanillas Bermúdez, 1997).

The agreement, the main points of which eventually passed into legislation, aimed principally at: reinforcing the contributory nature of the Spanish system of social security; raising social expenditure to the EU average; ensuring that the finances of the scheme were stable and extending universal programmes. The major reforms were a clear division between contributory social insurance (funded by both employers and employees), and universal non-contributory benefits (paid for through general taxation), provision for benefit uprating and procedures for review of the system. Contribution finance was to be fully in place by 2000, and contributions would be simplified, related more closely to salaries and increased annually in line with the expansion of the system. There would be two general regimes for paid labour and self-employed people: advantageous 'special regimes' would be brought into line with these. A reserve fund would be established from the annual surplus of the contributory system. Voluntary early retirement would be discouraged by reductions in pension entitlement, except in cases of industrial restructuring or after expiry of entitlement to unemployment assistance benefits. Disability pensions would be brought within the general scheme. Means-tested supplements financed from general taxation would be paid to families whose contributory pensions did not reach a minimum level, the cost to be reassessed after four years.

Pensions would be up-rated in line with price increases, taking the finances of the scheme into account. Voluntary and complementary private schemes have been encouraged through tax incentives for occupational provision. Pension calculations were to be based on a minimum contribution period of two years from 1997, raised to 15 by 2001. The rate applied in the calculation of pensions for the first 15 years of contributions was 50 per cent, rising to 80 per cent and 100 per cent for 20 and 25 years. Orphan pensions ages were raised and minimum benefits for widows under the age of 60 were increased.

A Permanent Committee with representatives of the government and the trade unions (UGT and CCOO) was established to monitor the implementation of the reforms. In order to maintain the climate of consensus achieved with the Toledo Pact, the Permanent Committee would present initiatives and proposals to the parliamentary commission responsible for social protection.

Institutional framework and policy responses

The Spanish 1978 Constitution was adopted by general consensus of the major political parties and approved by popular referendum.[4] The text reflects many of the tensions and political dilemmas that existed in Spain at the time, soon after the ending of a dictatorship of nearly 40 years. However, it also reflects a widespread desire to reach political agreement among all the political parties involved in the process of negotiation.

Spain is a constitutional monarchy which guarantees autonomy to each of the layers in its system of government. In line with the plural internal composition of Spain, which includes three 'historical nationalities' and 14 regions,[5] the 1978 Constitution established an open model of decentralization which paved the way for the establishment of a federalizing *Estado de las Autonomías* (State of Autonomies).

Universalization and targeting

Debates on universality and selectivity in welfare services and transfers have traditionally been related to issues of equity and redistribution. Spain characteristically combines universal and targeted services and has constructed a medium-sized system of social protection, compared with other EU countries (Moreno, 2000a; Moreno and Sarasa, 1992). The Spanish welfare state is fundamental to both social reproduction and political legitimization. Since its integration in the European Community (1986), Spain has followed a pattern of welfare convergence on three levels. First, universalization of social entitlements (education, health, pensions). Second, convergence in social expenditure patterns to the European median. Third, diversification in the provision of social services by private and 'third sector' organizations. In addition, regional home rule can be regarded as the most distinctive factor affecting welfare development in Spain. The decentralization process embodied in the 1978 Spanish Constitution has permeated all major areas related to both institutional framework and policy-making (see section below).

During the 1980s and 1990s, Spain confronted a period of constant increases in public expenditure at a relatively higher level than in most European countries. This was the result of providing the basis for new and costly social programmes, namely universal coverage in education, public health and the generalization of pensions. Growth of Spain's public spending has been designed to bring economic rationalization in line with the rest of the EU countries.

The move to a universal educational system has meant that the entire age group from four to 15 years old has access to nursery, primary and secondary schooling. About 12 per cent of public education spending goes to concerted private schools. These schools, together with non-concerted private education, covered 31 per cent of the total student population in 1990 (38.6 per cent pre-school; 34.5 per cent elementary; 28.7 per cent middle; and 8.1 per cent university). In 1992, relatively and absolutely, more women than men were in education in the 16- to 29-year-old age group. Among the 16–19-year-olds, 63 per cent of women were receiving formal education as against 53 per cent of men. Among 20–24-year-olds, the gender gap was more than 8 per cent (EPA, 1993).

The 1986 General Health Act set up a National Health Service, which guaranteed access to health care for all Spaniards and all foreign citizens resident in Spain. Coverage, already high in 1980 (83.1 per cent of all citizens and residents), was almost total by 1991 (99.8 per cent). (Almeda and Sarasa, 1996; Guillén, 2000).

Three quarters of the financing of Spanish health is public. Of the remaining one-quarter, 85 per cent are direct payments by individuals (mostly for private care and medicines). These figures remained stable during the 1980–1993 period. The most significant variation of this period was the shift of the financing of public expenditure from contributions to taxation. In 1980, as much as 82 per cent of the spending on health was met by social contributions, whereas in 1993 the corresponding figure was 20 per cent. This dramatic change is in line with the assumption that universalization of the public health service should be related to a system of general financing by taxation on the basis of a more equitable philosophy.

Public expenditure on health during the period 1980–1993 rose at a mere 0.5 per cent a year, indicating that universalization of coverage had not been matched by an equivalent improvement in standards of care. About 8 per cent of the population was covered by private health insurance (Freire, 1993). Some occupational schemes remain for groups in the well-protected core of the workforce.

Powers in the area of health provision have been decentralized to the seventeen *Comunidades Autónomas*. Some regions of these have implemented policies for the provision of services of a 'quasi-market' nature (Catalonia, Valencia) and have since faced problems in financing of their respective public health systems. Discussion of the adaptation of expenditure to socio-demographic changes has stressed the rationalization of health consumption, particularly of medicine, and especially for older people. Longer time-series are needed to evaluate properly the effects of these reforms on hospital management, financial restraint and the improvement of both efficiency and equality on health care.

The case of pensions and its implications for welfare financing is analysed below, but first we examine the most important factor affecting developments and reforms in the Spanish welfare state: the process of decentralization of power.

Table 5.1   *The territorial distribution of public spending in Spain (%)*

	1981[a]	1984	1987	1990	1992	1997	1999 (est.)
Central	87.3	75.6	72.6	66.2	63.0	59.5	54
Regional	3.0	12.2	14.6	20.5	23.2	26.9	33
Local	9.7	12.1	12.8	13.3	13.8	13.6	13

[a] Beginning of the process of devolution.
Source: Spanish Ministry of Public Administrations (MAP), 1997

Decentralization and federalization

In Spain there has been a growth of institutional 'stateness', or state pene-tration of the welfare sphere (Flora, 1986/87; Kuhnle, 1997). However, this should not be interpreted in Jacobin terms, by which central administra-tion and government are concepts synonymous to that of the state. In referring to 'stateness' we take into account all state institutions, i.e. central, regional and local. In fact, the *Comunidades Autónomas* (Autonomous Communities) have taken a leading role in the development of social assistance programmes and social services. Due to the growing importance of the regional and local levels in the provision of welfare pro-grammes, this is an area of increasing relevance for social policy researchers (Alber, 1995; Moreno and Arriba, 1999).

The construction of the *Estado de las Autonomías* in Spain had to follow a 'top-down' process of decentralization. This way of doing things is just one of the options available in the development of federal-like systems. The result at the beginning of the 21st century is not much more than a series of practices of a federal nature involving a series of politically con-current units (Moreno, 2000b). The decentralization process embodied in the 1978 Spanish Constitution has undergone a long period of consolida-tion. The degree of autonomy for the Spanish nationalities and regions is considerable. This is illustrated by the development of the distribution of public expenditure in Spain's three-tier system of government (Table 5.1).

The 1978 Constitution set in train the institutionalization of the social services in Spain. According to the Spanish *Carta Magna*, social assistance is a regional power in the 'exclusive competence' of the 17 Autonomous Communities (*Carta Magna*, art. 148, 1.20). Powers concerning the basic legislation and the economic regime of the social security system remain within the domain of the central government. However, the *Comunidades Autónomas* (Autonomous Communities) can exercise executive powers in the running of contributory programmes which can be decentralized to them (*Carta Magna*, art. 149; 1.17). The constitutional provisions neither define nor regulate the realms of social assistance and social services. All powers and responsibilities which are not listed as the 'exclusive compe-tence' of central government can be claimed and exercised by the Autonomous Communities (*Carta Magna*, art. 149.3).

As a consequence of the flexibility of the constitutional provisions, all *Comunidades Autónomas* claimed in their Statutes of Autonomy (regional constitutional laws) a large number of services and functions concerning social assistance, social services, community development, social promotion and welfare policies in general. The only services which remained outside the control of the meso-governments were those of INSERSO. However executive powers for running practically all INSERSO services were also transferred to the *Comunidades Autónomas* during the 1990s.[6]

During the period 1982–1993, the Autonomous Communities took the legislative initiative in their regional parliaments, and established regional systems of social services. In these pieces of legislation there were no references to social assistance as such. The implicit assumption was that social assistance was an 'exclusive' power of the Autonomous Communities, alongside social services. The main concern of the meso-governments in this period was to claim as many powers from the central administration as a flexible interpretation of the 1978 Constitution would allow. The *Comunidades Autónomas* have made extensive use of their constitutional prerogative for purposes of institutional legitimization.

A common basis for the legislation adopted by the regional parliaments to develop an integrated network of social services was the principle of decentralization. According to this, local governments would carry out the bulk of service provision, but the powers of legislation, planning, and co-ordination with the private and altruistic sectors would rest upon regional executives and legislatures.

All regional laws envisaged the social services as an integrated public system, open to all citizens without discrimination. Regional legislation on welfare provision was founded on the principles of universal and equal access. Traditional public welfare was to be 'updated' to avoid stigma. All things considered, the aim was one of modernization of the social services in line with other experiences of welfare provision in Western Europe. Such aspirations were in tune with the aim of rationalizing the provision of new social services.

On establishing the public systems of social services, the idea of the welfare 'mix' was also embraced enthusiastically by most Spanish meso-governments. Non-profit organizations, in particular, were incorporated in the general provision of social services, and many of them were subsidized by the regional public bodies.

The implementation of regional systems of social services in Spain did not proceed without some friction with central government. In 1986, a decision of the Constitutional Court (146/1986) established that, despite the 'exclusive' powers of the Autonomous Communities in this field, the central government could also develop programmes of social assistance guaranteeing equal treatment for all *Comunidades Autónomas*.

As a consequence of the process initiated in 1978, social assistance and social services are often treated as synonymous. Institutional fragmentation continues to be a defining trait of the Spanish welfare state, although the collaboration of the three layers of government may be seen as a

decisive factor in the rationalization of welfare provision. The process
of reform, however, is far from being over.

The approval of regional acts and the development of the *Plan
Concertado* have been carried out on universalistic grounds. Access is,
therefore, available for all citizens. Nevertheless, some programmes and
benefits – for example, those concerning minimum income guarantees for
non-contributory and disability pensioners – are targeted on the least-
favoured as social assistance. As a consequence, both social service culture
and the approach of the social workers balances both universalism and
selectivity (Serrano and Arriba, 1998).

The principle of decentralization advanced in regional legislation has
concentrated on the transfer of powers from central to meso levels. In fact,
the trend is to re-centralize the policy-making process towards the intermediate layer of government (the *Comunidades Autónomas*) to the detriment of the municipal locus of policy-making.

Important political decisions regarding the IMIs (*ingresos mínimos de
inserción*, programmes of minimum income of insertion) and the organization and planning of the services developed according to the *Plan
Concertado*, have reflected a higher degree of political dynamism by the
Comunidades Autónomas. They have also underlined the subsidiary role
played by local councils dependent to a great extent on regional financial
sources and political concerns. These have been articulated not only by
nationalist and regionalist parties, but also by the increasingly important
regional and federated branches of the main Spanish political formations
(PP, PSOE, and IU). Internal processes of power accommodation within
the parties have therefore contributed to the internalization of the shift
towards federal politics and policy-making. Only the big cities (namely,
Madrid and Barcelona) have been able to challenge meso-government as
the main protagonist in the development of social services.

Regional programmes of minimum income

The considerable expansion of both social services and social assistance
programmes has resulted in a *de iure* segmentation between the contributory (social insurance system for labour-market 'insiders') and social
assistance areas of welfare provision (for those excluded from the formal
labour-market). However, both domains are intertwined to produce the
sum-total of social provision. This has been inspired by the general principle of social citizenship and has thus expanded the grey areas between
social insurance and welfare assistance (Moreno and Sarasa, 1993).

The implementation of the public systems of social services by the
Spanish meso-governments has been coupled with the regional development of new social assistance programmes and the executive management of former social security services. This includes the assistance
subsidies inherited from the traditional schemes of public beneficence, the
management of the non-contributory pensions and the implementation of

the IMIs. Contingent and *ad hoc* benefits may also be granted to needy citizens. The 'safety net' providing the minimum means of sustenance and civic integration to those citizens and families who lack them rests to a great extent upon the network of regional systems of social services.

The process of policy innovation related to the programmes of minimum income started in September of 1988 with the announcement by the Basque Government of a regional *Plan de Lucha contra la Pobreza* (plan against poverty). This sparked off a regional mimesis, or 'demonstration effect', on the part of the other 16 *Comunidades Autónomas*. By the end of 1990, all Spanish meso-governments were engaged in the implementation of regional programmes of minimum income (Aguilar et al., 1995; Arriba, 1999; Ayala, 1997; Serrano and Arriba, 1998).

Some of the programmes were established mainly on the initiative of the regional governments as a result of combined action by both elected politicians and executive officials. In some other cases, the pressure exerted by the opposition parties in the regional parliaments was the main factor behind the elaboration of these programmes. Finally, a third path of policy-making was due to the mobilization of the regional branches of the main trade unions (CCOO and UGT) as well as some significant NGOs, such as Caritas.

Despite the different actors shaping the policy-making of the *ingresos mínimos de inserción*, the regional administrations are the main protagonists: prior to approval by the regional parliaments, no explicit popular demand was voiced in any of the territories of the *Comunidades Autónomas* for the implementation of these policies. The constitutional entitlement of the Autonomous Communities to exercise political autonomy underlay the development of the minimum income guarantee. 'Path dependency' was not involved, demonstrating that initiatives developed by sub-state communities with a perspective of 'cosmopolitan localism' can be more effective and efficient in social policy innovation (Moreno, 1999).

The regional programmes of minimum income are conditional quasi-universalistic entitlements, combining cash benefits with activation policies and programmes of social integration, mainly employment promotion and vocational training. Families are the units of reference even though individuals can be single beneficiaries; the means-tested threshold is set at a household income of about two-thirds of the minimum wage; there is a residence qualification of from one to ten years; and the benefit may be extended, provided that beneficiaries have complied with social insertion activities and their needs remain the same.

The central Ministry for Social Affairs showed reluctance to implement the regional minimum income programmes, due to concern about dependency and labour disincentives. Allegations that these new regional policies could affect territorial solidarity throughout Spain were among its criticisms (Ministerio de Asuntos Sociales, 1989). However, the newly created Ministry had already opted for making the generalization of non-contributory pensions its main priority, exhausting in this ambitious programme most of its political capital within the central government. The initiative taken by the *Comunidades Autónomas* left little room for the institutional manoeuvring of the central Ministry, and was based on the constitutional provisions safeguarding regional self-government. The Socialist government was unlikely to oppose the implementation of the regional minimum income programmes in this context.

Since the beginning of the process, the debate over the implementation of regional IMIs was unsophisticated (Aliena, 1991). The 'simplicity' of the arguments used by the Basque policy-makers illustrate the point. The IMIs were intended to reduce social marginalization and discourage labour passivity. Their development was supported by EU recommendations and other European experiences, such as the French *Revenu Minimum d'Insertion*. There was also a high degree of inter-party consensus and support from various Basque civil institutions.

Spanish meso-governments have benefited in terms of political legitimation as a consequence of the implementation of the IMIs. A clear message of policy innovation and political *aggiornamento* underlined their commitment to pursue the 'closure' of the system of social protection in Spain. The development was facilitated by the fact that they could afford such a highly targeted programme.

Regional governments followed a process of imitation in the implementation of minimum income programmes similar to that for social services legislation. Concerns about regional inequalities were not seriously considered. In fact, the effect of imitation by the different regions has arguably been to equalize the institutional output of the Spanish meso-governments, at least in terms of social policy innovation. This has resulted in the establishment of a differentiated arena of policy provision *vis-à-vis* the central government. At the horizontal level the *Comunidades Autónomas* have followed patterns of mobilization rooted in a self-perceived 'comparative grievance': no region wants to be left behind. These perceptions have interacted in a conflictual manner with the prerogatives claimed by the Spanish 'historical nationalities': the Basque Country, Catalonia and Galicia, who are particularly interested in maintaining a high degree of independence. The combination of these processes has resulted in a *de facto* policy equalization and in an incentive for policy innovation in those Spanish regions which have been traditionally lagging behind the 'modernized' ones.

Indeed, policy outcomes have resulted in some visible differences in benefit-levels and, above all, the nature of the 'insertion' programmes. Three groups of IMIs can be identified: workfare, where claimers must work for benefit: schemes linking the subsidy to labour-market re-entry; and discretionary social assistance benefits (Laparra and Aguilar, 1997). The impact of these innovative minimum income programmes has had an important effect in the debate about the completion of a 'safety net' in Spain. The Ministry of Labour and Social Affairs estimates that there were 211,221 beneficiaries in the whole of Spain (including dependent family members) by 1996, or around half of one per cent of the Spanish population.

Reforms and future scenarios

As a member of the Mediterranean family of nations, Spain shares with Greece, Italy and Portugal similarities in historical background, value-systems, and institutional characteristics. All four countries have had past experiences of authoritarian and dictatorial rule (for longer periods in the case of Portugal and Spain), and have suffered from economic and industrial 'delays' in the processes of modernization (except for early-industrialized areas in Italy and Spain). Religion has traditionally had a structuring role in all four countries, but the role of the Church as main organizer of social protection has diminished. This seems to correspond with a higher degree of secularization in the social practices of Southern Europe. The impact of Europeanization and globalization has brought about, respectively, increasing incentives to economic convergence with Northern and Central Europe (Economic and Monetary Union) and world-trade pressures to restrict social programmes. In broad terms, similar social-demographic trends, macroeconomic constraints and patterns of public policy can be observed in all four South European countries (Castles, 1998; Giner, 1986; Morlino, 1998).

As concerns the cultural and normative dimension of welfare development in Southern Europe, there is a self-perception of differentiated needs and lifestyles (intra-familial pooling of resources, home ownership, and heterogeneity of social reproduction). Also noticeable is a compelling household solidarity and a pre-eminent role for family inclusion and life-cycle redistribution (gift mechanisms, processes of age emancipation, proliferation of family companies and jobs). Cultural choices and practices have structured their civil societies in a characteristic mode resulting in heterogeneity of social reproduction, and particularistic practices in various kinds and degrees (social networking, patronage, clientelism, and group predation).

In institutional terms, there are fragmented systems of income guarantees and wide inter-generation disparities in cash benefits (for example, over-protection of the elderly in Greece and Italy).[7] The principle of status maintenance characteristic of the contributory systems in continental Europe links cash benefits to work position and the benefits are thus to be financed by both employers and employees. There is a preference for subsidiarity and an emphasis on the role of intermediary structures, but state organizations also play a significant role in the production and provision of social services.

Both the Mediterranean welfare mix and the gender/family/work nexus are adaptable and complementary. Analysis of politico-institutional development shows that the pivotal role of the family in social protection cannot be over-emphasized (Naldini, 1999). In Southern Europe the welfare state is to a large extent the Mediterranean welfare family. Intra-familial transfers are both material and through services: the involvement of women in the care of the elderly and children is crucial. However, the increasing participation of female workers in the labour force coupled with changes in the patterns of family formation and expansion raises major questions as to whether the system can survive in its current form.

Also characteristic of Southern European labour-markets is an apparent cleavage between 'insiders' (the well-protected core workforce), 'peripheral' (marginal) workers and 'outsiders' (precarious, 'left-outs', and 'junk' labourers). There are fragmented systems of income guarantees, and the informal 'tax-free' economies in Southern Europe are large.[8] This produces an uneven distribution of financial burdens across the various occupational groups.

In Spain labour policies are of the foremost importance since the unemployment rate is the highest in the European Union. This section focuses particularly on unemployment, as well as on pensions and the financing of social protection. All three areas are crucial to the future of welfare development.

Unemployment

According to the annual household survey, unemployment stood at 15.5 per cent or 2.5 million in September 1999, a sharp fall from 22.3 per cent only three years before. The active working population had also grown to approximately 16.5 million, about 41 per cent of the population. It is unclear whether the number registered as unemployed by the governmental job agencies of INEM (*Instituto Nacional de Empleo*) reflects the situation more accurately. INEM classifies as registered unemployed all those citizens who have filed a job application at any of its agencies and who legally qualify as unemployed: those in work, disabled people and students under the age of 25 are excluded. In order to be eligible for unemployment and social assistance benefits citizens must register. 9.5 per cent of the active working population was registered in September 1999.

Given the high rate of unemployment in Spain, some observers are puzzled by the stable social situation in the country, particularly for younger people: unemployment rates stand at about 40 per cent for men and 45 per cent for women aged 20–24 years. The lack of social tension may be explained by the relatively high public spending on unemployment benefits (4.8 per cent of the GDP in 1993, the highest percentage among EU12 countries) and the support of family and household networks of micro-solidarity.

The *Acuerdos sobre Estabilidad en el Empleo y Negociación Colectiva* (Agreements on Employment Stability and Collective Bargaining) were negotiated between the main employers' associations (CEOE and CEPYME) and trade unions (CCOO and UGT), and signed on April 1997. Subsequently, the PP government initiated the legislative implementation of the 'Agreements' with a law-decree, which was ratified by 94 per cent of Spanish MPs at the Congress of Deputies on June 6, 1997.

These labour reforms have had an ambivalent impact on job creation and employment stability in Spain. Employment growth has been steady since the implementation of such measures. By December 1999, two million stable jobs had been created according to the provisions set by the *Acuerdos* on 1997–70 per cent of all jobs created during the period. However, a third of these were temporary as against an EU average of 11 per cent. Simply to maintain the current proportion of temporary to permanent jobs, two permanent jobs must be created for every temporary job in the years to come.

Pensions

With the implementation of the Non-contributory Pensions Act in 1990, means-tested benefits for both old-age (over 65 years) and disabled citizens (over 65 per cent of disability) were established. By the late 1990s, there were nearly 8 million pensioners in Spain, of whom nearly 700,000 were non-contributory and around 200,000 were covered by the regional programmes of minimum income. The social security system ended the year with a surplus equivalent to 0.2 per cent of GDP in 1999, which enabled the government to establish, for the first time, a reserve fund. The pay-as-you-go pension system is expected to face a serious imbalance between workers and pensioners from 2005 onwards.

Spain's population is nearly 40 million and the annual growth rate has been a mere 0.2 per cent since the beginning of the 1980s. The main reason is the decline in fertility rates, which fell from 3.0 per cent in 1965 to 2.8 per cent in 1970, to 2.1 per cent in 1980 (below that required to ensure inter-generational replacement) and 1.07 in 1999 (the lowest in Europe). Projections for the year 2020 estimate that around 19 per cent of the total population of Spain will be over 65 years of age (European Commission, 1998).

Following the Toledo Pact, the *Acuerdo para la Consolidación y Racionalización del Sistema de la Seguridad Social* was signed between the Government and the two main trade unions (UGT and CCOO) on October 9, 1996. Subsequently, the Law on the Consolidation and Rationalization of the System of social security was passed on July 15, 1997. This legislation is designed to facilitate control of the expected increase in contributory pension spending. However, in 1998, 90,000 more pensioners joined than left the system (Chuliá, 2000). This figure is indicative of a trend towards a chronic social security deficit unless the growth in the creation of employment is maintained in the near future.

Political pressure on central government to raise minimum pensions mounted in 1999. Some regional executives participated actively in the demands and, in an early political decision, the *Junta de Andalucía* decided unilaterally to increase the rates for non-contributory pensioners and to meet the costs out of its own regional resources. The debate spread to other regions and paved the way to a new agreement between the PP government and the trade unions. Around three million of non-contributory, survivors', invalidity and minimum-income contributory pensioners

Table 5.2   *Social spending in the EC (EU12; % GDP)*

	1980	1985	1993	% increase 1980–1993
Belgium	28.0	29.3	27.6	−0.4
Denmark	28.7	27.8	33.2	+4.5
France	25.4	28.8	30.9	+5.5
Germany	28.8	28.4	31.0	+2.2
Ireland	20.6	23.6	21.4	+0.8
Luxembourg	26.5	23.4	24.9	−1.6
The Netherlands	30.1	31.7	33.6	+3.5
UK	21.5	24.3	27.8	+6.3
EU12	24.3	26.0	27.8	+3.5
Greece	9.7	15.4	16.3	+6.6
Italy	19.4	22.6	25.8	+6.4
Portugal	12.8	14.1	19.5	+6.7
Spain	18.2	20.0	24.0	+5.8

Note: Current expenditure at market prices.
Source: Eurostat, 1995: 16

Table 5.3   *Social expenditure by welfare regime (EC14; % GDP)*

	1980	1990	1995	% increase 1980–1995
Anglo-Saxon	21.5	24.3	27.7	+6.2
Continental	28.1	29.6	30.1	+2.0
Mediterranean	15.0	18.0	22.2	+7.2
Nordic	25.6	28.1	32.1	+6.5

Countries: Anglo-Saxon (UK); Continental (Austria, Belgium, France, Germany, The Netherlands); Nordic (Denmark, Finland, Norway, Sweden) and Mediterranean (Greece, Italy, Portugal, Spain).
Note: Unweighted averages.
Source: Kuhnle, 2000b: Table 1.1

benefited from the reform. The average increase of 5.4 per cent compared with the 2 per cent rise for other contributory pensioners.

Welfare financing

During 1980–1993, all Southern European countries increased their social expenditure at a higher rate than the EU12 average of 3.5 per cent (Table 5.2). According to Eurostat, social spending in Spain had already reached 24.0 per cent of the GDP by 1993, which compares with the EU12 average of 27.8 per cent. Data aggregated by welfare regimes shows that previous disparities in social spending fell between 1980 and 1995 (Table 5.3). The difference between continental and Mediterranean countries had been reduced by 5 percentage points. The EU states with the highest real growth rates of benefits per head were the four Southern European countries. Their average percentage increases were above 75 per cent, and in the case of Portugal about 140 per cent (Eurostat, 1997b).

Welfare transfers in Spain have been traditionally designed to secure 'income maintenance' for those citizens who have made contributions to the social security system during their working life. Employers' (53 per cent) and employees' (17 per cent) contributions meet the greater part of the financing of social protection spending. However, a significant shift has taken place in recent years with a gradual transferring of public money from the national budget to the social security accounts. In the not too distant future, and depending upon the renewal of the Toledo Pact in 2001, the contributory social security system will be entirely financed through employers' and employees' contributions. General taxation will then be responsible only for the cost of the non-contributory benefits and services.

Conclusion

Spain has achieved a very rapid and successful expansion of its welfare system since the period of transition to democracy (1975–1978) and subsequent integration in the EEC/EU (1986). Despite the substantial inequalities inherited from Francoism, the country has maintained sustained economic growth and distributed the benefits more equally. Spain's social structure has moved closer to that of neighbouring countries with a notable expansion of the middle classes. As regards welfare development, Spain has avoided the process of retrenchment that has affected the rest Europe for three main reasons: a higher degree of welfare spending has been possible because the country started at a lower level and because Spain's economic growth has been higher than in the rest of Europe. Second, the constitutional decentralization of powers and subsequent process of federalization has made available considerable autonomy to expand social policies and services at both regional and local levels. Third, and most important, the political legacy has given extra weight to the achievement of broad political and social consensus through negotiation between representative parties and social actors. It is remarkable that such a high degree of consensus has survived alongside decentralization.

The consensual approach adopted between the government and the social partners during the 1990s has had important repercussions for the consolidation of the system of social protection in Spain. It remains to be seen whether the consensus, which was renewed in the 'Agreement for the Consolidation and Rationalization of the Social Security System' of 1997, can be maintained in the future, especially in view of the anticipated pressures from the cost of pensions, the high level of unemployment and the declining birth rate.

After the 2000 General Election, which provided the incoming PP government with an absolute majority in parliament, the question was raised of whether a further liberalization of public services will mean the end of a climate of negotiation and agreement with the social partners. Neo-liberal groups within the PP are committed to the streamlining of the welfare state, while more centrist groups endorse the maintenance of the *diálogo social* (social dialogue) on welfare reform. This latter approach has also been renewed with the election in April 2000 of the new leader of the trade union *Comisiones Obreras* (CCOO), José María Fidalgo. He has insisted on the continuation of the practice of negotiation with the employers' associations and the government for the implementation of new policies and reforms. These will have to deal with four main areas of reform for the near future.

First, the public nature of social protection was reinforced during the 1990s. A multi-party consensus that social spending should keep pace with GDP growth was achieved. The reduction of previous levels of public debt together with a higher growth-rate than the EU average has allowed Spain to sustain its distinctive *via media* model of welfare development. A gradual separation of sources of finance is necessary to maintain this achievement. The non-contributory system of social assistance is based on the principle that the cost of universal benefits should be met by society as a whole and financed through general taxation. Contributory benefits are to be wholly financed from employers' and employees' contributions, although alternative complementary sources may be used in the future as national wealth increases (for example, a special charge for all taxpayers analogous to the French CSG – see Chapter 3).

Second, internal solidarity within the public pension system goes hand in hand with a reinforcement of its contributory nature. There is an observable emphasis on the actuarial principle of income maintenance linking cash benefits to be paid by social security more closely with total contributions made during working life. The automatic revaluation of minimum pensions and improvement of survivors' benefits is intended to provide a 'safety net', along with the non-contributory minimum income benefits of both national and regional programmes of social welfare. The latter are crucial in targeting social policies for the excluded and less-favoured social groups in a context where the 17 Spanish *Comunidades Autónomas* have full and 'exclusive' powers in the area concerning social assistance.

Third, social protection in Spain continues to rely heavily on the family as producer and distributor of welfare. The involvement of women in care for both older people and children has been crucial and has been traditionally considered a 'given fact'. However, the increasing participation of female workers in the labour force, coupled with new burdens on family formation and expansion, raise major questions as to whether the Spanish welfare system can survive. More institutional support for women is an essential precondition for the reversal of the worrying demographic trends in Spain. At the beginning of 2000, Spain's fertility rate was the lowest in Europe (1.07 per cent), and stood at about half the rate required to maintain population size.

Fourth, the role of the social partners, and especially of the trade unions and the employers' associations, has become more important. Their co-operation in the negotiation of the 'Agreements on Employment Stability and Collective Bargaining' of 1997 was crucial in steering legislative initiatives and governmental reforms towards the consolidation of the welfare state in Spain. The renewal of the Toledo Pact in 2001 is the major challenge in maintaining the *diálogo social* in the years to come.

In short, the achievements of Spain in expanding its welfare system and in maintaining a social consensus on the direction of reform during the last quarter century are unparalleled in the EU. The crucial question is whether the distinctive Spanish *via media* in welfare can be sustained in view of pressures from the cost of pensions for a rapidly ageing population; high levels of unemployment and temporary work; the low birthrate and rapid changes in family patterns; and increasing demands from regional authorities.

Notes

1 With the implementation of the 1959 Stabilization Plan public expenditure was reduced, the peseta was devalued, and investment controls were relaxed. Foreign holdings of up to 50 per cent in Spanish companies were permitted. The results of the *desarrollismo* were impressive, with GDP growing by an annual 7 per cent between 1960 and 1974.

2 On February 23, 1981, military officers stormed into Spanish parliament and kept hostage all members of the government and of both legislative houses until it became evident that the main bulk of Army commanders did not support the coup.

3 The ministry was formed by the General Directorate of Social Action, the INSERSO, the Institutes for the Women and the Youth, and the Board for the Education and Care of the Disabled. It also took responsibility of supervising the activities of NGOs, such as the Red Cross, the Blind Persons' Organization (ONCE, *Organización Nacional de Ciegos de España*), and other non-profit private charities.

4 On December 6, 1978, the Spanish Constitution received 87.9 per cent of 'Yes' votes, 7.8 per cent of 'No' votes, and 4.3 per cent of null or blank votes. 32.9 per cent of the electorate abstained.

5 The Basque Country, Catalonia and Galicia are constitutionally recognized as *nacionalidades históricas*. The rest of the *Comunidades Autónomas* are Andalusia, Aragon, Asturias, Balearic Islands, Canary Islands, Cantabria, Castile and Leon, Castile-La Mancha, Extremadura, La Rioja, Madrid, Murcia, Navarre and Valencia. The Spanish North African cities of Ceuta and Melilla have been also chartered local statutes of autonomy.

6 In 1996, this central governmental agency changed its name (i.e. *IMSERSO, Instituto de Migraciones y Servicios Sociales*, Institute for Migration and Social

Services). It has kept minor executive programmes regarding services for emigrants, as well as some co-ordination functions with EU programmes.

7 Italy and Greece are well above the EU mean percentage of 62.0 per cent for the per capita average pension (77.6 per cent and 78.8 per cent in 1991, respectively). This is not the case of Spain and Portugal (47.3 per cent and 42.1 per cent, respectively) with a more balanced inter-generation distribution of resources.

8 According to a much-criticized memorandum of the European Commission in March 1998, the 'underground' economy of Spain provided between 10 and 23 per cent of GDP. The European average varies between 7 and 16 per cent.

6 Switzerland: Stubborn Institutions in a Changing Society[1]

Giuliano Bonoli

The recent history of Switzerland's social and economic policy has shown that, in spite of its political isolation and relatively good macroeconomic conditions, the country confronts many of the problems that are torment-ing its European neighbours. In the 1990s, for the first time since the Second World War, Switzerland faced the problem of high unemploy-ment. Demographic ageing will hit the country over the next four decades, and is expected to put the pension system under severe financial pressure. At the same time, young entrants to the labour-market, mostly in the service sector, have to deal with job insecurity and low wages, and strug-gle to reconcile work and family life. The lack of state support tends to reduce the birth-rate, which worsens the demographic problem. In sum, even though Switzerland is commonly seen as an empty space at the centre of the map of Europe, its circumstances precisely reflect those else-where on the continent.

It is widely accepted that the Swiss welfare state requires extensive adaptation. First, there is an issue of sustainability in the face of demo-graphic ageing, but this is probably not the main problem. Switzerland, being a notorious welfare laggard, has the advantage of finding itself with an incomplete welfare state at a time when other countries need to retrench. The state welfare system is relatively cheap, and relies to a large extent on private forms of provision. The need to retrench is perhaps less pressing than elsewhere in Europe. However, a second issue is likely to trouble Swiss policy-makers over the next few years. This concerns the protection of the so-called 'atypical' workers, who were not really taken into consideration when most schemes were designed but whose num-bers are soaring. Related to this is the problem of supporting young fam-ilies, in order to avoid a descent into 'a low fertility equilibrium' (Esping-Andersen, 1999: 67). The Swiss welfare state might require some localized pruning, but above all it needs to respond to the current shift to a post-industrial economy and labour-market structure. It is in a way an enviable situation, as Swiss politicians may be spared the blame-generating exercise of implementing substantial welfare retrenchment.

There are several reasons to believe that the coming decade will be a crucial period for the development of the Swiss social, political and economic model. In the post-war years the country enjoyed unequalled levels of independence and, by the same token, isolation, which were accompanied by some of the highest levels of prosperity found in the Western world. The peculiarity of the country's political, economic and social structures, as well as its economic success, were responsible for the interpretation of its situation as a *Sonderfall*, a special case, which being successful, did not need to be abandoned nor modified. Since the 1990s, however, the capacity of the *Sonderfall* to last into the 21st century has increasingly been called into question. The process of European integration, from which the country has excluded itself, may damage the competitiveness of Swiss producers and restrict their access to European and world markets.

Moreover, the traditional instruments for dealing with socio-economic and political challenges developed during the post-war period seem ill-suited to the new international economic and political context. The Swiss post-war model was based on the integration of almost all social groups in power and wealth sharing, but excluded two of them: foreigners and women. The problem is that Switzerland now, and over the next few years, will need both of these groups. Because of demographic ageing, Switzerland needs women to have more children while working, and immigrants to compensate for the shrinking of the workforce. Social policies towards these two groups, however, are virtually absent from the welfare state repertoire and must be invented. This is likely to become a major policy challenge.

The Swiss post-war social model is under pressure that will increase during the next few decades. However, adaptation is likely to be extremely difficult, and, despite the government's commitment to modernize the welfare state, it is not at all certain that such reforms will eventually be adopted. The Swiss political system, in fact, allows the government comparatively little control over policy. The institutional arrangements of the country are such, that in order to legislate, a very large consensus is needed. Welfare state adaptation takes place in the context of the overall uncertainty generated by political institutions. The New Institutionalist claim that the link between socio-economic pressures and policy responses is neither linear nor direct is nowhere clearer than in the case of Switzerland, where the ability of the government to steer policy is very limited.

This chapter drives home this point. It starts by presenting the key features of the political system and policy-making process. It then looks at the main socio-economic pressures that are affecting state welfare, broadly understood to encompass social programmes, and also the relationship between the state, the (labour) market and the family. The discussion subsequently moves on to look at policy changes in selected areas: pensions, unemployment policy and fiscal policy related to welfare. Policy developments in each area show the difficulty that the government experiences in defining policy directions.

The state, the political system and the key actors

History has given Switzerland a weak state. Until the mid-19th century, Switzerland was a fairly loose federation of sovereign states, the cantons. The modern state was established in 1848, after a short civil war which opposed the more conservative Catholic cantons to the majority of Protestant, liberal states. The winners, the Liberal cantons, who supported the creation of a centralized state, were nevertheless willing to accept a compromise with the Catholics, who were keener to retain aspects of cantonal independence. As a result, the constitution, adopted in 1848, allowed individual cantons substantial powers in all areas of government policy, and enshrined the principle of subsidiarity. At no stage since its creation has the federal state been intended as the central locus of political power.

State structures

The federal structure of the state is certainly responsible for much of its weakness. Cantons have powers in all areas of policy that are not explicitly attributed to the federal state by the constitution. As a result, before the federal government can legislate in a new domain, it needs to modify the constitution. Federalism also means that in many policy areas substantial decision-making as well as managing powers are held by cantonal governments. This applies to education, fiscal policy and some social programmes, including social assistance and family benefits (Kriesi, 1995: ch. 3; Vatter, 1999).

Moreover the Swiss state, in particular parliament – but also the administration – is characterized by a high degree of influence of organized interests and particularly business associations. In the mid-19th century, these organizations were considerably more developed than the newborn federal state. As a result, the authorities had to co-operate with them in a range of economic and social policies, which included vocational training, the collection of statistics and the distribution of subsidies. The political role of interest organizations was further reinforced and institutionalized in more recent years, most notably after the Second World War. The standard policy-making process today includes consultation of all relevant interest groups, and often draft legislation is prepared by 'expert commissions' composed mainly of interest groups representatives (Bonoli and Mach, 2000; Mach, 1999; Papadopoulos, 1997).

The weakness of the Swiss state is reinforced by the political institutions that must be used to govern the country. The Swiss constitutional order includes a series of checks and balances which are meant to reduce the potential for the concentration of power with the central government. The most crucial concerns the provision for dissatisfied voters to call a referendum against any piece of legislation adopted by parliament[2]. Referendum politics, in fact, is notoriously different from parliamentary politics, as party discipline among ordinary voters is not as strong as it is among MPs. Typically, political parties issue voting recommendations for each referendum. However, a recent study shows that on average, 12.5 per cent of voters ignore party recommendations (Papadopoulos, 1996: 30). This figure might suggest that lack of party discipline is unimportant, since the government coalition can count on the support of some 80 per cent of the electorate. Nevertheless, it should be noted than many referendums are relatively uncontroversial which implies stronger compliance with party recommendations. On the other hand, in the case of controversial decisions, disregard of party guidelines is more widespread, with the result that voters may sometimes reject government proposals.

Consensual politics

The response of Swiss elites to the structural weakness of the state has been to develop what is known as a consociational type of democracy which pervades politics and policy-making. Its roots, however, go back to long before the establishment of democracy and of the modern state in Switzerland. Consociational practices of power-sharing between social groups emerged at the cantonal level soon after the Reformation, which split the country between Catholics and Protestants. In order to manage the diversity introduced by the new religious cleavage, several cantons developed forms of 'parity' representation in official bodies, involving power-sharing on equal terms between the two religious communities (Lehmbruch, 1993). In the following centuries, this method proved apposite to deal with other cleavages that affected the country, at the cantonal and at the federal level: most notably the linguistic division and, during the 20th century, the left–right cleavage in politics.

One of the most significant current features of Swiss consociational democracy is an oversized coalition government. The Federal Council, which has had the same composition since 1959, consists of a four-party coalition that includes the Christian Democrats, the Social Democrats and the Radicals (each with two ministers), and the Democratic Union of the Centre (with one minister). Together, these parties account for more than 80 per cent of MPs in the lower chamber of parliament, although the government could rule with the support of any three of the four. Because federal councillors are elected individually, they need the votes of other parties, and in this respect they tend to be selected among the more moderate individuals in each camp. This facilitates the consensual character of the government's operations, but reduces its control over parliament and over the electorate in referendums, as the most charismatic figures are unlikely to become federal councillors. Overall, the Federal Council's influence on policy-making is not comparable to that of governments in parliamentary systems.

A second important consociational practice is a policy-making process in which interest groups play a substantial role in the definition of policy

(Papadopoulos, 1997). Typically, legislative change is preceded by a lengthy and highly structured consultation procedure, which can be more or less encompassing, depending on the potential for the policy to generate controversy. Legislation is often drafted by 'expert commissions' which normally include representatives of all the relevant interest groups. During the golden age of the consensus model (1950s and 1960s) the agreements reached in this way were generally accepted by parliament with very little change, thanks also to the existence of an informal core of policy-makers who actually made most decisions (Kriesi, 1982, 1995). In more recent years, as will be seen below, parliament has become increasingly reluctant to ratify agreements reached by interest groups and, on various occasions, has imposed changes in a majoritarian way.

The Swiss consociational model has traditionally guaranteed political inclusion for influential groups: those whose power resources were sufficient to make effective use of the veto points provided by the political system. Inclusion was therefore not universal. Those who were left out were women, who were not granted the right to vote until 1971 at the national level, and foreigners who make up some 20 per cent of the population and do not have the right to vote at the federal level. This pattern of inclusion/exclusion in decision-making is to a large extent replicated in other areas of the Swiss social model: the labour-market and the welfare state. Both groups functioned largely as a labour-market buffer during recessions, allowing Swiss men to keep their jobs. Social policies targeted on either of these two groups are virtually non-existent in the Swiss welfare state, which has traditionally concentrated its efforts on the core workforce of male nationals (Cattacin and Tattini, 1999).

The party system

Thanks to an electoral system which guarantees proportional representation to political parties, these are quite numerous in Switzerland. The parliament elected in October 1999 includes members of 14 different parties. The big four, however, who form the ruling coalition, account for most of the votes and political influence. Together the Socialists, the Radicals, the Christian Democrats and the Democratic Union of the Centre obtained 81 per cent of the votes cast at the last general election and control 86 per cent of the seats in the lower house of parliament (in the upper house, because of the smaller number of candidates per canton, they control virtually all seats).

For most of the 20th century the Socialists (PSS) were the largest party in the country, but have lost their position to the Democratic Union of the Centre in the last election. The party has been a member of the ruling coalition since 1959, with two ministers. In government it often finds itself in a minority position on social and economic policy issues, as the representatives of the three remaining parties tend to have a common view in these areas of policy. That is why, in spite of being a government party, the PSS still periodically plays the role of an opposition party, campaigning against decisions taken by the government. At the last election the PSS obtained 22.5 per cent of the votes cast for the lower house and gained 51 seats.

The second largest party for most of the century have been the Radicals (PRD), a liberal party that because of its links with business and ability to build alliances is arguably the most influential in Swiss politics (Kriesi, 1980, 1982). On social and economic policy issues it follows a traditional liberal orientation, favouring limited state intervention in economic matters. In the 1999 election, the Radicals were chosen by 19.9 per cent of voters, giving them 43 seats in the lower house.

The Christian Democrats (PDC) have traditionally been a strong party, but have lost a significant share of the vote in recent years. In the 1990s, the PDC was unable to develop policy proposals that were acceptable to its working-class electorate, represented also by the Catholic unions, and its business wing. The current parliament contains 35 Christian Democrats, who were elected by 15.9 of voters.

Finally, the Democratic Union of the Centre (UDC), originally a farmers' party, has traditionally been the weakest of the big four, but recently it has successfully recycled itself into a populist, anti-foreigners and anti-Europe party, becoming the largest party in the country at the 1999 election, when it obtained 22.5 per cent of the votes and 44 seats in the lower house. With the exception of the last election, the Swiss party system has proved extremely stable over the years, with only small variations in relative party support throughout the last century (Ladner, 1999).

Organized interests

The Swiss system of organized interests is relatively fragmented. On the employers' side, there are five main associations. Large, export-oriented employers are represented by the Swiss Union of Commerce and Industry, known in Switzerland also as Vorort, and by the Union of Suisse Employers (UPS). Banks have a separate peak organization, the influential Swiss Association of Bankers. Small business is represented by a distinct employers' organization, USAM, which is certainly less influential than its larger counterparts but tends to be more anti-statist and vociferous. Finally, agricultural employers and self-employed farmers are represented by the Swiss farmers' union (Mach, 1999).

On labour's side, the key division is ideological. The USS, the largest peak association of workers, is close to the Socialist party. In fact many trade unionists are also Socialist MPs in the federal or in cantonal parliaments. In addition, there is an association of white collar workers (FSE) and a federation of Christian unions (CSCS). At 25 per cent, the unionization rate is rather low compared to most other European countries (Ebbinghaus and Visser, 1999).

The changing socio-economic context

As in other Western countries, socio-economic changes in Switzerland can be summed up as a shift from an industrial to a post-industrial economy and society. This development, which initially concerns the sphere of production, spills over into many other aspects of social, political and economic life. It changes the nature of employment, increasingly less characterized by stability and security. It facilitates access to employment for women, which in turn puts pressure on families as the locus of biological and social reproduction. All this, of course, is set against a background of increasing economic and political interdependence among nation states, which diminishes their ability to find national solutions to current problems. These developments constitute a powerful set of pressures on the Swiss social model.

External pressures

Because of the small size of its internal market, Switzerland has always had an internationally oriented economy. As far as products markets are concerned, Swiss manufacturing has had a global presence for decades, particularly in the main industrial sectors: engineering, and the chemical, watchmaking and textile industries. With regard to financial markets, Switzerland has never had capital movement controls, and has traditionally been able to retain investors since interest rates are lower than those in the major nearby alternative market, Germany. Given this relatively high degree of insertion in the world economy from the early post-war period, Switzerland can be expected to be comparatively less vulnerable to economic globalization than most of its European counterparts.

This view is probably accurate in a broad perspective, as Switzerland fared relatively well during the 1980s and the 1990s, the period in which economic globalization accelerated. Yet, especially in the 1990s, some sections of Swiss business significantly changed their behaviour both in the economic and in the political sphere. The explanation given for this change of direction is, invariably, economic internationalization and the need to remain competitive in the global economy. The changes concerned first the organization of production, with an unprecedented wave of restructuring in industry and services, but also in politics, where some sections of the export-oriented business abandoned their traditional consensus-oriented positions (Bonoli and Mach, 2000).

Labour-market changes

Historically, the Swiss labour-market has been characterized by comparatively high employment/population rates. Levels of employment remained high throughout the post-war period, with significant declines on two occasions: the mid-1970s and the early 1990s. Unemployment, however,

Welfare States Under Pressure

Table 6.1 *Labour-market indicators*

	Employment-rate (% of population aged 15 to 64 in employment)	Employ-ment-rate, women	Part-time employ-ment as % total employment	Women part-time employment as a % of female employment	Wage inequality (D9/D1)	Unemploy-ment
1970	76.8	52.3	12			0.4
1980	71.0	54.0	15			0.2
1990	76.1	59.2	19		2.7	0.5
1998	80.4	70.9	28.5	53.8	2.6	3.9 (March 2000: 2.3)

Source: OECD Statistical Compendium, Labour force statistics, 1997b; OFS, 2000 OECD, 1998b

remained virtually non-existent until the early 1990s (see Table 6.1). During the recession of the 1970s, a decline in total employment was to a very large extent absorbed by the reduction in the number of foreign workers and working women. Job losses were substantial: about 11 per cent of total employment, or 330,000 jobs, were lost between 1973 and 1976, and yet did not result in an increase in the unemployment rate. Over the same period, the female employment rate dropped by 3.3 percentage points to 50.8 per cent, by far the biggest decline of female employment among OECD countries. The number of foreign workers dropped from just under 900,000 in 1973 to 650,000 in 1977 (Armingeon, 1999).

The job-losses provoked by the recession of the 1990s, unlike the 1970s, have been accompanied by an increase in the unemployment rate. This time women did not withdraw from the labour-market, as female employment stagnated between 1990 and 1995, and increased thereafter. Similarly, the number of foreign workers decreased by around 30,000, a much lower decline than that experienced in the 1970s, and insufficient to compensate for the loss of male jobs. The labour-market buffer traditionally provided by foreigners and women seems to have stopped working since the 1990s. This explains the emergence of unemployment in a country which had previously managed to sustain full employment throughout the post-war years.

In the late 1990s, total employment picked up again. Between 1994 and 1998 total employment increased by 65,000. The increase concerned both male and female employment as well as part-time and full-time jobs, though the overall proportion of part-time employment continued to rise throughout the 1990s. New jobs were created in the sheltered sectors of the economy. At the low-skill end, 21,000 new jobs were created in the trade and tourism sector and 55,000 new jobs in the personal and social service sector. At the high-skill end, the financial/real estate sector saw an increase in employment of 48,000. Over the same period, the manufacturing and the construction industries continued to lose jobs.

At first sight, Switzerland seems to be moving towards a post-industrial employment structure along the American path, with a substantial expansion at both ends of the service economy. However, this job performance is combined with moderate levels of earnings dispersion, much closer to the continental European average than to English-speaking economies. In the mid-1990s, the ratio between the upper limits of the 9th and the 1st deciles of the earnings distribution (D9/D1) was 2.72 in Switzerland, 2.32 in Germany and 4.39 in the US. What is more striking, is the fact that such a moderate level of earnings dispersion remained stable throughout the 1990s, which, contrary to prevailing theories of post-industrial employment (for example Esping-Andersen, 1999; Iversen and Wren, 1998), has not prevented job creation in the low-skill service sector.

It has been noted, however, that while the expansion of employment of the late 1990s was not accompanied by increasing wage inequality, part-time jobs and self-employment have expanded rapidly. According to Flückiger (1999), the expansion of these less secure forms of employment is the Swiss functional equivalent of rising earnings inequality in English-speaking countries. Employers often resort to part-time work to save on the wage bill, because social contributions are proportionally lower for part-time workers. Below a given earnings level, which part-time workers rarely exceed, affiliation to a (costly) company pension fund is not compulsory.

The expansion of part-time employment seems to be an inevitable feature of the transition to a post-industrial employment structure in Switzerland. Employers like it because it is cheaper than the full-time equivalent. Women, and perhaps more generally, families, are also keen on it, because it helps them reconcile work and family life. Given the overall lack of support in this area of policy, part-time employment is often the only way out of the work–family predicament. Part-time jobs are taken up predominantly by women. In 1998, more than 50 per cent of the female workforce worked part-time.

Demographic change

Like other European countries, over the last few decades Switzerland has experienced a substantial drop in fertility rates accompanied by increasing life expectancy and stagnating migration, which, if current trends persist, will result first in a massive increase in the proportion of older people in the population over the next three to four decades and subsequently in population decline. This trend has potentially serious implications for various aspects of the economy and of society. First, it will put increased strain on the welfare state, which in Switzerland, has a strong pro-elderly bias. Second, population ageing and decline will result in a reduction in the size of the working age population, which given the current relatively high employment rates, is likely to result in labour shortage. Like the rest of Europe, Switzerland will probably soon face societal

Table 6.2　*Population projections according to three scenarios*

	1998	Projection	2010	2020	2030	2040	2050	Assumptions for 2030	
								Fertility rate	Foreigners as a % total population
%		Higher	17.4	20.2	23.1	24.0	23.9	1.8	23.9
aged	15.2	Central	17.5	20.5	23.7	24.9	24.9	1.56	21.9
65 +		Lower	18.1	21.6	25.6	27.2	27.1	1.2	17.8

Note: in 1998, fertility rate = 1.46; Proportion of foreigners in the population = 19.4 %.
Source: OFS, 2000

choices regarding whether to become an immigration country or an ageing and shrinking one.

The federal statistical office produces demographic projections until the year 2050, based on different assumptions. Table 6.2 reproduces the central as well as two extreme projections with regard to the assumptions they make on future fertility, migration and mortality trends. A massive increase in the proportion of older people seems inevitable, even in the most optimistic scenario, where the population aged 65 and over is expected to soar from the current 15.2 per cent to 24 per cent in 2040. Other, less optimistic scenarios present bleaker pictures. The central projection, which is still based on a moderately optimistic assumption concerning fertility rates (expected to rise from the current 1.46 to 1.56 in 2030), predicts a quarter of the population aged 65 and over by 2040. The lower projection, which assumes that fertility will decline further to reach current Southern European levels by 2030, expects older people to make up some 27 per cent of the population in 2040. In both the central and lower projection, absolute population size will start to decline, from 2015 and 2005 respectively.

Demographic change will also impact on the size of the working age population. In absolute terms, the number of people available for work will start declining from 2015 in the central projection, with the loss of nearly 400,000 potential workers by 2050 (or 10 per cent of the 1998 workforce). If the lower projection is followed, the shrinkage will start before 2005, and by 2050 the workforce will have lost 25 per cent of its workers. With the higher projection, the size of the working age population will continue to increase throughout the period.

These bleak scenarios may not happen. After all, how can it be possible to predict future developments over such a long time horizon? And yet demographic projections are very clear instruments: if the key parameters which determine the evolution of a population do not change – in other words if Swiss women continue to have fewer children and the current restrictive immigration policy is maintained – then the scenario becomes worryingly likely. For these projections not to materialize, something must change over the next few decades, and this can only be one of two things: either Swiss women will have more children, or more immigrants will be allowed into the country. These two groups, who have been neglected by the welfare state in previous years, can now play an essential role in the maintenance of an adequate demographic balance.

Families

Like the rest of Europe, Switzerland has seen substantial changes in family structures during the last few decades. Of these, the most important as far as its impact on social and economic policy is concerned, is certainly the massive entry of women in the labour force, and the implication of this development for other aspects of family life, such as social and biological reproduction. Together with the increase in the proportion of women in employment, Switzerland has witnessed a decline in its fertility rate. All this in an overall context in which families, and particularly women, are finding it extremely difficult to work and at the same time to fulfil socially and institutionally determined family obligations. Relative to some of their European counterparts, Swiss families enjoy little support from the state in their struggle to balance work and family responsibilities.

Responsibility for a child is a major obstacle to paid work for Swiss women. Employment rates for women decline sharply as the number of children increases. Female employment falls from 80 per cent for childless women to 57 per cent for those with one child, 51 per cent for those with two and 42 per cent for those with three or more (OFS, 1998: 146). The relationship between the number of children and employment is much closer to the German situation than to that found in the Nordic countries or in Britain (Hantrais and Letablier, 1995: 24). Even though the above discussion of the Swiss employment trajectory to post-industrial employment presents many similarities with the liberal model, it seems that with regard to the gendered division of labour, Switzerland is much closer to the conservative model typified by Germany.

In this context, Swiss families are experiencing severe difficulties in reconciling work and family life. Besides reliance on informal care, the strategy that seems to be used most often is women's part-time work. Swiss labour law does not restrict the use of part-time work, which has developed substantially over the last few decades (see Table 6.1). This situation, however, appears sub-optimal, in at least two respects. The first casualty is family size. Swiss women have on average 1.46 children each (in 1998). However, when asked about their desired number of children, the average answer is significantly higher, at 2.2 per cent. According to a recent national survey on the family, the gap between the number of children desired and achieved can to a large extent be attributed to the difficulties experienced in managing paid employment and childcare. Women who do not intend to have more children tend to agree with the statement that 'For a woman it is very difficult to work and have children' (58 per cent) (OFS, 1998). Current prevailing arrangements for dealing with family responsibilities do not seem to fulfil the needs of most women. In addition, they produce the low fertility rate which contributes to demographic ageing.

The current work–family arrangement has a second casualty: the pensions of currently working women. The Swiss pension system relies on a combination of three pillars, of which, for most current workers and future retirees, occupational pension is the most important. Occupational pension coverage is compulsory for employees earning above CHF 24,000 per annum: a threshold which is generally exceeded by full-time workers, but much less frequently by part-time employees (the threshold is not adjusted for time worked). The result is that occupational pension coverage is virtually universal for male employees, but reaches only 80 per cent for women. The part-time work-based strategy for reconciling work and family life adopted by many Swiss women has serious implications for their ability to gain an entitlement to a decent pension.

Foreigners

Switzerland has traditionally been an immigration country, particularly so after the Second World War. The integration of a foreign-born population has nevertheless proved problematic. The 1970s saw the emergence of a strong xenophobic movement, which resulted in a series of (failed) referendum attempts to impose a quota for the number of foreigners that can be allowed into the country. Xenophobic pressures faded away throughout the 1980s and early 1990s, but seem to have returned in the late 1990s, possibly in response to a change in the composition of the immigrant population. The xenophobic movements of the 1970s were directed mainly against Italian and Spanish residents, who, according to opinion polls, are now largely accepted by the native population. Current anti-foreigner discourse instead targets residents who migrated from the Balkans.

This situation is obviously worrying in itself and also in relation to the process of population ageing and decline, expected to occur over the next four decades. As seen above (Table 6.2), official demographic projections generally assume an increase in the number of foreign residents in the country (except in the most pessimistic scenario). If population decline is to be avoided, the influx of immigrants needs to be substantial. Of the three scenarios presented in Table 6.2, only the highest is not accompanied by population decline. It assumes an increase in the proportion of foreigners (from 19 to 24 per cent in 2030) but also an increasing fertility rate (1.8 in 2030). If fertility remains closer to current levels, then the number of immigrants needed to avoid population decline will be more substantial.

The authorities seem ill-prepared to manage the likely, and possibly inevitable, increase in the size of the immigrant population. Proactive measures to fight xenophobic attitudes and to favour integration are rare and often clumsy. The association agreement signed with the European Union, which includes the free movement of workers, might help improve the capacity of the country to integrate foreign workers and will allow Swiss employers to recruit workers from the whole EU more easily.

The Swiss trajectory to a post-industrial economy and society

The above discussion of current social and economic change in Switzerland suggests that the country combines features that are typical of the US trajectory towards a post-industrial economy and society with characteristics that are more akin to its German antithesis. Switzerland seems closer to the US with regard to institutions, particularly in the areas of labour-market regulation and welfare. Swiss labour law is unique in continental Europe for the extremely low extent of employment protection, making it akin to British or American legislation (Mares, 1996). Similarly, in the area of collective bargaining, Swiss practice in relation to the coverage of sectoral agreements and to their content is increasingly closer to the Anglo-Saxon model of decentralized industrial relations (Mach, 2000), although good protection through collective bargaining is still available to workers in the high-skill branches if the economy.

On the other hand, Switzerland looks much more similar to Germany with regard to the more culture-related aspects of its social model, particularly those which concern the work–family relationship and attitudes towards foreigners. Swiss women find it difficult to balance work and family life, with many deciding to give up on one or the other. Swiss families externalize little of their social reproduction tasks, and when they do it is most often to other extended family members (for example, child care being provided predominantly by grandparents).

This peculiar combination of liberal and conservative social characteristics confers a certain uniqueness to the Swiss socio-economic model. The problems it is facing are also likely to be unique and to require specific solutions.

Policy responses

Social policy-making in the early 1990s was characterized by a change in direction compared with previous years. Until the late 1980s, welfare reform generally meant expansion in the coverage or generosity of social programmes. In some respects, the Swiss welfare state was still catching up with its European counterparts in those areas in which it was underdeveloped. It was in the 1980s that occupational pension coverage and unemployment insurance were made universal. In contrast, since the early 1990s, the main theme in social policy reform is retrenchment and attempts to contain rises in public expenditure.

Given the fact that a fragmented political system, like that of Switzerland, requires substantial agreement in order to legislate, welfare retrenchment has proved to be extremely difficult. Those likely to lose out in a welfare reform tend to exploit the veto points provided by the constitutional set-up of the country to challenge government-sponsored legislation they regard as unsatisfactory. The 1990s thus witnessed a series of failed attempts at social policy legislation, with government proposals being turned down by voters on four occasions. A bill aimed at deregulating the labour-market was rejected in 1996 by 67 per cent of voters. One year later, a bill cutting unemployment benefits was also rejected, this time only by a small majority of voters (50.8 per cent). A third retrenchment-oriented reform was rejected in 1999. This time the cuts were to affect disability benefits, particularly those available to partially disabled people, and were opposed by 70 per cent of voters. Finally, the only attempt at expanding the welfare state made in the 1990s, a reform which would have intro-duced a maternity insurance scheme at the national level, was also rejected by 61 per cent of voters. Unilateral reforms, either in the direction of expansion or retrenchment, seem unfeasible in the current political con-text (Bonoli, 1999, 2000a; Obinger, 1998).

In contrast, the government has been successful in adopting new social legislation only when reform comprised elements of both retrenchment and expansion. This was a key feature of two reforms adopted in the 1990s: the 1995 pension reform, and the 1995 unemployment insurance reform, both of them discussed below. This strategy, which seems the only way to get round the institutional obstacles that exist in the policy-making process, is also likely to be pursued in future reforms.

Developments in pension policy[3]

As in other European countries, pension policy in the 1990s was made in a context characterized by concerns with the impact of demographic age-ing on pension expenditure and the sustainability of current arrange-ments. The main piece of legislation adopted during the decade, however, was only partly concerned with reducing or containing expenditure. The most recent pension reform, adopted in 1995, was designed to improve women's position within the basic scheme. However, the right wing of parliament was successful in forcing the inclusion of some moderate retrenchment. A new pension reform, meant to adapt the Swiss pension system to demographic change, is currently before parliament.

The pension system

The Swiss pension system is best described as a three-pillar system, each pillar catering for a distinct level of provision. The first pillar (AVS) is meant to cover the basic needs of retirees. It is partly earnings-related and provides a means-tested pension supplement (PC). The second pillar (LPP) has the task of providing retirees with a standard of living close to the one they had while working and consists of a compulsory system of occupational pensions. Finally, the third pillar, consists of non-compulsory private provision which is encouraged through tax-concessions. This functional division between three levels of pension provision is upheld by the federal constitution, and is widely regarded as an important constraint on policy change in this area.

The first pillar, introduced in 1948, provides universal coverage and is a fairly redistributive scheme, as there is no ceiling on contributions but the amount of benefit can vary between a floor and a ceiling, the upper limit being set at twice the lower. Within these limits the amount of the pension is related to the contributions paid while in work. In some respects the Swiss basic scheme is a compromise between the Bismarckian tradition of earnings-related contributory pensions and the Beveridgean flat-rate approach. Interestingly, in international comparisons the AVS is sometimes considered as a flat-rate pension scheme (Schmähl, 1991: 48). As far as financing is concerned, the AVS works on a pay-as-you-go basis. It has a fund which consists of roughly one-year outlays. The coverage is universal, so that those who are not working (like students) are required to pay flat-rate contributions or, if providing informal care, are entitled to contribution credits.

The scheme constitutes a good illustration of the focus of social protection on Swiss male employees: until the 1995 reform, married women were generally not entitled to a pension of their own, and entitlement to either insurance or means-tested benefits required a longer contribution record for foreigners (ten years) than for Swiss nationals (one year).[4]

The second pillar of the Swiss pension system consists of occupational pensions, which were first encouraged through tax concessions in 1916. They developed substantially throughout the 20th Century, but coverage remained patchy. In 1970 some 50 per cent of employees were covered by an occupational pension, but only 25 per cent of women. Since 1985, however, occupational pension coverage is compulsory for all employees earning at least twice the amount of the minimum AVS pension (CHF 24,000 per annum, or about 40 per cent of average earnings). Coverage is virtually universal among male employees but only around 80 per cent of female employees are included (OFAS, 1995: 10). A full occupational pension is granted to employees with an adequate contribution record (currently 37 years for women and 40 for men, the starting age being 25). Benefits vary according to the type of pension fund, though the law prescribes minimum requirements. As far as financing is concerned, occupational pensions are funded schemes. They are financed by employer/employee contributions, the former contributing at least as much as the latter.

The 1995 pension reform

The 1995 pension reform (see Bonoli, 2000b: ch. 4) illustrates the shift in the direction of social policy-making that has occurred since the early

1990s, and the political mechanisms which are being used to deal with the obstacle to policy change represented by institutional power fragmentation. Work on this reform started in 1979, with the intention of introducing gender equality in the basic pension scheme. Progress on the reform was slow, and it was only in 1990 that the government was finally able to present a bill to parliament. The bill made provision for the removal of any reference to gender in the pension formula, but did not take any proactive action in favour of women (such as contribution credits or sharing between spouses) as was advocated by various actors. A few years earlier, a number of organizations and political parties had published reports in which they had argued in favour of a system of individual pensions, granted regardless of gender and marital status and complemented by a contribution-sharing system between spouses. By the time the bill came to parliament, there was a relatively large consensus, most notably among the two largest parties (the Social Democrats and the Radicals) for a more proactive approach.

By 1993 the bill had been significantly modified by parliament, by adopting the measures suggested in the reports published a few years earlier. The bill, as amended by parliament, included the introduction of a contribution-sharing system between spouses and contribution credits for informal carers. Together with these measures, on which there was a relatively strong consensus, the new version of the bill also included the more controversial measure of raising the retirement age for women from 62 to 64 (the male retirement age is 65). This was imposed by the right-of-centre parliamentary majority, against the Social Democrats, allegedly in order to comply with the constitutional requirement of gender equality as well as to achieve some savings in view of the predicted worsening of the ratio between contributors and beneficiaries over the next few decades.

Outside parliament, the trade unions and some women's organizations attacked the proposed increase in retirement age for women by collecting the 50,000 signatures needed in order to call a referendum. The move was successful and the referendum on the pension bill was held in June 1995.

According to the constitution, referendums decide between the adoption and the rejection of a bill, but they cannot modify its content. Therefore the referendum called by the trade unions had to cover the age of retirement as well as the provision for gender equality, which had long been advocated by the trade unions and by the Left in the past. For the Left, this situation constituted a powerful dilemma. The decision on whether or not to support the referendum against the pension bill depended on what was seen as more important: gender equality on the positive side and the increase in women's retirement age on the negative one. The result was that the Social Democrats declined to join the unions in supporting the referendum against the pension bill, therefore reducing their chances of defeating it at the polls. In fact, the bill survived the referendum obstacle and is now law. The division within the Left obviously played an important role in making its adoption possible. To a large extent

Table 6.3   *Unemployment (% of active population) and the unemployment insurance fund (million CHF), 1988–1998*

	1989	1990	1991	1992	1993	1994	1995	1996	1997	1998
U. rate	0.5	0.6	1.2	2.6	4.6	4.8	4.3	4.6	5.2	3.9
Receipts	976	787	866	805	3556	3680	5488	5955	5680	5876
Outlays	442	503	1340	3462	5986	5921	5240	6124	7715	6208
Balance	534	283	−474	−2657	−2430	−2241	247	−168	−2135	−333

Source: Office Fédéral des assurances sociales, *Sécurité sociale*, various issues

the way in which the bill was designed encouraged the division, as it combined elements of retrenchment with measures that were among the key priorities of the Left.

Current pressures and reform plans

The Swiss pension system is facing two big challenges: population ageing and labour-market change. Current pension debates focus predominantly on these two issues. However, policy development is considerably more advanced in relation to the former. A pension reform which is currently being debated in parliament has the explicit objective of adapting the pension system to demographic change. It is expected to affect both the first and second tier of provision. In contrast, the issue of improving pension coverage for precarious and atypical workers, whose numbers are increasing rapidly, has not been included in the current reform despite the demands of trade unions and the Left.

Policies for unemployed people and low-paid workers

The unemployment rate remained very low until the early 1990s, when it soared from below 1 per cent in 1990 to 4.8 per cent in 1994. Since the mid-1990s job creation has restarted and the unemployment rate has declined to more manageable levels (see Table 6.3). This development has been accompanied by a shift in debates on policies for unemployed people. While the key concern in the first half of the 1990s was to limit spending, current debates focus more on incentives and on efficient activation programmes. In fact, many of the new jobs created in the late 1990s are part-time or precarious, which may generate poverty and unemployment traps.

Unemployment compensation is provided by two distinct tiers of provision: an unemployment insurance scheme, run by the federal government, and a social assistance system, which is managed by individual cantons and is administered by the communes. The insurance scheme is financed by employment-related contributions and government subsidies.

The replacement rate is 80 per cent or 70 per cent of gross earnings (see below) with a benefit ceiling equal to about 150 per cent of average earnings.

The Swiss social assistance system was conceived in a context in which it was used only by marginal, unemployable persons. However, partly as a consequence of higher unemployment, but also as a result of labour-market changes, social assistance is becoming an interface between work and welfare for an increasingly large number of people. For families, it sometimes substitutes for the weakness of family benefits, supplementing the incomes of low-paid breadwinners. However, it is widely accepted that most social assistance systems are wholly inadequate to take up this new role. First, social assistance recipients face effective marginal tax-rates of 100 per cent: every extra franc earned is deducted from the benefit. Second, in many cantons social assistance benefits are treated as loans which must theoretically be repaid once recipients get back to work. Finally, social assistance recipients are generally excluded from the federal active labour-market programmes available to insurance benefit recipients. This is why in several cantons, social assistance is being reformed or new programmes for the long-term unemployed are being introduced.

The reforms of the unemployment insurance scheme

The 1990s saw a radical transformation of unemployment insurance, which had previously been used mainly to deal with frictional unemployment. The initial stimulus for reform was the deficit resulting from the rise in unemployment in the early 1990s, which convinced the federal government to act with an urgent decree[5] in 1993. For those without dependent children the replacement rate was cut from 80 per cent to 70 per cent of insured salary but the entitlement period extended from 250 working days to 400. Contribution rates were increased and a stricter definition of 'adequate work' was introduced, whereby unemployed persons could be required to accept jobs at salaries lower than insurance benefits. These measures lasted until December 1995 in order to allow policy-makers time to introduce more substantial legislative change, which came in the shape of the 1995 unemployment insurance reform.

The reform was drafted by a joint group of representatives of employers and trade unionists, and accepted by parliament without major changes. As a clear compromise between different conceptions, it included divergent measures. On the one hand, the financial base of the scheme was strengthened and more funds were made available for labour-market programmes, such as vocational training and job creation. On the other hand, the maximum entitlement period was reduced to two years, whereas under the previous legislation benefits could be drawn practically indefinitely, provided the recipient was prepared to participate in labour-market programmes.

The joint contribution rate was raised to 3 per cent (1.5 per cent each for employers and employees), payable on earnings of up to 160 per cent of average salary. An additional contribution at a joint rate of 1 per cent is charged on earnings between 160 per cent and 400 per cent of average salary. This measure is temporary, in principle at least, until the debt accumulated by the scheme with the government is repaid. In addition, 5 per cent of current expenditure is financed by a federal subsidy. As far as benefits were concerned, the changes introduced with the urgent decree were maintained. The entitlement period was fixed at two years, and during this period unemployed persons are required to undertake retraining, to participate in a job creation scheme or take up temporary work.

The 1995 reform was successful in eliminating the deficit in 1995. However, at the time when the active labour-market programmes were introduced in 1996 and 1997, expenditure increased and the deficit re-emerged. The response of the federal government was to adopt a further urgent decree which included cuts in benefits of between 1 and 3 per cent, depending on their level, as well as the abolition of the subsidy paid to the unemployment insurance scheme by the government. This decree, unlike the previous one and unlike the 1995 reform, did not include measures to expand or improve provision. Probably for this reason, the decree was challenged by a local association of unemployed people, who managed to collect the 50,000 signatures needed to call a referendum on the legislation. The vote took place in September 1997 and saw the rejection of the decree by a small majority of voters (50.8 per cent): a surprising result given the fact the decree was openly supported by three of the four government parties (the sole opposition being from the Socialists).

Reforming social assistance systems

Reforms adopted in the broad area of unemployment compensation have also included changes in social assistance legislation in several cantons. Minimum income programmes have been introduced mainly in the French-speaking part of the country, which was particularly hard hit by unemployment. These are generally modelled on the French RMI (see chapter 3), and combine a cash benefit with support for labour-market re-entry. There is no requirement to pay back the benefit, and recipients have access to active labour-market policies such as training or job creation schemes, even though, in most cases, the objective of these schemes is to avoid the stigma of social assistance to long-term unemployed people, rather than directly promote employment. Other cantons have introduced cantonal unemployment benefits which kick in after entitlement to federal insurance benefits has expired. These remain essentially passive programmes, designed to avoid the stigma associated with social assistance. Finally, among the new developments, the Canton of Zurich is considering introducing a negative income tax programme for low-income families. The plan proposes to extend a means-tested benefit, distinct from

Table 6.4   *Financial indicators for the main social programmes*

	Contribution rates			Receipts	Expenditure
	Employer	Employee	% tax-financed	1997 % GDP	1997 % GDP
Basic pension	4.2	4.2	20	6.8	6.9
Invalidity insurance	0.7	0.7	50	1.9	2.1
Means-tested pension and invalidity benefit	–	–	100	–	0.5
Occupational pensions	6[a]	6[a]	0	12.7	7.3
Health insurance	individual premiums		12.4	4.8	4.8
Unemployment insurance	1.5/1	1.5/1	5	1.5	2.2
Social assistance	–	–	100	–	1.2
Family benefits	–	0.1–5.5	NA	1.1	1.1
Other federal benefits	1–2	0.2–17.2	0	1.9	1.8

[a] typical values (see text).
Source: recalculation of data from *Sécurité sociale* 1/2000, 42–43

social assistance, which is already available to pensioners and disabled people, to working families (*Le Temps*, 4 April, 2000).

The finance of welfare

The Swiss welfare state is mainly financed through employment-related contributions (Table 6.4). Rates have been roughly stable over the past decade, but additional welfare state finance has been provided through a 1 per cent increase in the standard rate of VAT. The current low level of VAT (7.5 per cent on most goods and services) allows ample scope for further increases, which may be needed to finance AVS and other social insurance programmes in the future. According to the government's own estimates, a VAT rate of 13.3 per cent (lower than the European average) would suffice to maintain the current level of welfare provision until 2010 (IDA FiSo 2, 1997). The key problem in financing welfare in Switzerland is not so much one of balancing dwindling fiscal resources with rising social demands. The incidence of taxation and social contributions and the distributional impact of the welfare state are more significant.

Besides various forms of taxation and social contributions, the Swiss welfare state is also financed through compulsory health insurance premiums that are not proportional to income. In 1996, health insurance premiums

Table 6.5   *Total taxation as % GDP, Switzerland and selected*
countries (around 1995)

	Older figures	Revised figures
Switzerland	34.6	53.8
France	45.4	48.2
Germany	39.2	45.9
Sweden	52.0	57.5
UK	35.9	37.2

Sources: Older figures OECD (1997e), Revenue Statistics, Paris, 1997. Revised
figures: OECD (1997e), National Accounts, Paris, 1998

amounted to 3.6 per cent of GDP, and constituted an important source of
revenue. Health insurance premiums are a particularly regressive form of
taxation: they are responsible for a substantial amount of inter-generational
redistribution but the contribution required from each individual is not
proportional to their capacity to pay. In fact, health insurance funds
are prohibited by law from charging different amounts in relation to the
level of risk of each member. As a result, younger members, regardless of
income, must subsidize older ones. For example, the actuarial cost of
insuring a 20-year-old is just over Euro 600 a year, but for an 80-year-old
it is about Euro 5600. Both, however, will pay the same amount in premiums, ranging between Euro 1000 and 3000, depending on the provider
they have chosen and the canton in which they live. The system hits the
lower middle classes particularly hard, since they are not entitled to the
means-tested voucher available to those on the lowest incomes but must
pay a premium (reduced for children under 18) which consumes a size-
able proportion of disposable income.

The fact that Switzerland relies to a large extent on private payments in
order to finance its welfare state is partly responsible for its comparatively
low rates of taxation. Recently released OECD figures have shown that, if
compulsory payments to occupational pension funds and health insurance
schemes are counted as taxation, it becomes the third greediest government in the OECD, after Sweden and Finland (Table 6.5). This result, surprising as it may be, has been confirmed by secondary analysis of national
data produced by the Swiss statistical office (Kriesi, 1999; Lane, 1999).

The revised OECD figures raise questions regarding what should be
considered as taxation and what should not. These questions are further
complicated by the fact that such payments include a compulsory component and a voluntary one. For instance, as far as health insurance is
concerned, residents are obliged to purchase a policy which provides only
basic health coverage, but it is common to buy additional provision as
well. Similarly, only a minimum level of occupational pension coverage is
mandated by law with pension funds being free to offer more. Currently,
available statistics do not distinguish between compulsory and voluntary

payments to either of these schemes, so that it is not possible to say what proportion of health insurance and occupational pensions contributions should be considered as analogous to taxation (Kriesi, 1999). The true figure for Swiss welfare state finance as a proportion of GDP lies somewhere between the two figures put forward by the OECD.

Overall, the Swiss welfare state probably costs as much as those of Central and Northern Europe (Armingeon, 2001), but with a substantial distributional difference: the fiscal instruments used to finance it are less progressive. Sixty per cent of social expenditure is financed by social contributions that are proportional to earnings and progressive direct taxation plays a relatively minor role. The last few years have seen an expansion in the use of VAT and this trend is likely to continue. In Switzerland, it has been estimated that this fiscal instrument is proportional up to an income of about CHF 100,000 per annum. Above that level, it becomes regressive. Finally, compulsory health insurance premiums are possibly one of the most regressive existing forms of taxation. If Switzerland matches its neighbours in terms of welfare spending, it still lags behind much of Europe in terms of 'welfare effort'.

In spite of this rather peculiar situation, current debates on the finance of welfare focus mainly on issues of affordability and cost containment, with only marginal political groupings taking up the distributional issues outlined here. The Socialist Party has launched a popular initiative which aims at making health insurance premiums earnings-related. The proposal, which will eventually be subjected to a referendum, has so far failed to gain the support of the government and of other parties. Previous initiatives in the same direction have consistently been rejected by voters.

Conclusion

Switzerland has gone through a series of transformations in the past decade in relation to its labour-market, family structures, position in the international community, and possibly, its domestic politics. The foundations of the Swiss post-war settlement, which (thanks largely to economic and political isolation) had been artificially sustained until the late 1980s, are increasingly undermined. The 1990s showed, for example, that the control of labour supply through restrictive immigration policies at times of recession is no longer an effective regulatory instrument. Women workers, who also functioned as a labour-market buffer during downturns, are no longer willing to play this role. All this takes place against the background of a rapidly ageing population. Some of these changes make Switzerland more similar to the rest of the continent. The difference lies in the fact that, in the Swiss context, these are new developments that will require essentially novel solutions.

Two aspects of the Swiss political economy seem crucial in determining the direction of current and future policy change. First, the socio-economic context and the resulting social problems share features typical of the liberal model of welfare capitalism, typified by the US, combined with other aspects more reminiscent of the German variant. Second, Switzerland has a peculiar set of state structures and political institutions which significantly limit the capacity of policy-makers to develop coherent and co-ordinated responses to socio-economic challenges.

The key socio-economic challenges reviewed above (population ageing, growth of atypical employment, a troubled work–family relationship, and the integration of immigrants), are in many ways interrelated, and could arguably be addressed with a comprehensive and coherent package of reforms. However, given the structure of the political system, such an outcome is unlikely. Adaptation is likely to take place by default, with citizens dealing with these problems at the individual level on the basis of the options available to them. One example of this trajectory of adaptation is the dramatic expansion of part-time work among women. This is virtually the only way to reconcile work and family life. Part-time and other forms of atypical employment will probably continue to play an important role, as the introduction of a full-scale welfare state for working families is unlikely. It is likely that the pressure to grant part-time and other atypical workers better working and social protection conditions will increase. The inclusion of these workers in the occupational pension system is arguably one of the key challenges that will need to be addressed. In addition, the fact that many of those who work part-time have a limited disposable income might raise the issue of negative income tax programmes. The strategy of improving the situation of atypical workers could be the Swiss route out of the low fertility equilibrium in which the country currently finds itself. Better social conditions for part-time workers would allow them to improve and strengthen their economic position, but they would still be able to fulfil social reproduction tasks within the family. At the same time, the extension of part-time employment will result in *de facto* work-sharing, making employment available to more people.

In order to be politically viable, reforms should be able to gain political support from the various sections of the political spectrum. Given the current balance of political forces, it is likely that successful reforms will need to combine these measures with others aimed at achieving savings. Consensus-generating reform packages would need to be crafted in such a way that at least three of the four main parties find them attractive. The improvement of working and social protection conditions for part-timers will need to be compensated with reductions elsewhere. Analysis of the reforms adopted or rejected in the 1990s suggests that such compromise is essential for legislation to succeed.

Notes

1 I would like to thank Yannis Papadopoulos for comments on an earlier version of this paper.

2 The Swiss constitution makes provision for various types of referendums. Constitutional change as well as accession to a supranational organization is automatically subjected to a referendum. Constitutional change can also be put forward by voters by means of a 'popular initiative', if they are able to back their proposal with 100,000 signatures. For these referendums to succeed, the double majority of voters and cantons is required. Voters can also challenge at the polls any act passed by parliament, if they are able to produce 50,000 signatures to that effect. In this case, a simple majority of voters is sufficient for the referendum to succeed (see Kobach, 1993 for a comprehensive account).

3 This section draws on collaborative work carried out with André Mach (Bonoli and Mach, 2000).

4 For nationals of countries which have signed a social security convention with Switzerland, the minimum contribution period is also one year. These are mainly EU member-states.

5 Urgent decrees differ from standard legislation because their enforcement cannot be delayed by a referendum.

7 Welfare Reform in the UK: the Construction of a Liberal Consensus

Peter Taylor-Gooby

The UK has made the most rapid and far-reaching welfare state reforms of any of the countries considered in this book. The bulk of pension provision has been transferred from state pay-as-you-go to privately funded schemes, unemployment benefit has been abolished and an extensive workfare scheme implemented. The government is able to introduce swift change because its constitutional system sets fewer constraints on the executive than exist elsewhere. Recent reforms have strengthened the centralization of power in the context of a weak trade union movement, and the opportunities that this offers have been grasped enthusiastically by self-consciously radical governments of both the liberal right (1979–1997) and the centre-left (1997 onwards). The policies of the two main parties, both committed to a broadly Beveridge-Keynes reluctant interventionist model of welfare from the 1940s to the 1970s, but diverging after the crisis of the mid-1970s towards liberal market and social democrat approaches, have again converged. The Labour Party discovered that it was impossible to win elections on a left-wing platform that included higher social spending, an expanded state sector and more generous social security. Both main parties now endorse cost constraint, the expansion of private provision and workfare.

The UK reforms are exceptionally precipitate and thorough-going but are undertaken in response to pressures from labour-market change, demography and globalization that are similar to but often less intense than those elsewhere. The experience of the country shows how a majoritarian policy-making framework facilitates the sustainability of a radical liberal-leaning reform programme in a West European welfare state by marginalizing losers. The groups most affected by the relatively high poverty levels (Table 1.4) are unable to exert much political influence. It also illustrates how different actors in a two-party system tend to diverge while seeking an electorally viable solution to problems, but converge on the 'middle ground' when a solution that attracts support is found.

This chapter examines developments in UK social policy in the finance of welfare, pensions and unemployment, and the political and policy-making machinery that produced them. The first section describes the framework in which policy is made – the political actors and the institutions within which they operate. The chapter then discusses the development of policy in each of the three areas, setting out the roles played by government, political parties and organized interests. A considerable measure of cross-party agreement on a broadly liberal programme evolved during the 1990s, dominated by concern for economic competitiveness, and including the moderation of taxes, retrenchment, targeting, a greater role for the private sector, a policy regime resembling 'trainfare' or 'workfare' for unemployed people and an emphasis on individual responsibility and opportunity.

The policy-making framework: political actors and institutional structure

The UK has a distinctive highly centralized policy-making apparatus, in which the party of government enjoys considerable power. Recent developments under both of the main parties have strengthened central authority. The influence of trade unions is in decline. Lijphart regards the UK, with its lack of a formal constitution or independent constitutional court, executive dominant over the legislature, oppositional parliament, weak second chamber, strong executive, strong party discipline, lack of parliamentary coalitions or corporatist consultational mechanisms and weak local government, as the polar case of majoritarian democracy (Lijphart, 1999: ch. 1; see Norton, 1998: ch. 1). Election is on a constituency basis with a first-past-the-post system that typically produces clear parliamentary majorities, although the winning party may have gained less than half the votes cast. Recent developments have strengthened the power of the party of government further. They include: an enhanced ascendancy of the Treasury with reforms that enable it to intervene actively in the spending departments which deliver policy; the modernization of the civil service and of the government machine to produce stronger links between different departments and enhanced central direction of policy; constitutional reform which has removed most of the non-elected members from the second chamber and weakened its powers, and also streamlined local government; increased centralization of Prime Ministerial control through expansion of the Cabinet Office and Prime Minister's Efficiency Unit and astute use of the media; Labour Party reform that weakened union influence, already damaged by declining membership; and the continued weakness of the parties in opposition. The only exception to the drive for central control is the devolution of some powers to regional assemblies in Scotland and, to a lesser extent, Wales.

Once elected, political parties can push through substantial reform programmes with little effective opposition, particularly if they have the large majorities of recent Thatcher, Major and Blair parliaments. Constraints on policy making arise chiefly through back-bench opposition, if MPs fear damage to their chances of re-election (as in the supplanting of Mrs Thatcher in 1990), second chamber defeats causing legislation to lose its place in the parliamentary time-table and effective lobbying by agencies to whom the government listens. In recent years the standing of unions has declined sharply and business is the major effective lobbying force.

Within this structure the chief actors are the two main political parties, the social partners and the civil service. New social movements, the voluntary sector, religious organizations and professional bodies find it difficult to exert effective pressure on policy, unless endorsed by these actors. Proposals for reform must be attractive to the groups in the electorate for whom the parties compete if they are to gain a place on the political agenda.

Conservative Party

This party formed the government under Thatcher and Major from 1979 to 1997. Historically it contained two elements: traditionalism, which valued Britain's imperial past, and commitment to business and financial interests. Thatcher managed to link both through commitment to the extension of free markets, which were presented as embodying the party's traditional values of individual responsibility and opportunity and at the same time reinforcing a vision of Britain as a nation distinguished through international leadership of a free market revolution. In recent years, tensions have centred around relationships with the EU and the growth of inequality as a result of free market policies. The party pursued a self-consciously ideological version of conservatism that abandoned the 'one nation' tradition and rejected Keynesian approaches to economic management. Its policies in the 1980s included radical retrenchment of public spending and 'rolling back the state', privatization and denationalization of state-owned industry and pursuit of market freedom. In practice, monetarism proved unworkable (the money supply continued to rise) and, after 1985, economic policy pursued intervention through manipulation of interest rates (Kingdom, 1999: 491–5). Relevant social policies included benefit and spending cuts, the sale of social housing to tenants, retrenchment of state pensions and a major review of social security. These enabled high profile cuts in direct taxation, particularly for higher income groups, although the pressures of population ageing and high unemployment precluded substantial spending reductions.

After 1987 the party moved towards the development of internal market and consumer empowerment policies in state services alongside the promotion of privatization, and introduced managerialist approaches within central government to reduce state bureaucracy and increase financial control. Most civil servants (half by 1992, over 80 per cent by 1996, Dunleavy et al., 1993: 187; Gray and Jenkins, 1998: 124) now work in agencies at arms length from the policy-making machine of the department, and operating on business lines.

Margaret Thatcher, Conservative prime minister from 1979 to 1990, alienated much of the business wing of the party by her refusal to contemplate closer links with Europe and lost popular support through the imposition of the local government Poll Tax. She was forced to step down by her cabinet in 1990. The new leader, John Major, pursued similar domestic policies, but negotiated UK entry into the ERM at a relatively high exchange rate. The weakness of the currency in the recession of the early 1990s forced an embarrassing devaluation and withdrawal in 1992. The UK refused to accept the Social Agreement of the Maastricht Treaty in 1992, despite concessions.

The Conservatives won the 1992 election aided by a Labour programme which included commitment to unpopular tax rises. However, economic pressures made it difficult to pursue the tax cuts of previous years. Major continued to stress the consumerist ethic of market empowerment through the Citizen's Charters – statements of service levels that could be expected from state sector providers. The party's standing was damaged by a series of corruption scandals. It suffered a sharp decline in popular support leading to internal divisions and electoral defeats in 1997 and 2001.

Labour Party

Labour developed as a working-class centre-left party promoted by the trade union movement in the early 20th Century. It has always faced problems in sustaining an adequate relationship with business and in capturing sufficient support from middle-class groups to gain a majority. These problems were most successfully managed in the 1960s and mid-1970s through an ideology that linked equality of opportunity with the claim that class-bound traditionalism impeded economic progress. However, the party was vulnerable to ideological attacks based on its association with unpopular high rates of taxation and inefficient public sector bureaucracies and local government in the 1980s. Successive leaders – Kinnock (1983), Smith (1992) and Blair (1994) – carried out a programme of internal 'modernization', weakening links with left-wing groups, unions and constituency parties, associating more closely with business and espousing a more market-oriented stance. The shift was symbolized in the struggle to rewrite 'Clause 4' of the party's constitution (which demanded widespread public ownership), to embrace 'the enterprise of the market'.

The long period out of office and the crushing defeat in the 1992 election forced members to accept that traditional commitments to the public sector, high rates of direct taxation and high-profile redistribution must be abandoned in order to secure power, so that state welfare policy was effectively remade to reflect the Conservative commitment to the centrality of the market. The party's influential Commission on Social Justice report stressed that 'Britain needs to change if it is to find its place in a changing world' (1994: 91), and part of that process must be a redirection of social policy effort to support economic competitiveness rather than promote social equality.

In office New Labour has followed many of the doctrines of the previous government, including spending restraint, the importation of market principles into the state sector, an emphasis on selectivity, individual responsibility and the role of work incentives in relation to benefits, and acceptance of the privatization of the greater part of pension provision. Redistribution is pursued discreetly through enhanced provision for lower-paid workers and (especially, after the 2001 election), lower-income families, and targeted benefit increases, and a range of measures which effectively increase the less visible taxes, especially for higher-income groups. The new government introduced a minimum wage, but symbolized its determination to limit economic interventionism by transferring responsibility for setting interest rates to the Bank of England, while the Treasury's role is confined to setting inflation targets.

Labour contains groups opposed to the EU as dominated by capital and groups enthusiastic for participation. Conflicts were initially resolved through a national referendum in 1975 following the renegotiation of membership. Since then, the leadership has supported participation. The party implemented the 1997 Amsterdam Treaty, managing internal opposition by deferring participation in monetary union. It also promoted constitutional reform in relation to the unelected second chamber, devolution and Northern Ireland. Policies which strengthen central government control over spending have simultaneously been pursued.

The executive and the government

The senior civil service – the 'mandarin' class – has traditionally had considerable power in policy-making in the UK. Three developments, pursued under both Conservative and Labour governments, have weakened its independence. First, the Prime Minister established an Efficiency Unit (1988) and expanded the Cabinet Office so that active intervention in the detailed operations and planning of government departments can be routinely pursued. Second, an increase in the number of cabinet committees (to over 40 – Kingdom, 1999: 435) offers a route for driving through reforms without exposing them to Cabinet or wider scrutiny. Third, the mechanism for overseeing public spending has developed from the traditional annual round between departments and the Treasury, in which cash limits would be set, through the Portillo reviews of 1993, in which the Treasury directly imposed spending cuts, to the three-year Comprehensive Spending Reviews (from 1998) in which every aspect of spending – and every possibility for savings – is scrutinized.

The Treasury has taken a particularly important and unusual role in policy in its involvement in the New Deal for unemployed people and in

Table 7.1   *Election results, 1979–2001*

	1979		1983		1987		1992		1997		2001	
%	Seats	Votes	Seats	Votes	Seats	Votes	Seats	Votes	Seats	Votes	Seats	Votes
Conservative	53	44	61	42	58	42	42	34	25	32	25	32
Labour	42	37	32	28	35	31	52	44	64	44	63	41
Lib/Lib-Dem	2	14	4	25	3	23	3	18	7	17	8	18
Other	3	5	3	5	4	4	4	6	4	7	2	9

Source: http://www.psr.keele.ac.uk/

minimum wage and tax credit policies. This facilitates welfare development (which had traditionally been promoted by the spending departments but opposed by the stronger Treasury) but also makes policy more vulnerable to a shift of direction in the Treasury (Deakin and Parry, 1998; Piachaud and Sutherland, 2001).

The social partners

The Confederation of British Industries represents manufacturing and the major service sector employers. It advocates domestic investment, removal of trade barriers and the development of EU links, and has tended to support state investment in infrastructure and services of direct benefit to business, but to oppose it vehemently elsewhere in the economy. The Institute of Directors is a smaller organization, vociferous in support for Thatcherism and the New Right, and more closely linked to the City of London and to the interests of finance capital. The Association of British Chamber of Commerce represents local businesses and advocates support for entrepreneurship through tax restraint and limits to minimum wage and similar policies (King, 1983).

Trade unions no longer have an effective voice in UK politics. Unionization declined as a result of anti-union legislation, the defeat of the 1984–1985 miners' strike, and the decline in the proportion of the labour force in traditionally highly unionized manufacturing sector and state sector employment. A series of new laws between 1980 and 1993 ended the closed shop, introduced postal ballots for the election of leaders and secret ballots for strike decisions, weakened the capacity to press for union recognition, and withdrew immunity from prosecution for those striking for any reason other than a tightly defined trade dispute and for secondary pickets (Savage et al., 1994: 101–5). Membership is now just under 30 per cent of the civilian labour force as against 53 per cent at the post-war peak in 1979 (ONS, 1997: 4.20; 2000: 4.27). Almost all unions are members of the Trades Union Congress. New Labour in government has severed the party's traditional links with the union movement, cutting off the main avenue for political lobbying by the TUC.

The context of policy-making: globalization, Europeanization and societal change

Globalization

The key theme has been international competitiveness, of particular importance in debates about the level of public spending, company taxation, education and training. The end of the period of confident post-war welfare state expansion was marked by the oil price rise of the mid-1970s, which forced the Chancellor to apply for an immediate IMF loan on the eve of the 1976 party conference. The significance of international competition is often understood in terms of the UK's dependence on trade. In fact, exports from the UK now account for only 21 per cent of GDP, comparable to other large EU countries, for example, France: 21.1 per cent; Germany 23.7 per cent (Held et al., 1999: 180). This contrasts with the situation in 1950 when UK exports were roughly double the percentage of GDP, compared with other European countries. However, trade with Europe has increased rapidly within this total, from 40 per cent of the UK's overseas trade in 1974 to 56 per cent by 1996 (HMSO, 1997; OECD, 1999f). International competitiveness is a bi-partisan issue, figuring in the manifestos of both main parties. In the early 1990s there was a strong contrast between Conservative and Labour views on policy in this area, but by the end of the decade they had converged.

The Conservative party argued consistently that its reforms, following a liberal agenda of deregulation, privatization and the weakening of trade union power, led the way in improving competitiveness. In 1993, the UK scored zero on a 6-point OECD index of labour-market standards, covering regulation of working time, minimum wages, employment protection, employee representation and fixed-term contracts, against 6 for France and Germany (OECD, 1994a: 154).

Labour in the early 1990s emphasized government-led investment rather than free market solutions (Labour Party, 1992: 11–13). However, by the 1997 and 2001 elections, party policy had shifted much closer to the Conservative position, embodied in the manifesto 'vision' of 'a Britain equipped to prosper in a global economy of technological change', and built on 'the dynamism of the market' and support for entrepreneurship (Labour Party, 1997: 3). Key differences between the parties are the stronger emphasis on training, the higher (but strictly targeted) social spending and the toleration of a higher level of regulation and employee protection in Labour's programme.

The social partners have tended to support policies designed to improve competitiveness. The CBI has supported the direction of state investment to areas where it benefits business, such as transport and telecommunications infrastructure, and has sought to oppose regulation, especially of small business. The TUC has argued ineffectively for state-led investment programmes on the lines of the 1992 Labour manifesto and repeatedly expressed disappointment at the party's shift away from such policies.

The European Union

The UK has pursued an inconsistent course in relation to Europe. The 1979–1997 Conservative government was officially strongly in favour of membership of an economic union, despite the UK's forced withdrawal from the EMU in 1992. It vigorously resisted any moves in relation to social policy, negotiating dilution of the ambitious programme contained in the 1989 Social Chapter and then opting out from the Social Agreement of the Maastricht Treaty in 1992. The parliamentary report on the UK presidency in 1992 stresses the competitive aspects of the EU: 'the key points for the presidency: ... creating conditions in which business and therefore jobs can be created without unnecessary regulation' (HMSO, 1993: 10.2). Opposition to social legislation continued. In 1996, a British challenge to a ruling limiting the normal working week to 48 hours (not part of the Social Chapter) was rejected by the European Court of Justice.

Although a minority on the Left of the party opposed EU membership, Labour was enthusiastic in support for the Social Chapter in opposition. After the 1997 election, the New Labour prime minister accepted the Amsterdam Treaty and social directives were adopted in the UK. However, Blair laid great stress on labour-market flexibility in his contributions to the Amsterdam debates and argued strongly for the 'shift from welfare to work' principles embodied in the EU Employment Guidelines agreed at the December 1998 Vienna European Council. Participation in monetary union was deferred until after the 2001 election. The Treasury and finance capital, but not the manufacturing sector, derive benefits from the strength of sterling.

Both TUC and CBI argued for ERM entry in 1990, and later complained that the exchange rate had been fixed at an uncompetitive level. Both supported re-entry after the crisis of 1992. The CBI has consistently opposed the social aspects of EU policy-making and endorsed calls for subsidiarity in this area. The TUC welcomed the Maastricht Treaty's Social Chapter and campaigned vigorously (and ineffectually) for its adoption.

EU involvement has had some direct effect on UK policy, despite the opposition of the Conservatives and the tendency of the Labour government to weak implementation and the promotion of labour-market flexibility. It may have a stronger long-term effect through the impact of pressures towards tax harmonization on a relatively low-taxed country and through policies which increase the influence of social partners.

Societal changes: the labour market and unemployment

The UK labour-market has undergone profound changes. The shift towards a post-Fordist economy is more thorough-going than in any of the countries discussed, with a greater manufacturing decline in employment (both skilled and unskilled) and stronger growth of the services sector (especially in finance – see Table 1.9 and Vickerstaff, 1999: 137).

These changes have been hardest on unskilled workers and create a demand – endorsed by both main parties and facilitated by the weakness of the unions – for more labour-market flexibility and a better qualified workforce. Unemployment has fallen more rapidly from 1993 onwards than in the other countries reviewed (see Table 1.8), although rates among young people remain relatively high, at about twice the overall rate (CEC, 1999: 127–49). Male unemployment is rather higher than that for women.

Issues of unemployment have figured prominently in political debate throughout the period, although UK politicians of both main parties have often exaggerated the gap between UK rates and those in other EU countries and claimed that the employment record vindicates the more liberal policy stance.

Societal changes: population shifts

In common with the other countries included in this study, the UK has an ageing population (Table 1.10 and ONS, 2000: 1.6). Anticipated demographic shifts have led to major developments in pensions policy and also concern about health and social care and about social security for lone parents. Population ageing is relatively slow, compared with the other countries discussed in this book. The impact of an ageing population on public spending is also substantially mitigated by the shift towards funded individually financed pensions (Falkingham, 1989: 230). However, the number over the age of 75 has increased steadily between 1961 and 1981 (from 4 to 6 per cent) and thereafter stabilized at 7 per cent between 1991 and 2001, after which it is expected to continue to rise to 9 per cent by 2021. This trend, coupled with the declining availability of the traditional care-giving group (middle-aged women not in full-time employment) gives rise to concern about health care and older care costs which has led to an unresolved debate about future policy. Family ties are as strong as ever (Finch, 1989; McGlone et al., 1996), but the capacity of the family to provide physical care has been weakened.

The policy context: key features

Changes in the environment in which policy is made have had two major impacts: first, all the main political actors are united in the belief that a stricter international competitive environment necessitates public spending constraint and tax moderation and that voters will reject any party proposing tax increases. The Labour leadership has used concern about globalization to defeat traditional Left demands for interventionism and to reshape its policy to appeal to a broader range of the electorate. The imperative of competitiveness is thus a powerful factor in the new liberal direction which UK welfare policy seems likely to follow in the medium-term future. Second, the influence of trade unions is in decline, as UK governments emphasize international competitiveness through flexibility and the less stable labour-market hampers recruitment. This contrasts with the role played by social partners in influencing EU policy-making and may lead to conflicts between the UK government and labour interests in Europe, mediated through EU directives and rulings. The factors that influence policy debate are broadly similar to those in other EU member countries. However, the UK response has been swifter and more thorough-going. There is no evidence that external factors are likely to lead to convergence between UK policy and that of other EU members.

We now turn to review policy developments in the finance of social welfare, unemployment and pensions. The key themes are:

- The abandonment of Keynes/Beveridge reluctant collectivism, as state second-pillar pensions are privatized, full employment policies are rejected, the benefit system moves towards activation through wage subsidy and workfare and policies to contain spending become more stringent.
- The development of a broadly bi-partisan party stance on these issues, with New Labour offering rather more targeted wage subsidies and more spending on training and the Conservatives leaning more towards the free market.
- The decline of trade union involvement in policy-making and the growth of central government and particularly Treasury authority under both parties.

The finance of welfare

Policy debates about the finance of welfare have been dominated by the determination of both main parties to cut spending and reduce personal taxation. The Conservative stance was summed up in the opening sentence of the 1979 Public Expenditure White Paper: 'Public spending is at the heart of Britain's present economic difficulties' (Treasury, 1979: para. 1). The determination to contain spending was reinforced by the humiliating expulsion from the ERM. The Portillo reviews were set up to identify areas 'where better targeting can be achieved or from which the state can withdraw altogether' (*Hansard*, 1993: col. 683). The reviews led to: the abolition of entitlement to national insurance unemployment benefit and the introduction of a conditional Job Seeker's Allowance; stricter tests for long-term sick and disabled people, which cut the numbers entitled to benefit by about an eighth (Glennerster, 1997: 262); the equalization of men's and women's retirement ages at 65 rather than earlier; the abolition of a guaranteed minimum requirement for portable pensions; and the ending of state second-pillar pension indexation and of means-tested assistance with mortgage payments for unemployed home-owners.

Labour, in opposition, at first argued for more investment in public services on traditional neo-Keynesian/Beveridgean grounds. The 1992 election was fought on an interventionist and redistributive programme. The defeat led to a fundamental rethinking of policy, culminating in the 1997 manifesto programme which stressed competitiveness, the market and entrepreneurship (Labour Party, 1997). This stands in sharp contrast to the party's national recovery programme of the 1992 election campaign, at a time of recession, which refers to 'intense competition' but offers a government-led investment programme as the solution (Labour Party, 1992: 11–13). The policy shift is summed up in a joint statement with German Chancellor Gerhard Schröder on the Third Way in June 1999: 'public expenditure as a proportion of national income has more or less reached the limits of acceptability' (Blair and Schröder, 1999).

Treasury involvement in the policy areas of other ministries has become more pro-active under governments of both parties. The Portillo reviews constitute a Treasury intervention into the territory of the spending departments, in contrast with the former reactive annual Public Expenditure Review system (Deakin and Parry, 1998). They presage the 1997 Labour Government's Comprehensive Spending Review, contributing to the extension of direct Treasury control of a widening range of aspects of social policy. Labour has taken the process further through enhanced Treasury involvement in provision via the increased prominence of tax credits, minimum wage policies, the New Deal and the privatization of pensions. An interesting development is the deliberate rejection of national policies in a number of high-profile areas by regional government in Scotland. The Scottish parliament has used its independent tax-raising powers to finance a 21 per cent pay rise for teachers, the abolition of university fees and free nursing care in residential accommodation for frail older people. It is at present unclear whether the regional challenge will influence the trajectory of national policy-making.

Throughout the rest of the UK, both parties have shifted policies and practice in a way that strengthens the centralizing tendencies of the UK polity and weakens the possibility of introducing a substantial redistributive tax-and-spend welfare system, to counter the secular trend to inequality. Trade union interests are side-lined and the CBI finds that the general drift of policy-making follows business interests.

Taxation and public spending

Cross-national comparisons reinforce the evidence presented in Chapter 1 (Tables 1.2 and 1.4), that the UK is a relatively low-taxed country with high poverty rates. The percentage of GDP accounted for by total tax revenues in the UK, at 35.3 per cent for 1997, falls well below the OECD and EU averages, and below comparable statistics for all EU member countries except The Republic of Ireland Portugal and Spain. A similar picture emerges in relation to take-home pay, although this is also slightly lower in Greece. EC comparative studies put the UK percentage at just under 38 per cent against an EU15 average of 42.4. (Eurostat, 1999: Table 2; OECD, 1999f).

The proportion of GDP allocated by government in the UK has fluctuated in relation to growth rates in the recession of the early 1990s and the later recovery, but is now at a level close to that of the beginning of the decade (House of Commons Library, 1999). Current spending plans seek to maintain this. Within the total, social security spending has risen, mainly as a result of improved provision for pensioners. Current plans envisage a shift in spending towards the most popular state services, education and health care. A public accounting manoeuvre ensures that the new tax credits are not included in the totals since they are accounted as tax foregone rather than revenue spent. The growth in health and personal social services reflects population ageing. Housing spending has fallen as a result of the sharp reduction in subsidies to social housing and the shift of support to means-tested rent benefits, which form part of the social security budget.

Election platforms provide a good indication of politicians' judgements of the importance of tax and spending issues in political debates. The 1987 Conservative manifesto stated baldly: 'there is a strong moral case for reducing taxation. Higher taxes deprive people of their independence ...' and celebrated the reduction in the basic rate of income tax (the most highly visible tax) from 33 to 27 per cent of income since 1979. The 1992 policy platform again included 'reducing the share of national income taken by the public sector' (Conservative Party, 1992: 7). Labour produced a carefully costed social programme (described by one senior backbencher as the 'longest suicide note in history'), which included increases in child benefit and retirement pensions and direct investment to provide employment, to be financed by tax increases for higher earners (Labour Party, 1992: 12). The taxation measures in the programme are widely believed to have cost Labour the election and resulted in the leadership's determination that Labour should never again be presented as the party of high personal taxation.

The Conservatives headlined Britain's 'Low Tax Economy' in their 1997 manifesto and promised a reduction of the basic rate from 25 to 20 per cent (Conservative Party, 1997: 7), while Labour promised 'no increase in the basic or top rates of income tax', offered the long-term objective of a 10 per cent starting rate and promised to hold to Conservative spending plans for the first two years in office (Labour Party, 1997: 4). Success in holding down taxes was highlighted in the 2001 manifesto.

The government kept to these plans. Spending was tightly constrained up to March 1999 and income tax cut, but the 1998 Comprehensive Spending Review (Treasury, 1998) incorporated substantial increases in spending on the two most popular universal welfare services, health and education. Spending rose to over £5 billion per year more than previously planned by 2001/2 (Hills and Lelkes, 1999), a real rise of over

5 per cent, later increased to 6.1 per cent from 2000 to 2004 for the NHS. This was financed through tax buoyancy resulting from growth and spending cuts for unemployed and disabled people (DSS, 2000b: Table B2).

Both main parties pursue cuts in visible taxes. The basic rate of income tax fell from 30 to 25 per cent in the late 1980s, and then to 22 per cent by 2000. Other direct tax cuts were the reduction of higher rate tax (paid by the top 10 per cent) from 60 to 40 per cent in the 1980s and the introduction of a lower rate of 20 per cent on very low incomes in 1992. The main business tax, Corporation Tax, also fell from 40 per cent in 1985 to 35 per cent and thence to 30 per cent currently, while the small companies rate has fallen from 29 to 20 per cent (Inland Revenue Statistics).

Expenditure taxes are now the most important generator of revenue (29 per cent), while National Insurance contributions (16 per cent) are a substantial direct personal tax, local taxation (4 per cent) has fallen in real terms, despite the political visibility of Poll Tax at the beginning of the 1990s, and capital and corporation taxes raise a relatively small but growing proportion of revenue. Despite the Chancellor's ingenuity in shifting taxation towards less obvious sources, the importance attached to low taxation means that it is not feasible to pursue policies which involve a major overall spending increase.

The impact on poverty and inequality

The chief trends in the distribution of incomes during the period are a move towards higher incomes in general, accompanied by greater income inequality (DSS, 2000a: 63). As a result, poverty thresholds have risen and the proportion falling below those thresholds has also increased. Thus, the proportion of households below half the median income rose from 5 per cent in 1979 to about 15 per cent by 1999 (DSS, 2000a: Figure 4.2). The main factors accounting for the increase in poverty have been to do with the labour-market (trends in the dispersion of pay, particularly between more and less skilled workers, in access to employment and in access to private and occupational pensions) and demography (an increase in the numbers of lone parent, retired and single person households – DSS, 2000b: 2; Hills, 1995: 61). The 1979–1997 right-wing government targeted the social assistance programme more tightly after the replacement of Supplementary Benefits by Income Support in 1987, and allowed benefit levels to fall behind wages. The 1979–1997 centre-left government was determined to constrain state benefit spending, expand the private sector and target benefits on particular groups. Spending is inadequate to counter the general trend for poverty to become more concentrated among families containing low-skilled or unemployed adults, while the proportion of some other groups (most notably pensioners) in poverty fell, because more members of those groups had access to savings or private pensions (DSS, 2000c: 9).

Despite the high-profile cuts in top-rate income tax, higher-income households have grown richer at a sufficient rate to ensure that they contribute a greater proportion of total tax, but the amounts involved are insufficient to mitigate the overall trend to inequality. The top fifth of tax-payers paid 36 per cent of total taxes in 1979. This had risen to 40 per cent by 1990 and 41 per cent by 1998 (Treasury, 1999). Conversely, the bottom fifth paid 6 per cent in the first two and 7 per cent in the third year. Widening income inequality meant the percentage of gross income paid by the top fifth fell (from 37 to 35 per cent) while that paid by the bottom group rose (from 31 to 38 per cent). The potential impact of the tax system on inequality has been diminished by the commitment of both parties to basic rate cuts, which benefit high earners who pay a greater proportion of income in tax, more than low earners.

The 1997 and 2001 governments have targeted their new measures on families of working age, and in particular on low-waged workers. Empirically based evaluation of these policies is not yet available but commentators predict mild vertical redistribution. IFS estimates that the fiscal reforms alone increased the net income of all the lower eight deciles with the highest gains for the poorest tenth (over 5 per cent – IFS, 2000); an estimate of the impact of new benefits suggests that income increased for the poorest tenth of the population by over 9 per cent on average (16 per cent for those in families with children), while slightly increasing taxation on the richest tenth (Hills and Lelkes, 1999: 2; Immervoll et al., 1999). The biggest gains have gone to families with children, single pensioners and low-waged families. These changes are insufficient to reverse the secular trend to income inequality (Piachaud and Sutherland, 2001: 114). Official figures show only a small reduction in the number of people on less than half average incomes between 1996/7 and 1999/2000, from 14.1 to 14 million (DSS, 2001).

A number of pressure groups linked to the traditional Left have criticized the 1997 government's spending constraints. Although the Prime Minister has made a commitment to end child poverty 'within a generation' (Blair, 1999) and has promoted a highly visible Social Exclusion programme, policy statements stress the 'Third Way' assumption that welfare goals are to be gained not primarily by spending but by activating individuals and communities. Benefits must be carefully targeted and justified by their contribution to economic competitiveness (DSS, 1998). The party treads a careful path between the limited and discreet redistribution discussed above and the presentation of a public face resolutely opposed to tax cuts.

The net result is that, in a context where changing labour-market and family patterns are likely to exacerbate inequalities, the policies of neither party will reverse this trend, although Labour may somewhat mitigate it. The highest levels of poverty will be among groups who are marginal in the labour-market. Those most affected by these developments are unable to gain a political voice within the UK framework.

Table 7.2   UK pension system, 1979–2000

First-Pillar	PAYG state pension (indexed to prices only 1980–1988)		
Second-Pillar state	PAYG SERPS (from 1979; cut back in 1988)		
Second-Pillar private		Funded occupational	
			Funded portable personal (from 1988)
Assistance	Means tested IS pension		

Pensions

Party policies differ, but have followed a common direction, away from state provision for the mass of the population and towards the expansion of the private sector. In this context, the pension industry and the Treasury have been the most powerful agencies shaping events.

As elsewhere, the main challenges to the stability of the existing system have been from population ageing and concern about future state commitments. The UK pension system includes a pay-as-you-go financed first-pillar state 'national insurance' pension, to which almost all workers are entitled, and a variety of state and private second-pillar schemes, plus means-tested assistance for poor minorities (Table 7.2). Reform has centred on policies to hold down first-pillar levels and expand privately funded second-pillar pensions.

The second-pillar consisted (until 1988) of the pay-as-you-go financed State Earnings Related Pension Scheme (SERPS), established in 1979, or membership of one of about 100,000 approved occupational schemes (subsidized through tax remissions) at the decision of employers.

Conservative reforms in the 1980s established the new portable personal pensions (intended to supplant SERPS, which was drastically cut back) and simplified the regulatory regime for private and occupational pensions. At the end of the 1980s some 40 per cent of workers were entitled to SERPS second-pillar pensions and 55 per cent to private, occupational or personal provision, so that about 15 per cent would be likely to have their first-pillar pension supplemented by means-tested assistance (Agulnik, 1999: 59; DSS, 2000c: ch. 2). By 1999, the proportion in SERPS had shrunk to about 20 per cent, 29 per cent were in personal pension schemes and 30 per cent in occupational schemes (House of Lords, 1999). Over 90 per cent of those on incomes at national average income level as against 40 per cent of those on one third of that level are in private or occupational schemes (Agulnik, 1999: 60). Most of those entitled only to first-pillar pensions would receive additional means-tested support.

The New Labour reforms at the end of the 1990s expanded assistance to provide a means-tested Guaranteed Minimum Pension at a rather higher level, introduced a new state funded pension regime for lower income people (the State Second Pension) and altered the regulation arrangements for the private sector, by creating Stake-Holder Pensions, intended to replace Personal Pensions for those without occupational cover. The intention is to expand private, occupational and stake-holder second-pillar cover even further, to perhaps 85 per cent of the work force, while the first-pillar pension continues to decline against earnings. Thus, both parties pursue the expansion of private and of funded pensions. The long-term impact on incomes depends on investment performance and industry policies. Since pensions will be more closely linked to contributions and thus to work record, outcomes are likely to reinforce the trend to inequality noted earlier (see DSS, 2000c: 65–6).

Conservative policies, 1979–1997: privatizing pensions

The initial proposal to privatize all second-pillar pensions was justified on demographic grounds. Population ageing would increase the costs to an unsustainable level: 'we shall put a halt to the enormous growth in pension expenditure in the next century which the continuation of SERPs in its present form would have entailed' (DHSS, 1985: 45). In fact, the UK demographic profile is more favourable than that of most EU countries (Table 1.10). Contribution rates (estimated to rise to 22 per cent by 2050 – Government Actuary, 1990), although high by comparison with UK experience, do not approach projected continental rates (Disney, 1996).

The Labour Party, the 'poverty lobby' and pensioners' groups opposed the proposal to cut back the state second-pillar pension (Hadjipateras, 1985). More effective opposition came from the government's own traditional supporters. The Secretary of State records 'I had against me almost the whole of the pension industry ... even more ominous both the CBI and the influential Engineering Employers' Federation ... moved against me' (Fowler, 1991: 222). The pensions industry opposed the changes because they wanted a secure market for occupational pensions and were concerned that small compulsory personal pensions with a 4 per cent minimum contribution would not be viable either for providers or for workers on low incomes, especially if they had interrupted contribution records. The contributions would not finance a satisfactory commission and provide a pension. The CBI and the employers' groups were concerned about the compulsory nature of the scheme and the implications for employers in terms of contributions (House of Commons Library, 1995, see Pierson,

1994: 61). The Chancellor opposed the compulsory second-pillar pension on the grounds that it would increase commitments to tax relief on contributions and would impose a burden on public and private sector employers (Timmins, 1996: 403). Fowler regarded the Treasury opposition as crucial. The CBI did not wish to defend SERPs in the longer term but were concerned about a rapid transition and about compulsion (CBI, 1984: 7).

The scheme that was embodied in the 1986 Social Security Act satisfied opposition by allowing SERPs to continue in a reduced form. At the same time personal pensions were introduced on an optional basis, but with a Treasury subvention of 2 per cent of National Insurance contribution. This made the scheme so attractive that by 1993 nearly five million rather than the half million originally estimated had moved to personal pensions and the cost to the Treasury in tax relief exceeded £2 billion, against an original estimate of £500 million.

The new legislation led to a rapid change in pension provision. However, many personal pensions are likely to be relatively small and will thus simply lift people on first-pillar state pensions above the means-tested IS level, so that the scheme effectively offers a private contributory substitute for state assistance.

Further cuts in SERPs entitlement were made in 1991 and 1995. The net effect is to reduce projected SERPs spending by about 25 per cent by 2020 and by nearly half by 2040. Meanwhile, a parallel process of privatization of short-term sick pay took place, with the support of the CBI, which saw it as providing opportunities to increase control over sick absence for work (*CBI News*, 1991: 16) and opposed by the TUC.

The regulation of the private pension industry became a prominent issue in the early 1990s, brought to a head by revelations that a leading newspaper owner, Robert Maxwell, had misappropriated occupational pension funds to shore up unsuccessful businesses in 1991. Scandals surrounding the 'mis-selling' of personal pensions to individuals encouraged to opt out of SERPS when it was not in their interests to do so emerged in the early 1990s. This problem is estimated by the government inquiry to affect nearly one million people, mainly older workers who were sold personal pensions by agents eager for commissions, although their contributions would have insufficient time to generate an adequate fund (Waine, 1995: 326–7; see also Goode Committee, 1994). The Goode Committee recommended stronger controls over private and occupational pensions and arrangements for the compensation of those who suffered as a result of mismanagement of funds. NAPF, the CBI, the TUC and the Securities and Investments Board endorsed these, and the CBI later succeeded in diluting the minimum solvency requirement and the ban on investment in the employers' own company. Some companies were fined for their unethical practices from the end of 1996 onwards, although it was not until 1998 that action was taken against the Prudential, the largest company and the one most prominent in mis-selling.

New Labour 1997 onwards: private pensions under new titles

The New Labour government held first-pillar state pension uprating to price inflation for its first year (in clear contrast to the party's 1992 election programme) and set up a fundamental review of social security under Frank Field who was encouraged by the Prime Minister to 'think the unthinkable'. Attempts to ensure that a full restoration of SERPs was included on the policy agenda had been decisively rejected by the Labour leadership at the 1996 party conference. Thus, the state-centred left of the party was rebuffed. Field, as Minister for Welfare Reform, initially experimented with the idea of compulsory stake-holder pensions which would be managed by their members as mutuals.

Treasury and industry opposition redirected Labour pension reform in the late 1990s, just as the same coalition had forced Conservatives to redesign their proposals in the mid-1980s. The Chancellor opposed the compulsory membership requirement of the new scheme on the grounds that this would imply a large Treasury subsidy and compulsory employers' contributions (*Economist*, 1998: 40). The pensions industry expressed concerns about compulsion while welcoming the idea of a greater role for the private sector (ABI, 1998: 6).

Labour increased the assistance pension (relabelled the 'Guaranteed Minimum Pension') in 1999 and 2000 beyond the rate of inflation, but has made no firm commitment about future increases. The main current proposals are to establish a new contributory funded State Second Pension with the expectation that it will eventually replace SERPs and a new privately funded 'Stake-Holder Pension' (which bears no relation to the Field proposal) from 2002, to replace personal pensions (see Table 7.3). Membership of neither of the two new schemes will be compulsory. The key features of the previous system – the expansion of funded private pensions for the better off, supported by means-tested assistance for the poor – are preserved, although there will be a new state second-pillar pension for lower earners and stricter regulation of the private sector.

TUC opposition to means-testing and to the dilution of the first-pillar unfunded state pension were ignored (TUC, 1999: 89). These features are endorsed by the CBI, which would prefer even more flexibility in occupational pensions (*CBI News*, 1998: 13). The shift from a system in which most people get the majority of their pensions through unfunded state schemes to one in which they get most of their pensions through funded private schemes is complete. The process of policy development illustrates the growing authority of the Treasury and the Executive, the convergence of party policies and the weakness of unions. Since outcomes depend in large part on stock market performance, they must remain uncertain. However, most analyses conclude that irrespective of the impact on aggregate pensions, the changes are likely to exacerbate

Table 7.3   *UK pension system, 2000 onwards*

First-pillar	PAYG state pension (indexed to prices only 1980–1998)			
Second-pillar state	PAYG SERPS (from 1979; cut back in 1988, and expected to decline)	Funded flat-rate SSP (to replace SERPS and only attractive to low earners)		
Second-pillar private		Funded SHP (from 2002)		
			Funded portable personal (from 1988; expected to decline)	
				Funded occupational
Assistance	Means-tested GMP			

inequalities, both on gender and class lines, since pensions are linked more tightly to contribution records (Liu, 1999; Williamson, 2000). Low income and poverty in working life continue into retirement.

Unemployment and the labour-market

Unemployment was a major political issue throughout the period. The main development is the convergence of party policy from opposing liberal and Beveridgean positions to a common emphasis on work incentives and on workfare.

The UK faced a rapid increase in unemployment in the early 1980s to levels not seen since the recession of the 1930s. The Conservative government decisively rejected the Keynesian commitment to full employment that had been the central feature of the policy-platforms of both main parties up to the mid-1970s. The main policy aims were to remove obstacles to the operation of a freer labour-market, through the weakening of labour unions and cut-backs in employment protection and benefit rights, and to promote job training especially for younger people. The government responded to the political salience of unemployment by changes to statistical methods – 19 between 1979 and 1988 – to reduce the count (Atkinson and Micklewright, 1989). The 1980 Social Security Act removed strikers' rights to benefit for themselves and uprated short-term benefits by 5 per cent below inflation. Benefits were taxed from 1982.

The means-tested wage supplement for low-paid workers with families was increased in 1986 and renamed Family Credit, and the gap in assistance benefits between those expected to work and unemployed, retired or disabled people widened. Universal Child Benefit was frozen between 1987 and 1989, with the explicit intention of strengthening work incentives, and the 'availability for work' test for those of working age on benefit was tightened. In the 1990s, further restrictions on benefit were introduced. After the Portillo reviews, Income Support claimers' entitlement to mortgage interest payments for the first nine months of unemployment was withdrawn, and the Job Seekers' Allowance (1996) replaced all unemployment benefits. This benefit is conditional on following an approved programme of work-seeking and employability-improving activities and is available for six months, renewable for a further six, after which the claimant must seek means-tested income support. National Insurance unemployment benefit was abolished.

The Manpower Services Commission, created in 1973 to promote a unified approach to training, set up a benefit-linked Youth Training Scheme in 1983. From 1987, young people who refused training placements could lose Income Support entitlement and, in 1988, all entitlement for 16- to 18-year-olds was withdrawn on the grounds that they would be in education or supported through Youth Training placements. About 200,000 people a year (the bulk of unemployed school leavers) entered the programme. In 1992 only 20 per cent of these gained a qualification at standard school-leaving level, rising to a third by 1997. Most trainees simply fail to complete their courses (ONS, 1999: Table 3.23) and the scheme has had little impact of the quality of the workforce. At the same time the Council for National Vocational Training was established. This body created a new unified system of vocational qualifications which gradually spread through further education as part of a programme to improve the skills of the workforce.

Labour offered a different approach to the unemployment crisis of the 1980s, based on the maintenance of benefit entitlements and a government-led investment programme to create jobs. However, the experience of repeated election defeats and the acceptance of the argument (vigorously promoted by the Commission on Social Justice, 1994: 91), that international economic competition demanded the redirection of policy to improve both incentives and the quality of the workforce, led to a remaking of party policy in this area as in pensions. Labour also began to develop the complex work support and incentive system designed to 'make work pay' that was introduced under the 1997 government, and is prefigured in Clarke's more limited 1994 'Workstart' scheme (Timmins, 1996: 516–17).

Table 7.4   *Low-paid working families receiving means-tested support*

Year	Nos (000)
1971	71
1985	199
1990	317
1995	600
1999	780
1999 (post Tax Credit)	1500

Source: Dilnot and McCrae, 1999

By 1997 unemployment levels were falling, mainly as a result of the economic upturn. The New Labour government's approach to unemployment is summed up in the Prime Minister's foreword to the Welfare Reform Green paper: 'Work for those who can, security for those who cannot' (DSS, 1998: iii). The government ignored campaigns by the poverty lobby and unions to restore national insurance benefits; by 1997 the proportion of unemployed people receiving means-tested assistance had reached 90 per cent, double the 1987 level (DSS, 1997: Figure 27). Current plans envisage an even stronger role for means-testing (DSS, 1999: Table 12).

The centrepiece of unemployment policy is the New Deal, providing jobs, education and training for unemployed people as a condition of receipt of benefit. Separate schemes cover young people, long-term unemployed, over-50s, disabled people, partners of unemployed people and lone parents. All schemes involve individual counselling and work or training placements at benefit levels of income. The most important is the young person's scheme which is compulsory for under 25s and is the only route to benefit for this age-group. It is effectively a Workfare/Trainfare scheme. The principle of confronting claimers with encouragement to train or work was extended to all of working age (including sick and disabled people and single parents, for whom it is voluntary) in April 2000. The 'make work pay' schemes widen the gap in living standards between those in and out of work. They include the new minimum wage and tax and childcare credits for low-paid working families, financed initially by a one-off levy on privatized utilities, while benefits for able-bodied unemployed people remain constant in real terms. Means-tested support to low-income families, provided they are in work, has risen to £5 billion a year – roughly double the level provided by the previous government (Table 7.4).

The New Labour programme is concerned to promote work incentives by improving the relative return from work and by making it difficult to sustain long periods on benefits. It also contains a commitment to upskill the labour force. It is based on an analysis of the problems of unemployment as partly behavioural (low incentives) and partly due to low employability. This contrasts with previous party policies which were designed to stimulate the supply of jobs. The previous government shared the commitment to stronger incentives and improvement of training, but devoted fewer resources to the area, and relied more on the liberal assumption that market forces, assisted by low benefits, should be permitted to price workers into jobs. Ambitions for this programme are considerable. More recently the Chancellor announced that a return to full employment was a real possibility. The official evaluation indicates that the problem may be less tractable, especially among older people. About 440,000 young people and 238,000 older people had been through the New Deal by February 2000. Only a third of the former and an eighth of the latter found jobs lasting more than six weeks. About half of these would have found work in any case (Millar, 2000).

The CBI has supported the development of a more active approach to the labour-market. Both the Director General of the CBI and the General Secretary of the TUC endorsed the Rowntree *Report on Income and Wealth*, which called for a greater emphasis on active labour-market measures and on 'benefits at work' (Hills, 1995). The CBI involvement meant that the organization was able to find common ground with the 1997 Labour government when it developed its Welfare to Work programme, although it opposed the Minimum Wage and stronger employment protection. The Learning and Skills Council which replace TECs remains predominantly business-led although it operates within a stronger framework of national strategic planning. The TUC has repeatedly expressed disappointment at a strategy that pays trainees at benefit rates, at the ending of National Insurance unemployment benefit and at the stricter 'availability for work' requirements attached to the Job Seekers' Allowance (TUC, 1994: 64, TUC, 1999: 86). Interestingly, it is concerned that the Working Families Tax Credit, unlike Child Benefit, is not paid directly to the carer of the children, but through the pay packet, so that less of the money supports children's needs. This reverses the position in the 1970s when unions opposed a shift from tax relief to higher child benefit on the contrary grounds, and reflects its abandonment of Fordist male breadwinner priorities. TUC opposition to many features of the current programme is ignored.

There is now substantial consensus between Conservative and Labour parties on the main policy directions: benefit entitlement strictly linked to training or work placements and a clear incentive regime which ensures that the benefits received by those out of work are substantially below the lowest market pay rates. The main differences are the amount of government investment, the extent of support for low-paid workers and the extent to which employers are involved in training. The Conservative approach represents a more liberal and the Labour approach a more state-centred activation programme.

Conclusion: swift reform and policy convergence

The UK governmental system is highly centralized. Recent reforms (weakening the second chamber, strengthening Prime Ministerial control of the executive and strengthening the interventionist powers of the Treasury) make it more so. Contingent factors (the weakness of opposition parties and of the trade union movement) reinforce the trend. The upshot is that the party of government has a freer hand to direct (or reverse) reform than elsewhere in Europe. More marginal groups (for example, unemployed people and those on low incomes) find it impossible to make their voice heard.

The policies of the two main parties diverged in liberal and social democratic directions in the 1970s, 1980s and early 1990s, but are now converging, driven by the commitment of both to economic competitiveness and the belief that low taxes are essential to electoral success. The traditional Keynes-Beveridge citizenship welfare state has no powerful advocates. There is widespread agreement on the retrenchment of spending, the promotion of privatization in areas like pensions, the targeting of benefits through means-testing and other restrictions and the importance of labour-market activation through incentives, training and what is effectively workfare. Areas of contention are: the minimum wage; the level of low-wage subsidy; the extent of interventionism in such programmes as the New Deal; the rates of first-pillar and means-tested pensions; and the scope of state involvement in second pensions. Conservative policies pursue negative activation of unemployed people through benefit constraint, New Labour is more inclined to combine this with opportunities for training. Much of this disagreement is on matters of degree rather than principle. Both main parties are determined to keep state spending – and taxes – low, and to direct welfare effort to sustain economic competitiveness.

UK political arrangements facilitate the stability of this consensus, because first-past-the-post voting makes it difficult for minority parties to exert an influence and because unions are too weak to contribute to policy-making. Since the groups whose interest are most damaged by the liberal-leaning consensus are unable to enter debate, the high levels of poverty and inequality noted in Table 1.4 are likely to persist.

The basic themes of recent theoretical debate have concerned both external and internal factors: do the forces of globalization, Europeanization, demographic shifts and high unemployment exert pressures that are sufficiently strong to overcome the inertia of national arrangements and propel policy-making in a common direction? In the UK, external pressures have played a strong role in policy debate. The response has been an effective political consensus, providing the foundation for stability. However, the UK continues along a policy trajectory that differs from that of its European neighbours. It spends less on welfare, is less concerned with state intervention and has little concern to involve the social partners (especially trade unions) in policy-making. The consensus is on a distinctive broadly liberal welfare agenda, and there is no obvious shift towards the more corporatist policy regimes that predominate in Europe.

8 Polity, Policy-Making and Welfare Futures

Peter Taylor-Gooby

This chapter examines the implications of the evidence reviewed in Chapters 1 to 7 for the future of the welfare state in Europe. The seven representative welfare states are used as markers to show how different welfare regimes and political configurations respond to current pressures. Reform so far has been a slow process and largely confined within the boundaries of regime type. However, shifts in institutional structure, political party positions and in the organization of welfare systems point the way to more rapid and radical change.

Patterns of welfare reform

The first chapter argued that the various welfare settlements in European countries face common pressures from a number of directions including technological shifts that reduce employment opportunities, especially for less skilled workers; economic globalization that strengthens pressure to ensure welfare policies enhance competitiveness at the same time as it weakens governments' ability to use export–import, capital and exchange rate controls to regulate their economies; European Monetary Union that exacerbates these pressures and compels governments to surrender the controls associated with national currencies and fiscal policy-making; changes in population structure that increase the likely cost of pensions and reduce the numbers of younger workers; and new family patterns associated with stronger demands for gender equality and for access to paid employment from women and a decline in the availability of unwaged domestic care. The principal evaluations of the impact of these changes on European welfare states paint a picture of the adaptation, evolution or recalibration of the welfare settlement rather than the decline or dismantling of state welfare (Ferrera and Rhodes, 2000a; Kuhnle, 2000a; Pierson, 2001; Scharpf and Schmidt, 2000). There is at present no strong evidence of overall convergence in the face of broadly similar pressures, and the different varieties of welfare state regime retain their distinctive characteristics.

This analysis is encouraging from a viewpoint that sees the welfare state as one of the great achievements of Europe, a strategy for combining the

Table 8.1 *Polity, welfare system and response to pressures*

	Policy-making system	Welfare system	Specific pressures[a]	Outcomes	Innovations[b]	Future issues: pressures for change
Finland	Coalition; strong consensus-building tradition	Universal citizenship	Economic crisis of early 1990s; competition affecting export industries; collapse of Russian market	Higher taxes, limited retrenchment, consensual pension and unemployment benefit reforms	New means-tested LMS benefit for unemployed; means-testing of universal state pension, in effect; other reforms negotiated within existing settlement	Settlement depends on maintenance of popular support and willingness to pay high taxes. Stronger divisions between social insurance and means-tested benefits. Possible shift towards a Continental corporatist solution
France	Strong executive; unions closely involved in social insurance	Social insurance + assistance	Globalization: high labour costs resulting from social insurance	Delays in reform due to weak state control of welfare; state gains more control of institutional levers	RMI; CSG; tax-subsidized, long-term saving scheme; 35-hour week	Reforms of social insurance finance and entitlement and expansion of incentives for private provision now more likely
Germany	Semi-sovereign federal state; strong consensus tradition	Social insurance + assistance	High cost of re-unification; contribution rates become politically unacceptable	Delays in reform due to obstacles to consensus; more confrontational welfare politics; 'neo-liberal turn' of the SPD enables pension and tax reform	Expansion of state-subsidized private funded pensions	Underlying agreement of the main political actors (despite party confrontations) opens the way to retrenchment in pensions and tax-reforms, and moves policy in a more neo-liberal direction
Spain	Decentralized federalizing structure; strong consensus tradition	Expanding social insurance + assistance	High rates of unemployment and temporary work; low fertility; changing family patterns	Consensus on welfare policy co-exists with political party competition and demands for decentralization by the regions	*Rentas Mínimas* (driven by regional government)	Unclear whether present rate of welfare expansion can be maintained without addressing future pension cost and provision for women workers and other marginal groups

(Continued)

Table 8.1 (Continued)

	Policy-making system	Welfare system	Specific pressures[a]	Outcomes	Innovations[b]	Future issues: pressures for change
Sweden	Minority single party; strong consensus-building tradition	Universal citizenship	Economic crisis of early 1990s; competition affecting export industries	Higher taxes, limited retrenchment, consensual pension and unemployment benefit reforms; introduction of funded pensions	Means-testing of universal state pension; mandatory funded pension; new lower benefits for young unemployed	Settlement depends on maintenance of popular support and willingness to pay high taxes; development of funded pensions may affect this. Possible shift towards a Continental corporatist solution
Switzerland	Weak, highly consensual, federal structure; some groups excluded	Limited social insurance + compulsory private	Historically high unemployment; inclusion of migrants and women workers in welfare settlements	Compromise solutions on pension reform and finance of welfare achieved	Contribution sharing between spouses in public pensions; more active labour market policies	Compromise policies for 'atypical workers' that can command support have not yet been developed
UK	Majoritarian government, strong executive; limited traditions of consensus-building	Liberal-inclined and individualist welfare system + universal health and education	Strong electoral pressure for low taxation	Major retrenchment and privatization of pensions; activation regime for unemployed	Abolition of unemployment benefit; shift towards means-tested state plus funded private pension regime	Bipartisan consensus renders neo-liberal reforms stable; exclusion of marginal groups may damage social cohesion

Notes: [a] Specific pressures which have played an exceptional role in national policy debate: similar common pressures from economic globalization, labour-market and family change and population ageing affect policy in all the countries reviewed.
[b] Specific innovations in the context of the national welfare system

dynamism of capitalism with a measure of social justice that renders it compatible with democracy and tempers the chaotic tendencies of markets within a framework of social cohesion. It also mitigates concern that the valued achievements of national welfare systems will be submerged by wider international processes of economic and political change. However, the analyses of the reform process in previous chapters (Table 8.1) indicates that changes in the organization of welfare now open the way to more radical reforms. Different welfare states start from different positions defined by political configurations and welfare regime. All are experiencing continuing and in most cases increasing tensions from the factors reviewed in Chapter 1, and all have introduced changes which will weaken political and institutional obstacles to the redirection of welfare.

Finland and Sweden

Both Finland and Sweden share a strong tradition of universal welfare provision, bound up with a commitment to the welfare state as an essential component in citizenship. They display the characteristics of the Scandinavian social democratic welfare regime. The Finnish welfare state was slightly less developed in a number of areas up to the late 1980s and only attained Swedish levels of social spending in the early 1990s as a result of the recession. A centralized governmental system gives the executive considerable authority in both countries, but this is combined with strong traditions of corporatism and consensus-building in policy-making. In Sweden, the political tradition is typically of single party minority government, and in Finland of coalition, but in both cases, government maintains close links with both employers and trade unions, the latter having a very close association with social democratic parties. As a result, social policy development tends to be negotiated with the relevant interests and policy enjoys a high degree of political support.

The importance of economic globalization and the ineffectiveness of traditional Keynesian control mechanisms were brought home by the fiscal crisis of the early 1990s (exacerbated in the case of Finland by the disruption of the export market to Russia associated with the collapse of the command economy). The centre-right governments elected in 1991 were unable to implement effective reform in either country and were replaced by the mid-1990s. Social Democrat and Social Democrat-led governments in Sweden and Finland respectively have responded to the pressures within the welfare consensus and increased taxes and social spending, while introducing some benefit cuts. Pension reforms with long-term implications for the living standards of the next generation of pensioners have been introduced (with an innovative funded element alongside state pay-as-you-go provision in Sweden).

Attempts by government to move beyond the traditional welfare system have been most marked in relation to unemployment. In both countries there has been a cautious expansion of means-testing and a strengthening of work incentives, but, when governments sought to introduce stronger controls on the insurance benefits for the core of the organized working class, they were vigorously opposed by trade unions and were unable to implement planned retrenchment. It is noteworthy that in Finland in 1996 the Social Democratic government was able to negotiate restrictions on unemployment benefits that the centre-right governments had been unable to establish, despite repeated efforts. In Sweden the attempt in 1996/1997 to extend the restrictions on unemployment benefit entitlement previously introduced by the centre-right failed as a result of public and trade union protest and the main policy changes of the Social Democratic government were to expand assistance.

The high quality, socially integrative welfare state in these countries has shown resilience to the shocks experienced so far, essentially because it enjoys strong popular support and because the policy-making system has the capacity to negotiate consensus on reforms with the groups who have political influence. How the settlement will respond to future pressures from EU calls for tax harmonization, which may diminish its revenue base, and from changes such as the growth of means-testing and the possible expansion of an individualized funded pension element in Sweden, which may undermine collective solidarity, is unclear. The pattern of social change includes elements likely to diminish social cohesion, and none likely to enhance it. One possible direction is towards a more strictly work-based system, with more stringent activation measures and the expansion of means-testing for those marginal to the labour force. This would retain the links between policy-makers and social partners in consensus-building, but take Finland and Sweden south, closer to the corporatist continental model – a trend which many citizens in these countries view with concern.

France

The French welfare tradition is based on a relatively generous social insurance system, which covers most workers. Together with Germany and Switzerland it serves as an example of the continental corporatist welfare regime. It enjoys a high level of popular support and is strongly defended by the trade unions, who are reluctant to surrender their entrenched role in the management of the system, since their power base in industrial relations is weak. Tax-financed means-tested welfare, directed at the needs of those not covered by social insurance, has developed rapidly since the late 1980s. The policy-making system combines relatively weak political parties with a strong executive and a president elected independently from parliamentary elections. In practice the ability of government to initiate change depends on political circumstances, and in particular the interactions between election-cycles for either parliament or president which may limit the capacity to pursue unpopular reform. The fact that the bulk of welfare is managed at arms length from the state and closely identified with the union movement exacerbates the difficulties of achieving change.

In this context the initial response to pressures on welfare provision in the 1980s was to increase social spending. However, economic competitiveness gained a particularly important place in welfare debate, reinforced by awareness of the implications of high social insurance contributions for labour costs. The failure of Keynesian experiments at economic management in the mid-1970s and early 1980s brought home the difficulties of ignoring international pressures. The response of government has been to seek welfare reforms which extend its control over the welfare system and contain expenditure without jeopardizing its electoral support. The role of taxation rather than social contributions in financing welfare has been broadened, the influence of unions and employers in certain social insurance schemes (for example, health care) weakened and the social insurance budget brought directly under parliamentary scrutiny.

The system does not facilitate the construction of consensus on policy changes. Private sector pensions were restructured in the early 1990s, but an attempt to introduce similar policies into the public sector was defeated by a national strike. Repeated efforts to introduce legislation directly promoting funded private pensions have been so far unsuccessful, although a tax-subsidized, long-term private saving scheme is under active discussion. However, labour-market activation policies, involving means-tested time-limited benefits and the promotion of training and work-experience have expanded substantially.

Welfare reform in France is now poised on a cusp: the changes in policy-making arrangements which will enable government to reform the system are in place, but radical new policies have not yet been introduced. The French welfare system faces the possibility of more substantial changes in the next decade than it experienced during the 1990s. These shifts are likely to involve the extension of state control within the corporatist framework, and may involve further conflicts with the traditional defenders of the French welfare settlement – trade unions and organized workers – as was the case in autumn 2000, when the state forced the social partners to renegotiate the collective agreement on the reform of social insurance three times.

Germany

The German policy-making mechanism is hedged about with moderating influences, located within a federal state and has always encouraged liaison with well-organized interest groups, so that the polity is often described as a 'semi-sovereign' state (Katzenstein, 1987). The established welfare system relies heavily on social insurance, built round a male breadwinner model and enjoying strong public support. It serves as a key example of the continental corporatist welfare regime. In addition to the common pressures of demography, rising costs and labour-market change, Germany also experienced the extra costs of reunification in terms of provision for unemployed people and transfers to subsidize the amalgamation of the former East German welfare system into the West German model. Policy debate has stressed the impact of greater demands on welfare in raising social insurance contributions to politically unacceptable levels, the significance of globalization for what has traditionally been regarded as the leading European economy with particular strengths in manufacturing, the problems of attracting investment exacerbated by the corporate and individual tax regime, and the expansion of part-time and low-waged work, not included within the social insurance framework.

The 1990s were characterized by political confrontations which resulted in deadlock and delay. However, the rejection of neo-Keynesian policies by the SPD after 1999, symbolized by the resignation of Lafontaine as Finance Minister in February, opened the way to radical reforms of pensions and taxation. Reforms are certainly a matter of bitter party debate and will require further modification, but an implicit consensus on a broadly neo-liberal direction of change underlies party conflict. The pension reform of 1989 was based on political consensus, but, by the mid-1990s, was seen as inadequate to meet the pressures of reunification and demographic shifts. The Kohl government was unable to secure consensus and imposed a further reform. New policies developed through hard-fought political debate by the SPD follow the general direction of constraint in state pensions and introduce state-subsidized privately funded pensions as a third pillar – a radical innovation in the German context, and one which has substantial implications for the future of state pensions. Kohl was unable to secure the support in both Bundestag and Bundesrat necessary to pass proposed tax changes but reform measures introduced by the SPD reduce taxes on higher incomes and on capital to encourage investment. In the area of unemployment, policy change has been limited, but has constrained benefits and pursued a moderate expansion of activation measures.

The German welfare settlement traditionally demonstrated all the positive characteristics of compromise and consensus. However, reform through the 1990s has been slow and marked by political controversy. The 'neo-liberal turn' of the SPD has enabled it to achieve reforms in pensions and taxation which will undoubtedly be subject to further modification, but which follow the broad policy direction favoured by the centre-right main parties. Thus, major aspects of welfare policy appear set in a new direction that implies a stronger role for the private sector and greater constraint of state welfare. Developments in relation to labour-market activation and meeting the needs of those excluded from traditional social insurance have been more limited. Whether attempts to promote more liberal policies will permanently undermine the traditional consensus-building system between unions, employers, welfare providers and central and local state is at present unclear.

Spain

The central feature of policy-making in Spain has been the emphasis on maintaining cohesion between social partners, political parties and the different regions of the country in the transition to democracy and afterwards, and the subsequent rapid expansion of social welfare provision. The commitment to consensus results from the experience of the transition from Francoist dictatorship to democracy and recognition of the necessity for compromise between different interests in order to integrate a country where strong decentralizing tendencies and economic pressures may threaten social cohesion. It is exemplified in the Moncloa and Toledo Pacts and appears likely to persist despite changes in the complexion of government. The system typifies the Mediterranean welfare regime.

The specific pressures experienced in Spain are the demands from the regions for greater control and independence in welfare, changes to traditional welfare provision through the family, the high rate of unemployment and temporary work, the strong demand to expand welfare spending towards the EU average and the sharp decline in fertility which exacerbates the impact of population ageing on pension spending. Welfare provision continues to grow and current regional and economic policies are making substantial progress in expanding job opportunities, although the bias towards temporary work remains. Regional governments took the lead in developing means-tested minimum income support, and central government responded by implementing a national scheme of means-tested non-contributory pensions. The pressures of demography, family change and unemployment on Spanish welfare systems remain severe. Demands for a restructuring of pensions to ensure that further expansion is financially viable, the introduction of stronger child support and nursery provision, and greater regulation of the labour-market may impose strains on the welfare consensus it will find hard to sustain.

Switzerland

The Swiss policy-making system is highly consensual, as a result of the constitutional weakness of central government and the wide range of opportunities for cantons and trade unions, employers' groups and the confessional divisions to represent their interests at all levels of policy-making, most clearly expressed in the capacity of organized groups to challenge reform through referendum. The outcome has been an underdeveloped social insurance system with a substantial role for private and occupational provision built into the welfare state through the compulsory inclusion of some groups of workers. It is closest to the continental corporatist welfare regime. Legislation is only possible through consensus-building and typically produces compromise policies which recognize diverse interests by offering different packages of advantages and disadvantages for various groups.

The main pressures recognized in the recent past have been globalization (brought home by an economic crisis in the early 1990s, which generated unemployment at a level moderate by European standards, but higher than that experienced in Switzerland for more than a generation, and which sent shock-waves through the highly successful Swiss economy) and the pressures of population ageing and family change. Consensual reforms to the pension system have been achieved. However, the pressures on employment and on the traditional family require recognition of the interests of groups not traditionally integrated into the welfare debate: women entering the labour-market and the migrant workers who have traditionally provided a buffer in times of economic downturn, but who will be increasingly necessary as the population ages. Possible reforms centre on the recognition of part-time work within the social insurance system, provision of child-care, the enforcement of equal opportunities legislation and the extension of citizenship to immigrants. The Association Agreement with the EU in 2000 may generate pressures for the adoption of policies comparable to those in surrounding countries.

These issues pose a particular challenge to the Swiss policy-making settlement, which is not well-equipped to include the interests most nearly affected by recent changes. The inclusion of a broader range of groups is likely to generate more extensive compromise reforms. It is difficult to see how agreement on the increase in state welfare spending necessary to match the EU average will be achieved, but there may well be a tendency to widen the inclusiveness of the system and the range of state responsibilities.

The UK

The policy-making system of the UK is unusually decisive in comparison with other European nations, as a result of first-past-the-post voting, a unitary state and strong party government with weak traditions of consensus-building. This tendency has been reinforced in recent years by changes in the organization of the executive, the ineffectiveness of both main parties in opposition and of the union movement, and the convergent trend between the welfare policies of the main political parties. Policy is dominated by spending constraint, with a strong role for means-testing and a large private sector. The welfare settlement is the closest in Europe to the liberal regime type.

The main issues recognized in debate have been the importance of economic globalization for the competitiveness of national industry and the implications of population ageing for pension spending. In both areas, there have been substantial reforms along lines endorsed by the main cross-national agencies (OECDb, 1994; OECD, 1995; World Bank, 1994): labour-market activation policies involving unemployment benefit cuts, trainfare, workfare and the enhancement of work incentives through subsidies to low wages have been introduced and the bulk of pension provision transferred to individually funded private schemes. Governments of both parties have been determined to hold down the already relatively low rates of tax. The outcome emphasizes the liberal elements in the UK system, moving it closer to that of the US, although bi-partisan commitment to a national health service remains. The resulting welfare settlement appears robust, because the broad policy framework is supported by both the main parties. Whether an essentially liberal solution to the problems of welfare at the end of the 20th century will undermine social cohesion in the 21st remains to be seen.

The overall picture

The above review shows how the various European welfare states have started from different places in reacting to the pressures they have experienced, and how the pace of reform has differed in the various national contexts. Three general points emerge:

First, as the research reviewed in the first chapter showed, European welfare systems are surprisingly resilient, at least so far as recent reform goes. The social democratic marker countries (Finland and Sweden) embrace changes that maintain their commitment to high-spending universal citizenship provision, the continental corporatist systems (France, Germany and Switzerland) in their various ways develop policies which continue the social insurance basis of their welfare states (with modification), the Mediterranean country (Spain) has committed itself to maintaining its mixture of universal and targeted, state and private provision, while expanding towards the EU average, and the liberal-leaning country (the UK) moves further in that direction through retrenchment and privatization. The different welfare regimes remain broadly distinct.

Second, national variations cannot simply be read off from regime type. Reform depends directly on the decisions made in national politics, and it is hardly surprising that national patterns of welfare policy-making can only be understood in the context of national politics, history and culture. For example, the relatively recent democratic transition in Spain underpins a commitment to consensus expressed in tripartite pacts on welfare, particular issues of national identity surround reunification in Germany and explain why voters in the West are willing to finance it, attachment to the 'people's home' is central to Swedish social democracy, and the National Health Service in the UK is protected by its historically entrenched status, while liberal policies are endorsed by the electorate in other fields of welfare. More immediately, particular events have acted as reference points for change in specific national settings – for example, the experience of the financial crises of the early 1990s in Sweden and Finland leading to centre-right governments that proved unable to contain welfare spending and were replaced with social democratic governments that could; the series of election defeats culminating in the 1992 debacle that compelled the Labour Party to remake its policies and abandon a centre-left position on welfare; the failure of Keynesianism in the 1980s in France leading to the conviction that a welfare reform trajectory which involved steadily increasing spending was not, in the long term, sustainable; and the failure of both main parties when in government to establish consensus on pension and tax reform in the 1990s in Germany leading to the policy-making departure of imposed solutions.

Third, while convergence between the different regime types identified in the mainstream of comparative social policy is so far limited, there are indications that radical changes are now probable in a number of states. This is the result of party political shifts, changes in welfare systems and the expansion of private provision. Most notably, the modernization of social democratic parties through the victory of the factions which abandon Keynesian approaches and accept the logic of the competitiveness imperative – the obvious cases are Germany and the UK – facilitates the construction of an implicit consensus which takes policy in a broadly neo-liberal direction, despite superficial party conflict. The capacity of social democratic parties to achieve neo-liberal reforms which conservative parties were unable to implement (the 1996 unemployment benefit cuts in Finland, the 2000 tax and 2001 pension reform in Germany, the introduction of subsidized private long-term saving schemes in France, the imposition of workfare/trainfare in the UK) by removing the possibility of effective opposition from the left, reinforces this development.

Institutional reforms have removed obstacles in France, as government acquires greater control over welfare provision and finance and in the UK through even stricter centralization. Changes elsewhere, such as the willingness of parties of government to impose major reforms without consensus in Germany, lead in the same direction. The growth of private pensions, the expansion of means-testing and similar targeting policies and new measures designed to activate dependent populations of working age, all tend to create tensions in the loose coalition of beneficiaries that provided the political endorsement of big welfare. The widespread acceptance of the competitiveness imperative as providing the overall framework for policy development does not lead directly to 'roll back the state' neo-liberalism. It reinforces activation and cost-containment everywhere and ensures that no government can respond to extra pressures on pensions, health care and unemployment provision simply by increasing taxes, social contributions and spending. Most European governments are now in a position where they can introduce reforms that would not have been politically feasible in the 1990s.

Understanding welfare states: resilience and sustainability

Almost all analysts group European welfare states loosely into categories that are broadly comparable to the regime model of Esping-Andersen (for a review see Abrahamson, 1999, or Pierson, 2001, concluding chapter). Accounts of regime differentiation were initially based on data from the 1970s and early 1980s (for example, Esping-Andersen, 1990: Tables 2.1 to 4.5) and focused on the analysis of the stable welfare frameworks that emerged during the post-war boom. The pressures that emerged as the pattern of economic growth became more unstable and welfare states matured provoked interest in the forces influencing welfare state change. In the context of economic globalization, the development of a common monetary and market system across the EU and anticipation that the expansion of the European Union will create a much broader and more politically diverse context for policy development, this interest focused particularly on questions of convergence, divergence or the possible abandonment of the welfare state tradition. This generated more sophisticated accounts of welfare state politics which received an added impetus from the necessity of coping with evidence of the resilience of welfare systems under stress. The new approaches also emphasize the point that the politics of welfare retrenchment differ fundamentally from the politics of expansion. Governments must now deal with the problem that the welfare systems which almost all experts agreed required reform are nonetheless hugely popular. It is now necessary to escape electoral blame for cut-backs, whereas previously government had welcomed credit for reform programmes based on expansion.

Pierson (1994) distinguishes between *systemic reform*, which entrenches change by weakening the interests which oppose it and creating constituencies committed to new policies, thus redirecting policy-making, and less fundamental *programmatic* changes which recalibrate policy instruments or alter the scope of particular aspects of policy (see also Hall, 1993; Ross, 2000; Visser and Hemerijck, 1997). The key issue is whether the changes in welfare systems taking place at present are in fact systemic or programmatic. If the former is correct, current policy changes will launch welfare states on new trajectories of reform leading to transformation or decline. Policy development will be cumulative and the impact of changes reach beyond current intentions. Welfare states may move between regime categories or the regime categorization may itself break down. From the latter perspective that understands change as programmatic, reform is to be taken at face value and is in principle reversible. If reforms currently amount to no more than a programmatic recalibration of welfare to meet changing circumstances, European welfare states will remain resilient into the future.

Systemic and programmatic change

The resilience thesis implies that systemic changes are insufficiently powerful to produce pressures for substantial and systemic restructuring. The framework that distinguishes the various regime types is thus stable. Changes that might be seen as systemic in the area of pensions are: the removal of the universal element in the Finnish and Swedish pension systems, and the shift from a 'defined benefit' to 'defined contribution' regimes and privatization (including the new, privately controlled funded element in Sweden, the private third pillar in Germany and the UK personal and stakeholder pensions); the weakening of the position of social partners in social insurance, development of new tax-subsidized long-term savings and the introduction of tax finance into schemes previously run on a social insurance basis through such devices as the CSG (France) for assistance pensions and the 'ecotax', intended also to contribute to environmental goals (Germany); and the downrating of annual pension increases to price rather than earnings indices, so that the contribution increases necessary to reinstate former levels of provision become electorally impossible (particularly marked in the UK). Other changes which involve adjusting entitlement and uprating formulae, extending the required number of contribution years, cutting early retirement pensions, increasing the recognition for time spent in child care and introducing demographic moderators, are, in principle, reversible (and therefore to be seen as programmatic), but require the commitment of resources on a scale which is politically unfeasible.

In relation to unemployment provision, the direction of policy, which has involved a retrenchment of entitlement and insurance-based benefits and an extension of means-tested assistance (even in Nordic countries), together with a greater emphasis on activation through training and workfare, pursued with differing levels of enthusiasm in different countries, tend to be shaped by the extent of government commitment to a more or less universal welfare system. In more universal systems the stress is on training schemes and positive support, whereas in less inclusive systems provision tends to workfare with strict entitlement conditions and low rates of benefit (Hvinden et al., 2000). These changes are not systemic and could in principle be reversed, although some, such as the reintroduction of insurance-based unemployment benefit in the UK or the development of an alternative to RMI in France, would require considerable redirection of spending. They tend to be sustained by a consensus constructed across the relevant social actors. However, the inclusion of groups not previously involved in the policy debate, such as women entering the labour-market or immigrant workers (in Spain and Switzerland), will involve systemic shifts, since it will then be impractical to exclude the interests of these groups from future policy debate.

Debates about taxation and the finance of welfare have led to a number of changes. The most significant in systemic terms are the introduction of privately funded pensions in Sweden and Germany, their expansion in the UK and the analogous saving scheme in France, creating an interest particularly concentrated among better-off groups that it will be difficult to curtail in future. Incentives for privately funded pensions through tax allowances and other means are on the statute book or under active discussion in all the countries. In addition, the incursion of non-traditional finance into social insurance (Germany, France) and its role in Spain entrenches the legitimacy of greater state involvement in the direction of these systems.

All these changes take place in a dynamic context. The intensification of international economic competition, as the single European market (including Switzerland by Association Agreement) develops and as the more recently industrialized nations progress in higher value-added market sectors, the probability of further technological changes, the impact of lower birth-rates on continuing population ageing and the impact of EU tax harmonization on welfare funding mechanisms will bring home the pressures for revision of welfare settlements. Although the Treaty of Nice (2000) did not make rapid progress in this direction, the move towards qualified majority voting in relation to social exclusion and the modernization of social protection systems is likely to increase pressures for co-ordinated action in other areas of social security and social welfare.

The inclusion during the next five or six years of some at least of the accession states who have applied for EU membership (most importantly the Czech Republic, Hungary, Poland and Slovenia, who started negotiations in March 1998 and Bulgaria, Romania and Slovakia, who started in 1999) will substantially increase the range of welfare systems and policy-making frameworks in the community. The immediate impact on wages, employment, migration and competition is likely to be limited, except in border areas, due to the relatively small size of these economies (Boeri and Brücker, 2000). In general, the impact of systemic changes and the difficulty of reversing programmatic changes in the context of enhanced competitive pressure means that welfare policies will receive fresh impetus in the direction in which they are already travelling.

The stability of reform

From a backward-looking perspective, welfare states are remarkably resilient. In all the countries reviewed, the welfare systems of the 1980s have 'weathered the storm' of the financial crisis of the early 1990s, the Maastricht Treaty, economic globalization and other pressures with considerable success, and retain recognizably the same outline in the early 2000s. From a forward-looking perspective that pays attention to the instabilities of current reform and the continuing pressures for change, the outlook is less settled. Three factors are of particular interest: first, while welfare policy in the EU is primarily national, regulated by the principle of subsidiarity, economic and fiscal policy certainly is not. The logic of a single market generates pressure for tax harmonization, with implications for national differences in the use of social insurance and direct taxation to finance differing levels of welfare spending (see Table 1.2). Second, labour-market changes driven by technological innovation and globalization demand strong policies to encourage the entry of new groups of workers in larger numbers, and welfare states are likely to develop strategies to accommodate these demands, with implications for the restructuring of consensus-building frameworks which at present focus mainly on the traditional social partners – employers and trade unions.

Third, welfare state settlements in a number of cases are incomplete and in all cases appear vulnerable to future pressures: it is unclear whether Finland and Sweden can continue to sustain a high tax regime and redistributive citizenship welfare or whether settlements which include a role for the private sector will, in the medium term, release pressures which undermine the distinctive welfare citizenship of those countries;

whether France, Germany and Switzerland, which have achieved current solutions in the areas of pension reform and the finance of welfare at the cost of some strain, can avoid further reforms which will generate conflict with the interests of the established social partners currently recognized in their consensual policy-making frameworks; whether Spain also will be able to manage emerging pressures from population, family and labour-market change while sustaining a consensus tradition; and whether the UK's liberal settlement, which would not comfortably generalize elsewhere in Europe, will exacerbate social divisions to the point where inequalities threaten social cohesion. The economic and demographic pressures on welfare states remain. Thus the resilience of established welfare systems is likely to be more severely tested, while the factors that have sustained resilience are weakened.

Achieving viable reform

Welfare state reform requires effective and stable solutions to complex problems, to be produced by the policy-making frameworks that have generated the welfare settlements which are currently under strain. One obvious problem is balancing the need to implement reforms that will meet the challenges faced by modern welfare states and the need to ensure that the solutions proposed are acceptable to the groups involved. Some countries are able to move more swiftly than others in dealing with identified problems.

The capacity to introduce rapid and far-reaching policy reform relates to factors that vary within the political configuration of individual countries. Most important in those reviewed here have been the authority of the executive and the ability of trade unions, other tiers of government and other actors to promote or oppose change. Thus, the UK, with a system that confers substantial power on the government, a strong executive and weak opposition, is in a good position to impose radical reforms. In France changes are more limited, due to the difficulties the executive, relatively powerful in other areas of policy, has experienced in exerting control over the welfare system, although recent reforms are likely to resolve this. In Spain, the issues that might threaten the highly valued consensus do not yet appear to be high on the political agenda, although a new government that felt confident in its majority might pursue them. In Switzerland, the groups most nearly affected by the transition to a post-Fordist labour-market and family patterns are not well represented in policy debates and change is difficult without cantonal agreement. In Germany, the traditional commitment to consensus and the necessity to gain the support of representatives of local state governments in the second house for decisions involving spending has in the past produced delay; recent pension and tax reforms imposed by the SPD appear to set a new policy course which reflects a neo-liberal consensus underlying party conflict.

The speed with which reform is introduced does not necessarily relate to its stability or its appropriateness, commensurate with the problem addressed, nor does innovation always flow out from the centre to other tiers of government. The reforms introduced in Finland and Sweden appear at present stable, due to strong support for state welfare, and appropriate to meet problems as they are currently identified. The changes to the policy-making framework in France may make stable reform possible in the future. The consensus-based reforms of the early 1990s in Germany failed to meet demands and efforts to construct a new reform consensus have so far been unsuccessful. Swiss reforms meet the problems of sustaining the current system, but are developed within a framework which does not facilitate recognition of the needs of some groups. The Spanish settlement remains politically sustainable, but may experience substantial pressure in the near future. In the UK, the liberal reforms are stable, but this is a new develop-ment arising from the convergence in party policies which has smoothed the traditional zig-zag trajectory of policy between successive governments from opposing parties. The reforms themselves seem to involve a degree of restructuring that is greater than that taking place elsewhere, and beyond what is necessary to secure the existing welfare system against the pressures it faces. The implication is that the decisiveness resulting from centralized executive authority is useful in producing solutions to problems (as in the Swedish, Finnish and UK cases), but that consensus-building frameworks are an important element in constructing stable and appropriate solutions, provided that the relevant interests are included within the consensus.

In countries with strong local tiers of government, decentralized author-ity typically acts as a brake on policy change. There are, however, a number of examples where local government has initiated reform. In Spain, the implementation of assistance benefits by the regions forced the central gov-ernment to concentrate attention on a national scheme of non-contributory pensions. In the context of the Mediterranean system, which tends to limit universal provision to health care and education and has a prominent role for insurance-based and for private provision, assistance is of particular importance. In Switzerland, there are substantial differences between cantons in the extent of support for unemployed people and other groups, with local assistance schemes on the lines of RMI, especially in the French-speaking areas, supplementary insurance benefits and experiments with a Negative Income Tax in the Zurich canton. The implementation of the innovative German social care insurance scheme was influenced by the desire to remove some of the financial responsibility for care from local government. Thus decentralization does not always block innovation.

Settlements that are currently stable may contain unresolved issues which can generate future difficulties. The key issues in the Finnish and Swedish cases lie in possible future shifts – EU tax harmonization, the expansion of private provision or the impact of more means-testing for par-ticular groups of jobless people, damaging social cohesiveness. Elsewhere, there are issues about the inclusion of all relevant groups in the policy-making framework: in France, unions and popular protests successfully opposed public sector pension reform in the mid-1990s, but may not be in a position to resist change now; in Germany, the political confrontations and the exercise of effective veto powers by opposition led to deadlock and a breakdown in the consensus-building system so that the imposed changes may become unstable with a change of government, and a number of issues remain unresolved; in Spain the interests of women in the transition from family to paid employment are not adequately represented in the policy debate; in Switzerland it is again the 'atypical workers' – women and immigrants – who are not included in consensus-building; and in the UK it is those excluded by or marginalized in the newly activated labour-market who face benefit cuts. A distinction must be drawn between the Spanish and Swiss cases, where economic changes create a demand for the inclusion of the groups at present excluded and will thus enhance pressure for their involvement, and the UK case where a sub-employed and politically unrepresented underclass with limited access to privatized welfare may have little leverage on policy-making. The capacity to include relevant groups seems essential to produce stable and successful resolution of the complex problems welfare systems face.

European welfare states need to balance the capacity to achieve a consensus on the direction of reform against the capacity to deliver appropriate policy changes with reasonable dispatch. The Swedish and Finnish approaches, which combine relatively strong unitary government with a consensus-generating approach pursued through tripartite negotiation and through the linkages between the dominant political party and interest groups appear most successful in finding solutions that maintain high levels of welfare. Centralized executive power is able to deliver decisions but not necessarily stability, while corporatist-leaning systems tend to produce more consensual policies; however, there is always the possibility that some relevant groups may be excluded from the dialogue, while decentralization sometimes, but not always, leads to inertia.

Conclusion

This study of the politics of reform in seven European welfare states representing the main regime types shows that recent changes tend to be located within the overall framework of the various existing national welfare settlements. The distinctive regimes have shown little tendency to converge and have displayed considerable resilience under the impact of current pressures. However, there are strong indications that the path is now open to more radical reform. The logic of the competitiveness imperative now underlies policy-making in most of the countries reviewed. The acceptance of this approach by 'modernized' social democratic parties promotes a neo-liberal direction in policy change. The varying significance of particular issues in different national contexts ensures that a marked shift towards policy convergence is unlikely, but the themes of labour-market activation, adaptation to meet new demands, cost-containment, the targeting of state support towards policies which assist economic competitiveness and support for the private sector are everywhere important.

Developments in the policy-making frameworks of the different countries lead, in different ways, towards the erosion of the balance of interests that sustained stable settlements. In Finland and Sweden the communality of interests that sustained universalism may be threatened by a greater role for private pensions and mean-tested welfare for younger unemployed people. In France, the alliance between social partners that supported high standards of contributory insurance is losing its pre-eminent role in the direction of social insurance and new forms of revenue give government greater power over welfare. In Germany, the political forces opposing retrenchment have suffered decisive reverses. In Spain, the pressures for continuing welfare expansion will conflict with the demands for inclusion by women and migrant workers and support may decline. In Switzerland, the needs of the labour-market demand a broadening of the groups included in consensus-building. In the UK the liberal-leaning settlement is entrenched through an established implicit consensus that endorses further targeting of the welfare state and expansion of the private sector.

The evidence presented in this book points to three conclusions. First, in relation to welfare policy-making, there are no obvious grounds for saying that a particular institutional or constitutional framework facilitates the most effective reform. Strong central control may lead to swifter change, but it seems likely that success in including the interests of the new groups emerging onto the welfare agenda through family and labour-market change is also essential to stable adaptation.

Second, in relation to welfare state theory, policy-making is a political activity and this is particularly true in the current context. Theory-building about European welfare trajectories must include shifts in party ideologies and the specific national political and institutional factors that shape or obstruct decision-making alongside the structural categories of regime theory in its analysis of how welfare states change. Otherwise there is a risk that the complex set of factors that influences the response to pressures on welfare in a given context does not receive due attention.

Third, in relation to the development of welfare provision in Europe, stability is ever impermanent. Welfare reforms and shifts in political alignments and welfare institutions seem to be opening opportunities for more radical changes in a number of countries. The recent past of the European welfare state is a story of resilience in the face of globalization, labour-market, population and family change and new political discourses about the role of government. The various factors that in different contexts mitigate pressures to shape welfare around the pursuit of economic competitiveness have been weakened. The past does not offer a helpful guide to the future.

Bibliography

Aaberge, R. et al. (1997) *Unemployment Shocks and Income Distribution: How Did the Nordic Countries Fare During Their Crisis?*, Discussion Paper 201, Statistics Norway.

ABI (Association of British Insurers) (1998) *Stake-holder Pensions – A Consultation Document*. London.

Abrahamson, P. (1999) 'The welfare modelling business', *Social Policy and Administration*, 33(4): 394–415.

Adema, W. (2000) 'Revisiting public expenditure across countries', OECD *Economic Studies*, 30, 2000/01: 191–6.

Agranoff, R. (1993) 'Las relaciones intergubernamentales y el Estado de las Autonomías', *Política y Sociedad*, 13: 87–105.

Aguilar, M., Gaviria, M. and Laparra, M. (1995) *La caña y el pez: El salario social en las Comunidades Autónomas 1989–1994*. Madrid: Fundación Foessa.

Agulnik, P. (1999) '*Pension tax reforms and the Green paper*'. Casepaper 24. LSE.

Alber, J. (1995) 'A framework for the comparative study of social services', *Journal of European Social Policy*, 5(2): 131–49.

Alber, J. and Standing, G. (2000) 'Social dumping, catch-up or convergence? Europe in a comparative global context', *Journal of European Social Policy*, 10(2): 99–119.

Aliena, R. (1991) 'RMI, le Gouvernement espagnol à contre-courant', *Revue Française des Affaires Sociales*, 45: 81–97.

Almeda, E. and Sarasa, S. (1996) 'Growth to diversity', in V. George and P. Taylor-Gooby (eds), *European Welfare Policy: Squaring the Welfare Circle*. London: Macmillan. pp. 155–76.

Andersson, J-O., Kosonen, P. and Vartiainen, J. (1993) *The Finnish Model of Economic and Social Policy*, Åbo: Nationalekonomiska Institutionen (Series A: 401).

Armingeon, K. (1999) 'Swiss labour market policy in comparative perspective', in U. Klöti and K. Yorimoto (eds), *Institutional Change and Public Policy in Japan and Switzerland*. Zurich: IPZ. pp. 179–94.

Armingeon, K. (2001) 'Institutionalizing the Swiss welfare state', *West European Politics*, 24(2).

Arriba, A. (1999) '*Rentas mínimas de inserción en España: Procesos de implantación y dinámicas sociales*'. PhD thesis. Universidad Autónoma de Madrid Facultad de Ciencias Económicas y Empresariales.

Atag, Ernst and Young Consulting (1999) *Evaluation des ORP: Rapport final*, Berne.

Atkinson, A. and Micklewright, J. (1989) 'Turning the screw: benefits for the unemployed, 1979–88', in A. Dilnot and I. Walker (eds), *The Economics of Social Security*. Oxford: Oxford University Press.

Ayala, L. (1997) *Ánálisis económico de los sistemas de rentas mínimas en España desde una perspectiva comparada*. PhD thesis, Universidad Complutense de Madrid, Facultad de Ciencias Económicas y Empresariales.

Baldwin, P. (1990) *The Politics of Social Solidarity: Class Bases of the European Welfare State, 1875–1975*, Cambridge: Cambridge University Press.

Beck, W., van der Maesen, L. and Walker, A. (1998) *The Social Quality of Europe*. Bristol: Policy Press.

Becker, S. and Falk, J. (1999) 'Nichtnormalarbeitsverhältnisse: Eine Gefahr für die gesetzliche Rentenversicherung?', *Deutsche Rentenversicherung*, (5): 273–97.

Bedau, K.D. (1999) 'Zur materiellen Situation der Senioren in West- und Ostdeutschland', *DIW-Wochenbericht* 66(37): 667–79.

Bieback, K.J. (1997) 'Der umbau der Arbeitsförderung: Das neue Sozialgesetzbuch III – Arbeitsförderung – von 1996/97', *Kritische Justiz*, 30(1): 15–29.

Beltrán, M. (1992) *El régimen jurídico de la acción social pública.* Oñati: IVAP.

Bichot, J. (1997) *Les Politiques Sociales en France au 20ème Siècle.* Paris: Armand Colin.

Blair, T. (1999) 'Beveridge Revisited' in R. Walker (ed.), *Ending Child Poverty.* Bristol: Polity Press. ch. 1.

Blair, T. and Schröder, G. (1999) *Europe: The Third Way – die Neue Mitte.* London: Labour Party and SPD.

Boeri, T. and Brücker, H. (2000) *The Impact of Eastern Enlargement on Employment and Labour Markets in the EU Member State, Final Report.* Brussels: EC Employment and Social Affairs Directorate.

Bönker, F. and Wollmann, H. (2000) 'Sozialstaatlichkeit im Übergang: Entwicklungslinien der bundesdeutschen Sozialpolitik in den Neunzigerjahren', in R. Czada and H. Wollmann (eds), *Von der Bonner zur Berliner Republik: 10 Jahre Deutsche Einheit.* Opladen: Westdeutscher Verlag. pp. 514–38.

Bonoli, G. (1997) 'Pension politics in France: patterns of co-operation and conflict in two recent reforms', *West European Politics*, 20(4): 160–81.

Bonoli, G. (1999) 'La réforme de l'Etat social en Suisse: Contraintes institutionnnelles et opportunités de changement', *Swiss Political Science Review*, 5(3): 57–78.

Bonoli, G. (2000a) 'Political institutions, veto points and the process of welfare state adaptation', in P. Pierson (ed.), *The New Politics of the Welfare State.* Oxford University Press. pp. 238–64.

Bonoli, G. (2000b) *The Politics of Pension Reform. Institutions and Policy Change in Western Europe.* Cambridge: Cambridge University Press.

Bonoli, G., George, V. and Taylor-Gooby, P. (2000) *European Welfare Futures.* Polity, Cambridge.

Bonoli, G. and Mach, A. (2000) 'Switzerland: adjustment politics within institutional constraints', in F.W. Scharpf and V. Schmidt (eds), *From Vulnerability to Competitiveness: Welfare and Work in the Open Economy.* Oxford: Oxford University Press. pp. 131–74.

Bonoli, G. and Palier, B. (1996) 'Reclaiming welfare: the politics of social protection reform in France', *Southern European Society and Politics*, 1(3): 240–59.

Bonoli, G. and Palier, B. (2000) 'How do welfare states change? Institutions and their impact on the politics of welfare state reform', *European Review*, 8(2): 333–52.

Börsch-Supan, A. (2000) 'A model under siege: a case study of the German retirement insurance system', *Economic Journal*, 110(2): F24–45.

Boss, A. (1998) 'How Germany shouldered the fiscal burden of the unification'. Working Paper No. 851. Kiel: The Kiel Institute of World Economics.

Bradbury, B. and Janatti, M. (1999) *Child Poverty across Industrialised Nations.* Economic and Social Policy paper no. 71. Florence: UNICEF International Child Development Centre.

Bradshaw, J. (1999) 'Child poverty in comparative perspective', *Journal of European Social Security*, 1(4): 383–404.

Buch, H. and Rühmann, P. (1999) 'Atypical work as a form of low-wage employment in the German labour market', in S. Bazen, M. Gregory and W. Salverda (eds), *Low-Wage Employment in Europe*. Cheltenham, UK/Northampton, MA: Elgar. pp. 111–26.

Cabanillas Bermúdez, J.M. (1997) *El Pacto de Toledo. Análisis descriptivo del Sistema Nacional de la Seguridad Social en España*. Madrid: Tecnos.

Carlin, W. and Soskice, D. (1997) 'Shocks to the system: the German political economy under stress'. *National Institute Economic Review*. 159: 57–76.

Carta Magna (1978) *Spanish Democratic Constitution*.

Casado, D., Aznar López, M., Casado de Otaola, D., Gutiérrez Resa, A. and Ramos Feijó, C. (1994) 'Acción social y servicios sociales', *FOESSA, V Informe Sociológico sobre la situación en España: Sociedad para todos en el año 2000*. Madrid: Fundación FOESSA. pp. 1735–880.

Castles, F. (1998) *Comparative Public Policy: Patterns of Post-war Transformation*. Northampton, MA: Elgar.

Castles, F. and Mitchell, D. (1990) 'Three worlds of welfare capitalism or four?'. Graduate Programme in Social Policy, paper no. 21. ANU.

Cattacin, S. and Tattini, V. (1999) 'Les politiques sociales', in U. Klöti, P. Knoepfel, H. Kriesi, W. Linder and Y. Papadopoulos (eds), *Handbuch der Schweizer Politik*. Zurich: NZZ Verlag. pp. 807–40.

CBI (1984) 'Evidence to the Government Special Enquiry into Pensions Provision'. April. London: CBI.

CBI News (1991) April.

CBI News (1998) April.

CEC (Commission of the European Community) (1996) *Ageing and Pension Expenditure in the Western World*. European Economy: Reports and Studies 3. Luxembourg: Office for the Official Publications of the European Communities.

CEC (Commission of the European Community) (1998) *Social Protection in Europe, 1997*. DGV. Luxembourg: Office for the Official Publications of the European Communities.

CEC (Commission of the European Community) (1999) *Concerted Strategy for Modernising Social Protection*. Brussels: COM 1999, 347.

CEC (Commission of the European Community) (2000a) *The Community Work Programme for 2000*. Brussels: COM 2000, 155.

CEC (Commission of the European Community) (2000b) *Social Protection in Europe, 1999*. DG for Employment and Social Affairs. Luxembourg: Office for the Official Publications of the European Communities.

Charpin, J.-M. (1999) *L'Avenir de nos Retraites*. Paris: La Documentation Française.

Chuliá, E. (2000) 'El Pacto de Toledo y la política de pensiones'. ASP Research Paper 33(a)/2000. Madrid: Analistas Socio-Políticos.

CIS (1996) *Estudio 2.213*. Madrid: Centro de Investigaciones Sociológicas.

Clasen, J. (2000) 'Motives, means and opportunities', *West European Politics*, 23(2): 89–112.

Commission on Social Justice (1994) *Social Justice: Strategies for National Renewal*. London: Vintage Books.

Conservative Party (1987) *The Next Moves Forward*. Conservative Central Office: London.

Conservative Party (1992) *The Best Future for Britain*. Conservative Central Office: London.

Conservative Party (1997) *You Can Only Be Sure with the Conservatives*. Conservative Central Office: London.

Cox, R.H. (1999) 'The social construction of an imperative: why welfare reform happened in Denmark and the Netherlands, but not in Germany'. Mimeo, Department of Political Science, University of Oklahoma.

Cram, L. (1997) *Policy-making in the European Union: Conceptual Lenses and the Integration Process*. London: Routledge.

Crouch, C. (1993) *Industrial Relations and European State Traditions*. Oxford: Clarendon Press.

CSO (1999) *Social Trends 29*. London: HMSO.

Czada, R. (1998) 'Vereinigungskrise und Standortdebatte: Der Beitrag der Wiedervereinigung zur Krise des westdeutschen Modells', *Leviathan*, 26(1): 24–59.

Dagens Nyheter (1996a) February 13.

Dagens Nyheter (1996b) October 10.

Dagens Nyheter (1996c) November 11.

Dagens Nyheter (1999) June 14.

Daly, M. (1997) 'Welfare states under pressure: cash benefits in European welfare states over the last ten years', *Journal of European Social Policy*, 7(2): 129–46.

Deakin, N. and Parry, R. (1998) 'The Treasury and social policy'. Social Policy Association annual conference, July.

DHSS (1985) *Reform of Social Security*. Cmnd 9517. London: HMSO.

Dilnot, A. and McCrae, J. (1999) *Family Credit and the Working Families Tax Credit*, Briefing Note 3/99, Institute for Fiscal Studies.

Disney, R. (1966) *Can we afford to grow older? A perspective on the economics of ageing*. Cambridge, MA: MIT Press.

Ds (Departementsserien) (1992) *Ett reformerat pensionssystem – Bakgrund, Principer och Skiss*. Stockholm: Allmänna förlaget.

DSS (1997) *Departmental Report, 1996/7 to 1999/00*. Cmnd 3613. London: HMSO.

DSS (1998) *A New Contract for Welfare*. Cmnd 3805. London: HMSO.

DSS (1999) *Social Security Departmental report 1999/2000*. Cmnd 4214. London: HMSO.

DSS (2000a) *Households Below Average Incomes, 1994/5–1998/9*. London: HMSO.

DSS (2000b) *The Changing Welfare State*. Social Security Paper no. 1. London: HMSO.

DSS (2000c) *The Changing Welfare State: Pensioners' Incomes*. Social Security Paper no. 2. London: HMSO.

DSS (2001) *Households Below Average Incomes 1996/7–1999/2000*. London: HMSO.

Dunleavy, P. et al. (1993) *Developments in British Politics 4*. London: Macmillan.

Dupuis, J.-M. (1989) 'La Réforme Du Financement De La Protection Sociale, Inventaire Bilan'. Lere, Rapport pour la Mire, Convention N°310/88.

Ebbinghaus, B. and Visser, J. (1999) 'When institutions matter: union growth and decline in Western Europe, 1950–1995', *European Sociological Review*, 15(2): 135–58.

Economist (1998) 'Field of dreams' March 28. pp. 39–41.

Eitrheim, P. and Kuhnle, S. (2000) 'Nordic welfare states in the 1990s', in S. Kuhnle (ed.), *Survival of the European Welfare State*. London: Routledge. pp. 39–57.

EPA (1993) *Eucuesta de Población Activa*. Madrid: Instituto Nacional de Estadística.

Esping-Andersen, G. (1990) *Three Worlds of Welfare Capitalism*. Cambridge: Polity.

Esping-Andersen, G. (ed.) (1996) *Welfare States in Transition: National Adaptations in Global Economies*. London: Sage.

Esping-Andersen, G. (1999) *The Social Foundations of Post-Industrial Economies*. Oxford: Oxford University Press.

Estefanía, J. and Serrano, R. (1987) 'Diez años de relaciones industriales en España', in A. Zaragoza (ed.), *Pactos sociales, sindicatos y patronal en España*. Madrid: Siglo XXI. pp. 17–42.

European Commission (1998) *Social Protection in Europe 1997*. Luxembourg: MISSOC.

Eurostat (1995) *Eurostat Yearbook 1995: A Statistical Eye on Europe, 1983–1993*. Luxembourg: OOPEC.

Eurostat (1997a) *Poverty in EU Member States*. Statistics in Focus, Population and Social Conditions, no. 6. Luxembourg: OOPEC.

Eurostat (1997b) *Eurostat Yearbook 1997: A Statistical Eye on Europe 1986–1996*. Luxembourg: OOPEC.

Eurostat (1999) *General Government Accounts*. Rapid Reports, 36/1999. Luxembourg: OOPEC.

Eurostat (2000a) *Social Benefits and their Redistributive Effects in the EU*. Statistics in Focus, Population and Social Conditions, no. 9. Luxembourg: OOPEC.

Eurostat (2000b) *Persistent Income Poverty and Social Exclusion in the EU*. Statistics in Focus, Population and Social Conditions, no. 13. Luxembourg: OOPEC.

Eurostat (2000c) *Income Poverty in the EU*. Statistics in Focus, Population and Social Conditions, no. 12. Luxembourg: OOPEC.

Falkingham, J. (1989) 'Dependency and ageing in Britain', *Journal of Social Policy*, 18(2): 211–34.

Feist, H. and Schöb, R. (1999) 'Workfare in Germany and the problem of vertical fiscal externalities'. CESifo, Working Paper No. 185, Munich.

Ferrera, M. (1996a) 'The Southern Model of Welfare in Social Europe', *Journal of European Social Policy*, 6(1): 17–37.

Ferrera, M. (1996b) 'Modèles De Solidarité, Divergences, Convergences: Perspectives Pour L'europe', *Swiss Political Science Review*, 2(1): 55–72.

Ferrera, M. and Rhodes, M. (2000a) 'Building a sustainable welfare state', *West European Politics*, 23(2): 257–82.

Ferrera, M. and Rhodes, M. (2000b) 'Recasting European welfare states', *West European Politics*, 23(2): 1–10.

Financial Times (1996) November 11.

Financial Times (1999) November 15.

Finch, J. (1989) *Family Obligations and Social Change*. Cambridge: Polity.

Flaquer, L., Giner, S. and Moreno, L. (1990) 'La sociedad española en la encrucijada', in S. Giner (ed.), *España: Sociedad y Política*. Madrid: Espasa Calpe. pp. 19–74.

Flora, P. (1986/87) *Growth to Limits. The European Welfare States Since World War II*. Berlin: De Gruyter.

Flora, P. (Dir.) (1986–1993) *Growth To Limits: The European Welfare States Since World War II*, Berlin-New York: De Gruyter. 5 Volumes.

Flückiger, Y. (1999) 'Inégalité, bas salaires et working poor en Suisse', unpublished manuscript: University of Geneva.

Fowler, N. (1991) *Ministers Decide*. London: Chapman & Hall.

Freire, J.M. (1993) 'Cobertura sanitaria y equidad en España', *El impacto de las políticas sociales: educación, salud, vivienda*. Madrid: Fundación Argentaria. pp. 113–38.

Gaxie, D. (et al.) (1990) *Le 'Social' Transfiguré*. Paris: Puf.

George, V. and Taylor-Gooby, P. (1996) *European Welfare Policy – Squaring The Welfare Circle*. London: Macmillan.

Gerlach, I. (2000) 'Politikgestaltung durch das Bundesverfassungsgericht am Beispiel der Familienpolitik', *Aus Politik und Zeitgeschichte*, 50(3/4): 21–31.

Geyer, R. (2000) *Exploring European Social Policy*. Cambridge: Polity.

Giddens, A. (2000) *The Third Way and its Critics*. Cambridge: Polity.

Giner, S. (1986) 'Political economy, legitimation and the state in southern Europe', in G. O'Donnell and P. Schmitter (eds), *Transitions from Authoritarian Rule: Prospects for Democracy*. Baltimore: Johns Hopkins University Press.

Glennerster, H. (1997) *Paying for Welfare – towards 2000*. Hemel Hempstead: Prentice Hall.

Goode Committee (1994) *Pensions Law Reform*. Cmnd 2342-1. London: HMSO.

Government Actuary (1990) *National Insurance Fund: Long-Term Financial Estimates*. London: HMSO.

Gray, A. and Jenkins, W. (1998) 'British Government and Administration, 1996–7', *Parliamentary Affairs*, 51(2): 111–30.

Guillén, A. (2000) *La construcción política del sistema sanitario español: De la postguerra a la democracia*. Madrid: Exlibris.

Hadjipateras, A. (1985) 'The Reform of Social Security: A Checklist of the Responses of 60 Key Organisations'. London: CPAG.

Hagen, T. and Steiner, V. (2000) *Von der Finanzierung der Arbeitslosigkeit zur Förderung von Arbeit. Analysen und Handlungsempfehlungen zur Arbeitsmarktpolitik*. Baden-Baden: Nomos.

Hall, P. (1993) 'Policy Paradigm, Social Learning and the State: the Case of Economic Policy in Britain', *Comparative Politics*, April: 278–9.

Hall, P. and Soskice, D. (eds) (2000) *Varieties of Capitalism: The Institutional Foundations of Comparative Advantage*. Cambridge: Cambridge University Press.

Hall, P. and Taylor, R. (1996) 'Political science and the three new institutionalisms', *Political Studies*, 44(5): 936–57.

Hansard (1993) February 8.

Hantrais, L. and Letablier, M.-T. (1995) *La relation famille-emploi: Une comparaison des modes d'ajustement en Europe*. Paris: Centre d'Etudes de l'Emploi, Dossier No. 6.

HE 143 (1991) Hallituksen esitys Eduskunnalle laeiksi työttömyysturvalain ja työttömyyskassalain muuttamisesta sekä työttömyyskassalain 19 §:n väliaikaisesta muuttamisesta.

HE 110 (1992) Hallituksen esitys Eduskunnalle laiksi valtion eläkelain muuttamisesta.

HE 242 (1992) Hallituksen esitys Eduskunnalle laiksi kunnallisten viranhaltijain ja työntekijäin eläkelain muuttamisesta.

HE 289 (1992) Hallituksen esitys Eduskunnalle laeiksi työttömyysturvalain ja työttömyyskassalain muuttamisesta.

HE 337 (1992) Hallituksen esitys Eduskunnalle laiksi työttömyysturvalain muuttamisesta.

HE 338 (1992) Hallituksen esitys Eduskunnalle laiksi työttömyysturvalain muuttamisesta.

HE 359 (1992) Hallituksen esitys Eduskunnalle laiksi työttömyysturvalain muuttamisesta.

HE 235 (1993) Hallituksen esitys Eduskunnalle työmarkkinatukea koskevaksi lainsäädännöksi sekä laiksi työttömyysturvalain muuttamisesta.

HE 118 (1995) Hallituksen esitys Eduskunnalle yksityisalojen työeläkejärjestelmän uudistamista koskevaksi lainsäädännöksi.

HE 172 (1995) Hallituksen esitys Eduskunnalle laiksi työmarkkinatuesta annetun lain muuttamisesta.

HE 72 (1996) Hallituksen esitys Eduskunnalle laiksi työttömyysturvalain muuttamisesta.

HE 75 (1996) Hallituksen esitys Eduskunnalle laiksi työmarkkinatuesta annetun lain muuttamisesta.

HE 217 (1997) Hallituksen esitys Eduskunnalle laiksi toimeentulotuesta sekä laiksi sosiaalihuoltolain ja-asetuksen eräiden säännösten kumoamisesta.

Heinelt, H. and Weck, M. (1998) *Arbeitsmarktpolitik: Vom Vereinigungskonsens zur Standortdebatte*. Opladen: Leske & Budrich.

Heinze, R.G. (1998) *Die blockierte Gesellschaft: Sozioökonomischer Wandel und die Krise des 'Modell Deutschland'*. Opladen: Westdeutscher Verlag.

Held, D., McGrew, A., Goldblatt, D. and Perraton, J. (1999) *Global Transformations*. Cambridge: Polity.

Helsingin Sanomat (1995a) October 4.

Helsingin Sanomat (1995b) November 11.

Helsingin Sanomat (1997) September 3.

Hills, J. (1995) *An Inquiry into Income and Wealth*. 2 Vols. New York: Joseph Rowntree Foundation.

Hills, J. and Lelkes, O. (1999) 'Social security, selective universalism and patchwork redistribution', in Jowell et al., *British Social Attitudes: the 16th Report*. Dartmouth: CNR. pp. 1–22.

Hinrichs, K. (1998) 'Reforming the public pension scheme in Germany: the end of the traditional consensus?' Zentrum für Sozialpolitik, ZeS-Arbeitspapier Nr. 11/98, Bremen.

Hinrichs, K. (2000) 'Elephants on the move', *European Review*, 8(4): 353–78.

HMSO (1993) *Development Report on the UK Presidency, July to December, 1992*. Cmnd 2168. London: HMSO.

HMSO (1997) *Development in the EU: January to July 1997*. Cmnd 3802. London: HMSO.

House of Commons Library (1995) 'Social security reforms'. Reference sheet no. 85/6.

House of Commons Library (1999) 'The burden of taxation'. Research paper 99/67.

House of Lords (1999) 'Welfare reform and pensions bill: explanatory notes', session 1998–99, HL Bill 62-EN, Internet: http://www.dss.gov.uk/hq/wreform/bill/progress.htm.

Huber, E. and Stephens, J. (2001) *Political Choice in Global Markets: Development and Crisis of Advanced Welfare States*. Chicago: Chicago University Press.

Hvinden, B., Heikkla, M. and Kankare, I. (2000) 'Towards activation? The changing relationship between social protection and employment in Western Europe', in M. Kautto, B. Hvinden, J. Kvist and H. Uusitalo (eds), *Nordic Welfare States in the European Context*. London: Routledge. pp. 168–97.

IDA FiSo 2 (1997) *Analyse des prestations des assurances sociales*, Berne: IOA.

IFS (Institute for Fiscal Studies) (2000) *Distributional Consequences of Fiscal Reform since May 1997*. http://www.ifs.org.uk/budgets/index.shtml/

IMF (1997) 'Germany: selected issues'. Staff country report no. 97/101. Washington, DC.

IMF (1999a) 'Germany'. Staff country report no. 99/129. Washington, DC.

IMF (1999b) 'Germany: selected issues and statistical appendix'. Staff country report no. 99/130, Washington, DC.

IMF (2000) 'Germany: Selected Issues'. Staff country report no. 00/142, Washington, DC.

Immergut, E. (1998) 'The theoretical core of the new institutionalism', *Politics and Society*, 26(1): 5–34.

Immervoll, H., Mitton, L., O'Donoghue, C. and Sutherland, H. (1999) 'Budgeting for fairness? The distributional effects of three Labour budgets'. Microsimulation Unit Research Note 32, University of Cambridge.

Iversen, T. and Wren, A. (1998) 'Equality, employment, and budgetary restraint: the trilemma of the service economy', *World Politics*, 50(4) (July). pp. 507–46.

Jessop, B. (2000) *The Future of the Welfare State*. Cambridge: Polity.

Jobert, B. (1991) 'Democracy and social policies: the example of France', in J. Ambler (ed.), *The French Welfare State*. New York: University Press. pp. 232–58.

Join-Lambert, M.-T. (Dir.) (1997) *Politiques Sociales*. Paris: Presses De Science Po Et Dalloz. 2ème Édition.

Katzenstein, P. (1987) *Policy and Politics in West Germany: The Growth of a Semisovereign State*. Philadelphia: Temple University Press.

Kautto, M. et al. (1999) *Nordic Social Policy: Changing Welfare States*. London and New York: Routledge.

King, R. (1983) *Capital and Politics*. London: Routledge and Kegan Paul.

Kingdom, J. (1999) *Government and Politics in Britain*. 2nd edn. Cambridge: Polity.

Kitschelt, H. (2001) 'Partisan Politics', in P. Pierson (ed.), *The New Politics of the Welfare State*. Oxford/New York: Oxford University Press. pp. 265–304.

Kobach, K. (1993) *The Referendum: Direct Democracy in Switzerland*. Aldershot: Dartmouth.

Köppe, O. (1999) 'Neoliberale Steuerrechtslehre und Bundesverfassungsgericht', *Kritische Justiz*, 32(1): 15–31.

Korpi, W. (1983) *The Democratic Class Struggle*. London: Routledge and Kegan Paul.

Kosonen, P. (2000) 'Activation, incentives and workfare in Nordic welfare states', in MIRE (ed.), *Comparing Social Welfare Systems in Nordic Europe and France*. Paris: MSH Ange-Guélpin.

Kosunen, V. (1997) 'Lama ja sosiaaliturvan muutokset 1990-luvulla', in M. Heikkilä and H. Uusitalo (eds), *Leikkausten hinta: Tutkimuksia leikkauksista ja niiden vaikutuksista 1990-luvun Suomessa*. Helsinki: Stakes. pp. 45–101.

Kriesi, H. (1980) *Entscheidungsstrukturen und Entscheidungsprozesse in der Schweiz*. Frankfurt: Campus.

Kriesi, H. (1982) 'The structure of the Swiss political system', in G. Lehmbruch and P. Schmitter (eds), *Patterns of Corporatist Policy Making*. London: Sage. pp. 133–62.

Kriesi, H. (1995) *Le système politique suisse*. Paris: Economica.

Kriesi, H. (1999) 'Note on the size of public sector in Switzerland', *Swiss Political Science Review*, 5(2): 105–7.

Kuhnle, S. (1997) 'La reconstrucción política de los Estados del Bienestar europeos', in Moreno, L. (ed.), *Unión Europea y Estado del Bienestar*. Madrid: CSIC. pp. 31–65.

Kuhnle, S. (2000a) 'The Scandinavian welfare state in the 1990s: challenged but viable', *West European Politics*, 23(2): 209–29.

Kuhnle, S. (ed.) 2000b, *The Survival of the European Welfare State*. London: Routledge.

Kvist, J. (1999) 'Welfare reform in the Nordic countries in the 1990s: using fuzzy-set theory to assess conformity to ideal types', *Journal of European Social Policy*, 9(3): 231–52.

Labbé, D. (1996) *Syndicats Et Syndiqués En France Depuis 1945*. Paris: L'harmattan.

Labour Party (1992) *It's Time to Get Britain Working Again*. London: Labour Party.

Labour Party (1997) *Because Britain Deserves Better*. London: Labour Party.

Ladner, A. (1999) 'Das Schweizer Perteisystem und seine Parteien', in U. Klöti, P. Knoepfel, H. Kriesi, W. Linder, and Y. Papadopoulos (eds), *Handbuch der Schweizer Politik*. Zurich: NZZ Verlag. pp. 213–60.

Lane, J.-E. (1999) 'The Public/private Sector Distinction in Switzerland', *Swiss Political Science Review*, 5(2): 94–104.

Laparra, M. and Aguilar, M. (1997) 'Social exclusion and minimum income programs in Spain', in MIRE *Comparing Social Welfare Systems in Southern Europe*. Vol. 3. Paris: Mission Recherche et Expérimentation (MIRE). pp. 515–35.

Lehmbruch, G. (1984) 'Concertation and the structure of corporatist networks', in J. Goldthorpe (ed.), *Order and Conflict in Contemporary Capitalism*. Oxford: Clarendon Press. pp. 60–80.

Lehmbruch, G. (1993) 'Consociational democracy and corporatism in Switzerland', *Publius: The Journal of Federalism*, 23(1): 43–60.

Lehmbruch, G. (1998) *Parteienwettbewerb im Bundesstaat: Regelsystem und Spannungslagen im Institutionengefüge der Bundesrepublik Deutschland*. 2nd edn. Opladen: Westdeutscher Verlag.

Leibfried, S. and Pierson, P. (1995) *European Social Policy*. Washington: Brookings Institute.

Leibfried, S. and Pierson, P. (2000) 'European social policy', in H. Wallace and W. Wallace (eds), *Policy-Making in the European Union*. 4th edn. Oxford: Oxford University Press.

Leibfritz, W., Büttner, W. and van Essen, U. (1998) 'Germany', in K. Messere (ed.), *The Tax System in Industrialized Countries*. Oxford: Oxford University Press. pp. 128–58.

L'État de la France (2000) Paris: La Découverte.

Lijphart, A. (1999) *Patterns of Democracy: Government Forms and Performance in 36 Countries*. New Haven and London: Yale University Press.

Lijphart, A. and Crepaz, M. (1991) 'Corporatism and consensus democracy in eighteen countries: conceptual and empirical linkages', *British Journal of Political Science*, 21(2): 235–56.

Lindlar, L. and Scheremet, W. (1998) 'Germany's slump: explaining the unemployment crisis of the 1990s'. DIW, Discussion Paper No. 169, Berlin.

Liu, L. (1999) 'Retirement income security in the UK', *Social Security Bulletin*, 62(1): 23–46.

LO (1999) *LO-medlemmarnas röster - analys, utvärdering och uppföljning av valet 1998*. Stockholm: LO Press.

Mach, A. (1999) 'Associations d'intérêt', in U. Klöti, P. Knoepfel, H. Kriesi, W. Linder, and Y. Papadopoulos (eds), *Handbuch der Schweizer Politik*. Zurich: NZZ Verlag. pp. 299–336.

Mach, A. (2000) 'Les relations industrielles en Suisse dans les années 90: une lente évolution vers le "modèle anglosaxon?", in Klaus Armingeon and S. Geissbühler (eds), Gewerkschaften in der Schweiz. Herausforderungen and Optionen. Zurich: Seismo. pp. 153–90.

Majone, G. (1996) *Regulating Europe*. London: Routledge.

Makinen, T. (1999) 'Structural pressures, social policy and society', *International Social Security Review*, 52(4): 3–24.

MAP (1997) *Estudio sobre reparto del gasto público en 1997 entre los distintos niveles de administración*. Madrid: Ministerio de Administraciones Públicas.

Mares, I. (1996) 'Firms and the welfare state: the emergence of new forms of unemployment'. WZB Discussion Paper No. FS I 96–308. Berlin.

McGlone, F., Park, A. and Roberts, C. (1996) 'Relative values', ch. 3 in R. Jowell (ed.), *British Social Attitudes, the 13th Report*, SCPR/Dartmouth.

Merkel, W. (1999) *The Third Ways of European Social Democracy at the End of the Twentieth Century*. Heidelberg: University of Heidelberg.

Meyer, T. (1998) 'Retrenchment, reproduction, modernization: pension politics and the decline of the German breadwinner model', *Journal of European Social Policy*, 8(3): 195–211.

Millar, J. (2000) *Keeping Track of Welfare Reform*. York: Joseph Rowntree Foundation.

Ministerio de Asuntos Sociales (1989) 'Informe sobre diferentes prestaciones sociales en la CEE y España'. Mimeo.

Ministry of Social Affairs and Health, Finland (1995) *Tulonjako noususuhdanteesta laman pohjalle: katsaus tulonjaon kehitykseen vuosina 1988–1993*. Helsinki: Ministry of Social Affairs and Health.

Ministry of Social Affairs and Health, Finland (1996) *Toimeentuloturvakatsaus 1996*. Ministry Publications 3/1996. Helsinki: Ministry of Social Affairs and Health.

Ministry of Social Affairs and Health, Finland (1998) *Social Protection in Finland 1996*. Publications 1998: 1 eng Helsinki: Ministry of Social Affairs and Health.

Ministry of Social Affairs, Sweden (1998) *Frågor och svar om det nya pensionssystemet*. Stockholm: Regeringskansliet.

Ministry of Social Affairs, Sweden (1999) *Välfärdsfakta social*. Stockholm: Regeringskansliet Offsetcentral.

Mishra, R. (1999) *Globalisation and the Welfare State*. Elgar, Cheltenham.

Möller, T. (1999) 'The Swedish election 1998: a protest vote and the birth of a new political landscape?', *Scandinavian Political Studies*, 22(3): 261–76.

Moreno, L. (1999) 'Local and global: mesogovernments and territorial identities', *Nationalism and Ethnic Politics*, 5(3/4): 61–75.

Moreno, L. (2000a) 'Spanish development of Southern European welfare', in S. Kuhnle (ed.), *Survival of the European Welfare State*. London: Routledge. pp. 146–65.

Moreno, L. (2000b) *The Federalisation of Spain*. London: Frank Cass.

Moreno, L. and Arriba, A. (1999) 'Welfare and decentralisation in Spain'. Working Paper EUF No. 99/8. Florence: European University Institute.

Moreno, L. and Sarasa, S. (1992) 'The Spanish 'via media' to the development of the welfare state'. Working Paper 92–13, Madrid: IESA-CSIC.

Moreno, L. and Sarasa, S. (1993), 'Génesis y desarrollo del Estado del Bienestar en España', *Revista Internacional de Sociología*, 6: 327–69.

Morlino, L. (1998) *Democracy between Consolidation and Crisis: Parties, Groups and Citizens in Southern Europe*. Oxford: Oxford University Press.

Myles, J. and Quadagno, J. (1997) 'Recent trends in public pension reform', in K. Banting and R. Boadway (eds), *Reform of Retirement Income Policy*. Kingston, Ontario: Queen's University, School of Policy Studies. pp. 247–72.

Naldini, M. (1999) 'Evolution of social policy and the institutional definition of family models: the Italian and Spanish cases in historical and comparative perspective'. Ph.D thesis. Florence: European University Institute.

Norton, P. (1998) *Parliament and Government in Western Europe*. London: Macmillan.

Nugent, N. (1999) *The Government and Politics of the European Union*. London: Macmillan.

Nullmeier, F. (1996) 'Der Rentenkonsens – Eine Stütze des Sozialstaates in Gefahr?', *Gegenwartskunde*, 45(3): 337–50.

Nullmeier, F. and Rüb, F.W. (1993) *Die Transformation der Sozialpolitik: Vom Sozialstaat zum Sicherungsstaat.* Frankfurt/M. and New York: Campus.

Obinger, H. (1998) 'Federalism, direct democracy, and welfare state development in Switzerland'. ZeS-Arbeitspapier Nr. 8/98. Bremen.

OECD (1988) *Reforming Public Pensions.* OECD Social Policy Studies, No. 5. Paris: OECD.

OECD (1994a) *The Jobs Strategy: Evidence and Explanations.* Vol. II. Paris: OECD.

OECD (1994b) *New Orientations For Social Policy.* Paris: OECD.

OECD (1995) *The OECD Jobs Study: Implementing the Strategy.* Paris: OECD.

OECD (1996) *Economic Outlook.* No. 56, December 1994. Paris: OECD.

OECD (1997a) *Economic Surveys – Finland.* Paris: OECD.

OECD (1997b) *Statistical Compendium (Labour Force Statistics).* Paris: OECD.

OECD (1997c) *Historical Statistics 1960–1995.* Paris: OECD.

OECD (1997d) *Implementing the OECD Jobs Strategy: Member Countries' Experience.* Paris: OECD.

OECD (1998a) *A New Social Policy Agenda for a Caring World.* Paris: OECD.

OECD (1998b) *Labour Force Statistics, 1977–1997.* Paris: OECD.

OECD (1998c) *The Caring World: An Analysis.* Vol. 2. Tables and Charts. Paris: OECD.

OECD (1999a) *Employment Outlook (June 1999).* Paris: OECD.

OECD (1999b) *OECD Observer.* No. 216, March. Paris: OECD.

OECD (1999c) *OECD Observer.* December. Paris: OECD.

OECD (1999d) *Benefit Systems and Work Incentives.* Paris: OECD.

OECD (1999e) *A Caring World: The New Social Policy Agenda.* Paris: OECD.

OECD (1999f) *Economic Outlook.* 66. Paris: OECD.

OECD (1999g) *Germany: Economic Survey.* Paris: OECD.

OECD (2000a) *OECD in Figures.* At http://www.oecd.org/publications/figures/

OECD (2000b) *Economic Outlook.* No. 68, December 2000. Paris: OECD.

OECD (2000c) *OECD Observer.* May. Paris: OECD.

OECD (2000d) *Employment Outlook.* August. Paris: OECD.

OECD (2000e) *Reforms for an Ageing Society.* Paris: OECD.

OFAS (Office Fédéral des Assurances Sociales) (1995) *Rapport du Département fédéral de l'intérieur concernant la structure actuelle et le développement futur de la conception helvétique des trois piliers de la prévoyance vieillesse, survivants et invalidité.* Berne: OFAS.

OFS (1998) *L'enqûete suisse sur la famille,* Berne: OFS.

OFS (2000) *Annuaire statistique de la Suisse,* Berne: OFS.

Olli, Å. (1996) *Arbetsmarknadspolitiskt kalendarium.* Stockholm: Arbetsmarknadsdepartementet.

Onoli, G. (1997) 'Classifying welfare states: a two-dimensional approach', *Journal of Social Policy,* 26(3): 351–72.

ONS (1997) *Social Trends.* No. 27. London: HMSO.

ONS (1998) *New Earnings Survey 1998.* London: HMSO.

ONS (1999) *Social Trends.* No. 29. London: HMSO.

ONS (2000) *Social Trends.* No. 30. London: HMSO.

Orloff, A.S. (1993) 'Theorising European welfare systems', *American Sociological Review,* 58(2) pp. 303–28.

Outin, J.-L. (1997) 'Les politiques d'insertion', in M. Vernières (Dir.), *L'insertion Professionnelle: Analyses Et Débats.* Paris: Economica.

Palier, B. (2000) '"Defrosting" The French welfare state', *West European Politics,* 23(2): 113–36.

Palier, B. and Bonoli, G. (1995) 'Entre Bismarck et Beveridge: crises de la sécurité sociale et politique(s)', *Revue Française de Science Politique*, 4(45) Août: 668–99.

Palier, B. and Bonoli, G. (2000) 'La Montée en puissance des fonds de pension', *L'année de la Régulation*, 4: 71–112.

Palme, J. and Wennemo, I. (1997) 'Swedish social security in the 1990s: reform and retrenchment'. Centre for Welfare State Research Working Paper No. 7. Danish National Institute for Social Research.

Papadopoulos, Y. (1996) 'Les mécanismes du vote référendaire en Suisse: l'impact de l'offre politique', *Revue Française de Sociologie*, 37(4): 5–35.

Papadopoulos, Y. (1997) *Les processus de décision fédéraux en Suisse*. Paris: L'Harmattan.

Pfaller, A., Gough, I. and Therborn, G. (1991) *Can the Welfare State Compete?* London: Macmillan.

Piachaud, D. and Sutherland, H. (2001) 'Child poverty and the New Labour government', *Journal of Social Policy*, 30(1): 95–118.

Pierson, P. (1994) *Dismantling the Welfare State? Reagan, Thatcher and The Politics of Retrenchment*. Cambridge: Cambridge University Press.

Pierson, P. (1998) 'Irresistible forces, immovable objects: post-industrial welfare states confront permanent austerity', *Journal of European Public Policy*, 5(4): 539–60.

Pierson, P. (2000) 'Increasing returns, path dependence, and the study of politics', *American Political Science Review*, 94(2): 251–67.

Pierson, P. (ed.) (2001) *The New Politics of the Welfare State*. Oxford: Oxford University Press.

Prop. (1994/95) 150 Reviderad finansplan m.m. (Bilaga 1 till kompletterings-proposition).

Prop. (1996/97) 124 Ändring i socialtjänstlagen.

Rabe, B. and Schmid, G. (1999) 'Eine Frage der Balance: Reform der Arbeitsmarktpolitik', *Aus Politik und Zeitgeschichte*, 49(37): 21–30.

Rhodes, M. (2000) 'The political economy of social pacts: "competitive corporatism" and European welfare reform', in P. Pierson (ed.), *The New Politics Of The Welfare State*. New York and Oxford: Oxford University Press. pp. 165–96.

Rhodes, M. and Ferrera, M. (1999) 'Building a sustainable welfare state', *Conference for the Programme: Governance in the 21st Century*, EUI, Florence, 20 November.

Rodríguez-Cabrero, G. (1989) 'Política social en España: realidades y tendencias' in R. Muñoz (ed.), *Crisis y futuro del Estado del Bienestar*. Madrid: Alianza. pp. 183–204.

Ross, F. (2000) 'Interest and choice in the 'not quite so new' politics of welfare', *West European Politics*, 23(2): 11–34.

Rostgaard, T. and Ffridberg, T. (1998) *Caring for Children and Older People*. Copenhagen: Danish National Institute for Social Research.

Ruellan, R. (1993) 'Retraites: l'impossible réforme est-elle achevée?', *Droit Social*, 12: 911–29.

SAF (Swedish Employers' Confederation) (1994) *Sacred Cows and the Future – On the Change of System in the Labour Market*. (Håkan Lundgren). Stockholm: Norstedts Tryckeri.

SAF (Swedish Employers' Confederation) (1999) *Towards a more entrepreneurial labour law* (Christian Bratt), photocopied document, SAF, August 1999.

SAP (1996) Snabbfakta No. 22, October 1996. 'Utredning om ny arbetslöshets-försäkring'.

SAP (1997a) Snabbfakta No. 3, February 1997. 'Lagrådsremiss om ändringar i socialtjänstlagen'.

SAP (1997b) Politisk redovisning No. 6, February 1997. 'Frågor och svar om förslaget till ny socialtjänstlag'.

SAP (1997c) Politisk redovisning (Arbete) No. 16, December 1997. 'Steget in i 2000-talet'.

Sarasa, S. (1993) *El servicio de lo social*. Madrid: Ministerio de Asuntos Sociales.

Savage, S., Atkinson, R. and Robbins, L. (1994) *Public Policy in Britain*. London: Macmillan.

Scharpf, F. (1999) 'The viability of advanced welfare state in the international economy: vulnerabilities and options'. Working paper 99/9. Max Planck Institute for the Study of Societies, Cologne.

Scharpf, F. (2000) 'Globalisation and the welfare state'. Paper presented at the EU COSTA15 Annual Conference, University of Cologne.

Scharpf, F. and Schmidt, V. (2000) *Welfare and Work in the Open Economy*. Oxford: Oxford University Press. Vols I and II.

Schmähl, W. (ed.) (1991) *The Future of Basic and Supplementary Pensions Schemes in the European Community – 1992 and beyond*. Baden-Baden: Nomos.

Schmähl, W. (1999) 'Pension reforms in Germany: major topics, decisions and developments', in K. Müller, A. Ryll, H.-J. Wagener (eds), *Transformation of Social Security: Pensions in Central-Eastern Europe*. Heidelberg: Physica. pp. 91–120.

Schmid, G. (1996) 'Reform der Arbeitsmarktpolitik: Vom fürsorgenden Wohlfahrtsstaat zum kooperativen Sozialstaat', *WSI-Mitteilungen*, 49(10): 629–41.

Schmidt, V.A. (1999) 'The EU and its member-states: institutional contrasts and their consequences'. Working Paper 99/7. Max-Planck-Institut for the Study of Societies, Cologne.

Schmidt, V.A. (2000) 'Values and discourse in the politics of adjustment of advanced welfare states: does discourse matter?' Mimeo. Department of International Relations, Boston University.

Sell, S. (1998) 'Entwicklung und Reform des Arbeitsförderungsgesetzes als Anpassung des Sozialrechts an flexible Erwerbsformen? Zur Zumutbarkeit von Arbeit und Eigenverantwortung von Arbeitnehmern', *MittAB*, 31(3): 532–49.

Serrano, A. and Arriba, A. (1998) ¿*Pobres o excluidos? El Programa del Ingreso Madrileño de Integración en perspectiva comparada*. Madrid: Fundación Argentaria-Ministerio de Trabajo y Asuntos Sociales-Editorial Visor.

SESI (annual) Service des Statistiques des Etudes et des systèmes commion des comptes de la protection sociale. Paris: INSEE.

SESI (annual) Commission des comptes de la sécurité sociale. Paris: INSEE.

SFS (Svensk författningssamling) (1997) 313 *Lag om ändring i socialtjänstlagen*.

Siegel, N.A. and Jochem, S. (2000) 'Der Sozialstaat als Beschäftigungsbremse? Deutschlands steiniger Weg in die Dienstleistungsgesellschaft', in R. Czada and H. Wollmann (eds), *Von der Bonner zur Berliner Republik: 10 Jahre Deutsche Einheit*. Opladen: Westdeutscher Verlag. pp. 539–66.

Socialstyrelsen (1992) *Allmänna råd från Socialstyrelsen*. Stockholm: Socialstyrelsen.

Socialstyrelsen (1999) *Socialbidrag 1998*. Stockholm: Socialstyrelsen.

SOU (1996) 113 'En allmän och aktiv försäkring vid sjukdom och rehabilitering'.

SOU (2000) 3 'Kommittén Välfärdsbokslut – Delbokslutet 'Välfärd vid vägskäl'.

Speech by Sirkka Hämäläinen, Director of the Bank of Finland, 7.6.1986.

Spicker, P. (1991) 'The principle of subsidiarity and the social policy of the European Community', *Journal of European Social Policy*, 1(1): 3–14.

Ståhlberg, A.-C. (1995) *The Swedish Pension System: Past, Present and Future*, Reprint Series No. 456, Swedish Institute for Social Research, Stockholm University, June 1995.

State Council (Finland) (1991a) 31.10.1991 Periaatepäätös hallituksen toimenpiteistä kustannustasoa alentavan työmarkkinaratkaisun yhteydessä, *Valtioneuvoston pöytäkirjat*. 24.-31.10.1991, 336.

State Council (Finland) (1991b) 29.11.1991 Periaatepäätös hallituksen toimenpiteistä työmarkkinaratkaisun yhteydessä, *Valtioneuvoston pöytäkirjat*. 21.11.-4.12.1991, 287.

Statistics Finland (1998) *Statistical Yearbook of Finland*. Vol. 93. Hämeenlinna: Karisto.

Statistics Sweden (1996) *Statistical Yearbook of Sweden*. Vol. 82. Stockholm: Statistics Sweden.

Strange, S. (1996) *The Retreat of the State: Diffusion of Power in the World Economy*. Cambridge: Cambridge University Press.

Streeck, W. (1996) 'Public power beyond the nation state – the case of the EU', in R. Boyer and D. Drache (eds), *States against Markets*. London: Routledge.

Sykes, R., Palier, B. and Prior, P. (2001) *Globalisation And European Welfare States: Challenges And Changes*. Basingstoke: Palgrave.

Taylor-Gooby, P. (2000) 'Risk, contingency and the third way: evidence from BHPS and qualitative studies'. Social Policy Association Annual Conference. University of Surrey at Roehampton, July.

Teague, P. and Grahl, J. (1998) 'Institutions and labour market performance in Western Europe', *Political Studies*, 46(1): 1–19.

Timmins, N. (1996) *The Five Giants*. London: Fontana.

Timonen, V. (1999a) 'A threat to social security? The impact of EU membership on the Finnish welfare state', *Journal of European Social Policy*, 9: 253–61.

Timonen, V. (1999b) 'The defence of the welfare state: welfare state restructuring in Finland and Sweden in the 1990s'. Paper presented at 'Western Europe in an Age of Globalisation' workshop, Harvard University, 26–28 February 1999.

Treasury (1979) *The Government's Expenditure Plans, 1980–81*. Cmnd 7746. London: HMSO.

Treasury (1997) *Public Expenditure: Statistical Analyses 1997/8 to 1999/00*. Cmnd 3601. London: HMSO.

Treasury (1998) *Modern Public Services for Britain: Investing in Reform*. (First Comprehensive Spending Review). Cmnd 4011. London: HMSO.

Treasury (1999) *Public Expenditure: Statistical Analyses 1999–2000*. Cmnd 4201. London: HMSO.

TUC (Trades Union Congress) (1990–99) *Annual Report to Congress*. TUC.

Ukkola, A. (1999) 'Social assistance as a wage of too many people during and after the recession'. Paper presented at the University of Turku Summer School, May 1999.

Van Den Broucke, F. (1999) 'The active welfare state: a European ambition'. Den Uyl Lecture, Amsterdam.

van Kersbergen, K. (1995) *Social Capitalism: A Study of Christian Democracy and the Welfare State*. London: Routledge.

Vatter, A. (1999) 'Föderalismus', in U. Klöti, P. Knoepfel, H. Kriesi, W. Linder and Y. Papadopoulos (eds), *Handbuch der Schweizer Politik*. Zurich: NZZ Verlag. pp. 77–108.

Vickerstaff, S. (1999) 'Education and Training', in J. Baldock, N. Manning, S. Miller and S. Vickerstaff *Social Policy*. Oxford: Oxford University Press. pp. 132–53.

Visser, J. and Hemerijck, A. (1997) *A Dutch Miracle: Job Growth, Welfare Reform and Corporatism in the Netherlands*. Amsterdam: Amsterdam University Press.

VNP (1995) Valtioneuvoston päätös toimeentulotuen yleisistä perusteista annetun valtioneuvoston päätöksen muuttamisesta, Valtioneuvoston pöytäkirjat 21.12.1995, 232.

Waine, B. (1995) 'A disaster foretold? The case of personal pensions', *Social Policy and Administration*, 29(4): 317–34.

Williamson, J. (2000) 'Social security privatisation: lessons from the UK'. Paper Centre for Retirement Research.

World Bank (1994) *Averting the Old Age Crisis: Policies to Protect the Old and Promote Growth*. New York: Oxford University Press.

World Bank (2000) World Bank Pensions Web Pages at: http://www.worldbank.com.

Zohlnhöfer, R. (1999) 'Die große Steuerreform 1998/99: Ein Lehrstück für Politikentwicklung bei Parteienwettbewerb im Bundesstaat', *Zeitschrift für Parlamentsfragen*, 30(2): 326–45.

Zohlnhöfer, R. (2000) 'Der lange Schatten der schönen Illusion: Finanzpolitik nach der deutschen Einheit, 1990–1998', *Leviathan*, 28(1): 14–38.

Index

Page numbers in *italics* refer to tables